Purity Crusade

Purity Crusade
Sexual Morality
and Social Control,
1868-1900

David J. Pivar

CONTRIBUTIONS IN AMERICAN HISTORY
NUMBER 23

GREENWOOD PRESS, INC., *Westport, Conn. / London, England*

Library of Congress Cataloging in Publication Data

Pivar, David J
    Purity crusade: sexual morality and social control.

    (Contributions in American history, no. 23).
    Bibliography: p.
    1. Prostitution—United States. 2. United States—
Moral conditions. I. Title.
    HQ125.U6P57   363.4'0973   70-179650
    ISBN 0-8371-6319-6

Library of Congress Catalog Card Number: 70-179650

ISBN: 0-8371-6319-6

First published in 1973

Greenwood Press, Inc., Publishing Division
51 Riverside Avenue, Westport, Connecticut 06880

Printed in the United States of America

To

Morton Herskovitz

Let the memory of Brook Farm never be a bygone. Its lesson is a lesson for our time. It was another serious and high endeavor to do what puritanism tried to do at the beginning—to organize human society definitely according to divine law, to make the aim and duty of the Christian the same, to do God's will on earth as it is done in heaven. Such a theocracy, such a commonwealth, larger and better than Brook Farm, is the goal which is set before us. The American who has lost his vision of it has lost his character. The New Englander who is not working for it, as George Ripley worked for it, is false to the Puritanism of which he was born. The Church which is not preaching it is living in denial of its master.

"A Christmas Lesson from Brook Farm,"
New England Magazine, quoted in
Woman's Journal, December 25, 1897

Contents

Acknowledgments

The process of manuscript preparation is a long and, at times, difficult one. I have incurred far too many debts to acknowledge them all. I can, however, list those persons and institutions who have provided most assistance.

I am especially obligated to Mr. Lauren Selden, who, during the formative stages of the conceptualizing phase in dissertation writing, worked with me in an exercise in content analysis. Professors Thomas C. Cochran and Morton Keller guided the dissertation and encouraged me to investigate the unexplored domains of historical knowledge. Other members of the University of Pennsylvania History Department listened sympathetically and prodded me into more detailed analysis with their questions. Charles E. Rosenberg, Wallace E. Davies, Gabriel Kolko, Richard Dunn, and James Davis rendered such help.

Like most historians, I owe a special debt to librarians, who make it possible to do research. Without the continuing assistance of the University of Pennsylvania library staff, this book would have never been written. Librarians at the Library of Congress, the National

Woman's Christian Temperance Union, Radcliffe College, Columbia University, the Historical Society of Pennsylvania, the Baptist Historical Society, and Swarthmore College and Haverford College were more than willing to extend themselves in the search for relevant source materials.

I am grateful to Professor Oscar Handlin who read the doctoral dissertation and made recommendations for revisions in the preparation of the book. Professor John C. Burnham commented on the manuscript and generously made some research notes available to me.

I gratefully acknowledge the financial assistance of the Samuel Fels Foundation. Through their generosity I spent an unencumbered year completing the doctoral dissertation. The American Philosophical Society provided a grant-in-aid that permitted me to make use of English source materials. I am grateful, as well, to the Foundation at California State University, Fullerton, for the small grants that enabled me to travel and revise my earlier work.

During the preparation of the manuscript, Miss Margaret King not only contributed editorial advice but expedited preparation by contributing her typing skills. Misses Pauline Han and Susan Parker also deserve thanks for their secretarial skills.

Portions of this book appeared in my article "Theocratic Businessmen and Philadelphia Municipal Reform, 1870-1900," *Pennsylvania History* 33 (1966): 289-307.

Lastly, I am indebted to Phyllis, my wife, who freed me from daily tasks of domestic economy so I could complete the manuscript.

Purity Crusade

Introduction

Until the twentieth century, Americans tended to refrain from public discussion of sex. Victorian morality dictated that civilized men and women engage only in polite conversation. When urban Progressives introduced a variety of sex reforms into American life after the turn of the century, many Americans were shocked. With vice commission investigations, the passage of the Mann Act, public campaigns against venereal diseases, and regulated prostitution for the military, Progressives unveiled the many faces of American sexuality.

Americans were little prepared for the parade of sex reformers who appeared in search of public support. A conservative consensus concerning the place of sex in society had, until then, existed among reformers. In 1912, that stalwart consensus, which had already begun to crack, was permanently shattered. Americans who had been disturbed by women suffragettes were still more rudely shaken by Margaret Sanger's ideas on birth control. In the United States it seemed that only a coterie of Greenwich Village intellectuals—excluding scholars, of course

3

—dared even to explore the teachings of Freud, which sometimes appeared to include so much sex as to be labeled pansexual.[1]

Today, when public discussion of every sexual aberration seems commonplace, we tend to underestimate the emotional responses that discussion of such subjects initially aroused. But once the Progressives discovered Freud, prostitution, free love, and birth control, external and internal restraints against public discussion of sex were broken. American sexual attitudes then changed so rapidly that the liberal ideas of nineteenth-century feminists Susan B. Anthony and Elizabeth Cady Stanton soon came to seem conventional.[2]

These changes in sexual attitudes pervaded the Progressive movement. John C. Burnham has demonstrated that progressives in politics and economics and reformers in psychiatry and psychology shared common assumptions, and he has recently extended his views to include sex reformers as well.[3] Since sexual attitudes affected the Progressives' idea and ideal of personality, reexamination of sex theories contributed greatly toward their new idea of civilization.

The abruptness of America's rite of passage was, in some respects, more apparent than real. For decades, reformers had been conducting a continuing debate among themselves, and occasionally with the public, on numerous sex issues. Before the Civil War, John Humphrey Noyes and other sexual radicals had used the public mails to stimulate a vigorous public debate on free love. The Comstock Act of 1873 ended the use of the mails for these purposes, but reformers persisted in discussing theories of sex among themselves and occasionally initiated public campaigns on less controversial sex issues.

Victorian moralists, moreover, moved beyond the utopian speculation and communitarian experimentation of earlier antebellum reformers. They retained a lively interest in theory, but, being influenced by, and in communication with, the reform agencies of the woman's movement, they were more concerned with the actual reform of American sexual practices—a distinctly pragmatic aim. Raising new issues to enlist the support of enthusiastic women, these sex reformers sought the construction of new social institutions and the transformation of older ones. Abandoning the luxury of free-wheeling speculation and committing themselves to practical action, they experienced, in practice, the difficulties of conserving the ideal of individualism of an old era as they journeyed toward greater social collectivity in the new. The danger inherent in the process of transformation was the promotion of social conformity at the expense of individual freedom.

This sketch of Victorian morality suggests that the two-sided view of the Victorians inherited from historians should be modified. According to the traditional image, Anthony Comstock was a Victorian prototype—a Calvinistic prude, a moral policeman ferreting out panderers, prostitutes, and pornographers to punish the destroyers of American virtues. In contrast to this austere and stern image of the American moral reformer, historians have revealed Victorians with secret lives, holding this foil of actuality against the professed ideals of the era, and pointing to the hypocrisy so widespread in the pre-Progressive era. This dual emphasis—on excessive moral repression on the one hand, and persistence of illicit and subterranean sex on the other—ignores a more complex reality. Moderate social and moral reformers confronted the serious problems emerging from new sex relationships in a changing society. Far removed from sensationalism, men and women investigated the nature of sexuality and applied their understandings to the problems of the transformation of society in its new urban character. In the process, two impulses forged the reformers' program: an unstated utopian vision and the concrete new social realities of the city.

The backbone of the woman's movement was formed by moderate and conservative women reformers, such as the members of the Women's Christian Temperance Union and the General Federation of Women's Clubs—social feminists who committed themselves to numerous social and moral reforms of astounding range.[4] Historians have applauded them, quite correctly, for their contributions to social betterment. One of their activities, however, was less appealing and more controversial, and it has escaped the historians' attention. Women joined with moral reformers in an all-out attack upon prostitution, commercialized vice, and the white slave traffic. This campaign, beginning in the late 1860s and cresting in the Progressive era, was a major effort with international ramifications. Despite a slow start—for even women with the do-everything philosophy of the WCTU initially shrank from this reform—the woman's movement had identified itself by the 1880s with the crusade against prostitution.

Serving as a policy-forming committee for the woman's movement, though hidden from immediate view, was a small group of former abolitionists. After the Civil War they became moral educationists and interested themselves in sex reform, child rearing, sexual criminality, and prostitution. They addressed themselves to seemingly dissimilar reform interests, developed action programs, and infused the woman's movement with their spirit of opposition to legalized prostitution in American cities. Initially vigilance societies were formed to concentrate on the rejection of licensed prostitution, but in the mid-1880s these societies were reconstituted as social purity alliances, having a broad range of interests, including moral education, child rearing theories, sex education programs, organizations for the protection of women travelers and workers, vocational education, social hygiene, and, especially, the abolition of prostitution. The new abolitionists, who served as social theorists and technicians in these alliances, were joined by other reformers, women physicians, and philanthropists. Their active inquiry into the relationship between prostitution and social organization led them to interpret their function as the purification of society itself—the fomenting of moral or religious revolution.

Dissatisfied with, and fearful of, random change, the new moralists hoped for the reconstitution of society upon a new cultural foundation. They envisioned a new social character for urban man. In the act of freeing the prostitute they, through the woman's movement, would raise a higher standard of civilization that would require of men the same standards of purity previously demanded of woman alone. The iniquities of the city might be mastered, even eliminated, by proclaiming and realizing a new system of values.

Former abolitionists dominated the leadership of the crusade against prostitution and exercised substantial control over the social purity movement as it turned to more universal reform. Habitually willing to accept the most onerous moral responsibilities, these abolitionists now envisioned themselves as new abolitionists dedicated to the emancipation of the white slave—the prostitute. Their immediate objectives of eradicating prostitution and ending the white slave traffic expanded tremendously, however, once they actually encountered the institution and its "fallen women." Preventive social reforms based on child rearing and education became their broader objective. While they retained a negative goal—the eradication of sin and evil—they added a positive goal—the reconstruction of American society through its children.

Aware that the building of modern society required basic transformations and eager to effect them, these reformers were guided by what they considered permanent in Christianity—its value system. Their eagerness to institutionalize a new morality led them beyond the limited goal of abolishing prostitution to a twofold program. Its repulsive side was remedial—rescuing prostitutes and closing brothels; its shiny and attractive promise was contained in its thrust toward social reconstruction—purifying society.

New abolitionists, as a modernizing elite, worked, then, for the transformation of society while conserving its religious foundations. How was one to bridge over the chasm between centuries of natural development by years of artificial education? How might the masses be raised to the standards of civilization preached by the clergy? These were their pressing enquiries. Civilization was, for the new abolitionists, an aggregate of the social characteristics of individuals. Traditional habits, a legacy from agrarian America, were inadequate for an urban society. (Purity reformers, unlike Frederick Jackson Turner, located the promise of American life on the urban frontier). Accordingly, the role of civilization was to free man from instinct; thus, if urban society were to be civilized, a new social character had to be molded through social conditioning. The reformers worked toward a system of democratic social control to eliminate a need for external coercion and authority. In articulating their social goals, reformers challenged traditional ontologies while at the same time adjusting themselves to social realities and reaffirming traditional cultural values.

The influence of a small band of purity leaders, headquartered in New York City, on the development of American social life was far out of proportion to its numbers. The leaders interpreted and transmitted European reform news on prostitution. They devised a strategy for combatting prostitution and discovered techniques for popularizing their reform proposals. Their audience was national. By coordinating the programs in local committees, they standardized and rationalized moral education and lent support to the woman's movement campaign to reform the republic through the child. Theirs was an unbridled reform movement maturing into a national effort against prostitution at a rate unprecedented in American social history.

Prostitution, obviously, was not a uniquely American institution. Still, its American character was somewhat distinct, as it never had the scope, and rarely had the forms, of the European institution. It was not a system of commercialized vice during the colonial period. While bawdy houses had flourished, there was little traffic in prostitutes, and municipal vice was localized and isolated. Vice followed the trade routes; as economic development created affluence and transportation revolutions shrank distances, prostitution grew at a proportional rate. Merchants of vice borrowed organizational models from the business community, plying their trade in damaged goods with relative impunity. A recently emerged, and still unregulated, national market could be exploited by both legitimate businessmen and merchants of vice.

Early in the 1860s, European social reformers (English reformers supported by Continental sympathizers) began a campaign against regulated prostitution in their major cities. By 1876, Americans joined this international movement. Their interest in the international movement for the abolition of prostitution continued, and they attended European congresses, corresponded with European reform notables, and received European reform leaders. American reformers devoted themselves mainly to the domestic aspects of this social reform, but they owed much to the intellectual leadership of their European confreres.

Purity reform has been largely unexplored by American historians. The basic objective of this book is to trace the major contours of the movement, including its accomplishments, the events in which purity reformers participated, the social functions of purity reform in the woman's movement and urban Progressivism, and its effects upon the development of the social hygiene movement. Multidimensional, yet apparently unified, the social purity movement pressed in different directions and possessed various possibilities for potential development. Although, in the nineteenth century, these divergences did not result in organizational cleavages, they did foreshadow various paths of development in the twentieth century.

Purity reform, enthusiastically greeted by Frances Willard as the "latest and greatest crusade," underwent many changes as it was communicated through the woman's movement and applied locally. At the start, since purification meant various things to various reformers, a discrepancy between theory and practice developed. But the imprecision of the purity symbol proved useful, as it permitted an appearance of unity among, at times, divergent factions within the movement. Clearly the movement had no philosophical consistency and might be considered, because of its character as an aggregation of social values, a social religion.

The language used by purity reformers changed with the changing nature of the movement. The appellation "new abolitionist" had a specific meaning, reflecting the original function of the movement. The new abolitionists pursued the abolition of prostitution, the eradication of the brothel, and the suppression of the white slave traffic. They derived from the old antebellum antislavery party. As used in this study, "new abolitionist" refers specifically to the narrower reform, which constituted the original, but not the expanded, goals of the movement. "Purity reform" refers to the broader effort at social reconstruction. New abolitionism converged with moral education groups to become the social purity movement early in the 1880s.

In discussing the woman's movement, emphasis is placed upon social feminism. As allies of the purity movement, suffragists did not always formally belong to a purity organization. If they pursued purity work, however, they are referred to as purity reformers in this study. While the purity leadership was a well-defined group, purity workers were unified not only by institutional but by symbolic bonds. They identified with the objectives defined by the purity leadership without necessarily knowing that such a leadership existed. Because of their influence within the woman's movement and their access to reform agencies, purity leaders could transmit their ideas rapidly through the institutional channels of the woman's movement. They were consulted as authorities on purity subjects by feminist leaders and, later, by national political leaders.

Purity reform has had an enduring effect, and Americans may discover in purity thought familiar expressions and admonitions. As the movement fragmented, it contributed social ideas that have persisted to this day. While it may be impossible to ascertain the full extent of its influence on contemporary American culture, a study of purity reform permits at least a minimal assessment of that influence. Much of purity reform thought is casually accepted, and one suspects it is basic to the American character. By examining the institutional forms of the purity movement, we may evaluate its significance as an objective phenomenon, not merely as a compilation of subjective attitudes. In a time of cultural challenge, a study of purity reform may contribute to an understanding of our contemporary condition.

NOTES

1. For an analysis of Greenwich Village intellectuals, see Christopher Lasch, *The New Radicalism in America, 1889-1963: The Intellectual as a Social Type* (New York: Alfred A. Knopf, 1965).

2. For an analysis of women's leaders more liberal than most purity reformers, see Aileen S. Kraditor, *The Ideas of the Woman Suffrage Movement, 1890-1920* (New York: Columbia University Press, 1965).

3. John Chynoweth Burnham, "Psychiatry, Psychology and the Progressive Movement," *American Quarterly* 12 (1960): 457; and "The Medical Inspection of Prostitutes in America in the Nineteenth Century: The St. Louis Experiment and its Sequel," *Bulletin of the History of Medicine* 45 (1971): 203-18.

4. The phrase "social feminism" was coined by William L. O'Neill in *Everyone Was Brave: The Rise and Fall of Feminism in America* (Chicago: Quadrangle Books, 1969), pp. ix-x. He distinguished between hard-core feminists, who worked primarily for the vote, and social feminists, who subordinated women's rights to broad social reforms believed more urgent. Social purity reformers in the woman's movement were, given this rule of thumb distinction, "social feminists."

1

The Genesis of Purity Reform

Although prostitution is only one aspect of social organization, it has profoundly influenced social relationships,
women's status, and family development in the Western
world. To write about this institution is to touch upon the
history of human society itself. The management of
prostitution has varied according to time, place, and circumstances; the determination of state policy, however,
has depended upon the ordering of three factors—economic, moral, and hygienic—to harmonize
policy with the culture of the legislating nation. The ordering of these factors in the policies of Germany, Venice, and
England after the late Middle Ages may provide insights
into the official response to prostitution and the influence
of the response on social organization.

THE EUROPEAN HERITAGE

Emile Durkheim, a historical sociologist especially interested in the history of social institutions, thought he had

located a pivotal change in the history of the family in the
emergence in Germany of licensed municipal brothels. He
interpreted the appearance of legalized prostitution,
therefore, as the defeat of free love and a victory for the
conjugal family. A nascent middle class had discovered in
legalized prostitution a device for the protection of
domestic purity. Since the medieval church had long con-
doned prostitution, townsmen who legalized the practice
were not overly troubled by conscience, but the prostitutes
had their own interests to defend and, after organizing
themselves into a guild, petitioned for equal status with
other crafts.[1] It may be safely assumed that their petition
was denied, for the subsequent history of the prostitute was
one of declining status until she had become a member of a
pariah class, required to wear clothes and insignia to dis-
tinguish her from the wives and daughters of the burghers.

Venetians expressed other motivations in formulating
their state policy. Prosperity allowed for a growing population of prostitutes in the Renaissance, some imported from
foreign lands to protect the status of Venetian citizens. The
Venetian Great Council was forced to take the problem
under consideration in the thirteenth century when they
became alarmed over the practice of keeping "female
slaves" for illicit purposes. In 1266, they levied large fines
to discourage this practice. Fines, however, were ineffec-
tual deterrents. Before the century ended, Venetians
resigned themselves to the persistence, even expansion, of
prostitution by designating a residential district for brothels
where they could be kept under governmental surveillance.
Like the Germans, the Venetians hoped to protect themselves against venereal diseases, especially after syphilis
was introduced into their city, but they were also interested
in preserving the Venetian reputation for economic and
religious liberties. Accordingly, the Venetian Grand Council acted, in 1438, to prohibit the selling of women into

slavery for purposes of sex. Thus, the Council reconciled sex with political economy. As years went by, the Venetian courtesan gained in status at home and abroad.

Although England experimented with licensed prostitution, its history varies appreciably from Germany's and Venice's. In the twelfth century Henry II gained the dubious distinction of introducing legalized prostitution into England on a grand scale. His program did not meet with universal acclaim, as both yeoman farmers and London merchants resisted this policy. In 1381, during Ball's Rebellion, insurgents destroyed the licensed houses on the outskirts of London. Moreover, London merchants persistently resisted the Council's attempts to introduce licensed brothels into the city. Indeed, it was under pressure from the Puritans, and after an epidemic of syphillis, that Henry VIII withdrew state sanction for legalized vice.[2]

Neither monarchs nor popes possessed an unblemished moral record in the management of prostitution. Occasionally both resorted to regulation as a means of replenishing their depleted coffers. Religious principles did, nevertheless, encourage their efforts for the redemption of "fallen woman." The medieval church had maintained asylums for reformed women and had persistently urged its adherents to rescue prostitutes. With the memory of Mary Magdalene to encourage them, churchmen made provision for the repentant by establishing Magdalene Homes—the Viennese founded their famed home early in the fourteenth century and the Venetians theirs in the sixteenth.[3]

No clear policy toward prostitution emerged during the late Middle Ages or Renaissance. Religious and secular attitudes toward the institution were ambiguous; only a reformation of religious life clarified Christian thought on issues directly and indirectly affecting prostitution. As Protestant movements gained ascendancy in Northern Europe, and the Council of Trent (1545-1563) reformed Catholicism internally, Christians reexamined their ideals of social organization and enhanced the role that the family was to play in the future. Among Protestant reformers, Huldreich Zwingli, John Calvin, and Martin Luther opposed compulsory chastity, rejecting the pre-Reformation ideal of abstinence and substituting for it the ideal of the conjugal family. Martin Luther declared marriage divinely sanctioned, while Calvin, not as therapeutic as Luther, denied that sexual intercourse was unclean or inspired by the Devil. Despite these obvious advances over former sexual attitudes, Protestants remained ascetic in their general point of view. Although marriage became a civil institution, Protestants were not issuing a license for lewd or licentious living.[4]

The Reformations, Protestant and Catholic, accelerated the transformation of the family, which had previously proceeded almost imperceptibly. As Philippe Ariès emphasized in his seminal work *Centuries of Childhood: A Social History of Family Life*, he was reconstructing the triumph of the modern family over types of human relationships that hindered its development, and, hence, the very emergence of modern society.[5] If Professor Ariès' general proposition is correct, then reconstructing changing attitudes toward prostitution and concomitant attitudinal changes toward women and the family may be equally important in understanding the emergence of the modern family.

In the eighteenth century, physicians, medical reformers, and governmental officials increasingly emphasized the hygienic aspects of prostitution. English writers advocated operating public brothels to protect wives and children from the dangers of private vice—venereal diseases. In fact, Central European nations, enmeshed in the patterns woven from absolutism and mercantilism, turned to "medical police" for the sanitary control of prostitution. This policy of reglementation—the segregation and quarantine of the ill and the compulsory medical inspection of prostitutes—found particular favor among cameralistic nations. Britain and the United States, without an authoritarian or paternalistic tradition of economic development, were spared the full impact of reglementationist thought in the later eighteenth and nineteenth centuries.

During the French Revolution, the Directorate discovered new pretexts for the enforcement of reglementation. Virtuous Louis XVI and chaste Marie Antoinette had turned to it, but its full force was not felt until the Revolution. Yves Guyot, with the hindsight of a nineteenth-century historian, attributed reglementation to the "dechristianization" begun with the Revolution and accelerated, after 1802, by Napoleon who relied upon the system to protect the health of his soldiers. Reglementation was boldly sanitarian, and France, according to Guyot, was unable to invoke morality or religion to justify the *police de moeurs*. The anticlerical thrust of the Revolution had placed the *police de moeurs* in the position of protecting prostitutes. They, not the displaced clergy, were the new guardians of morality. In practice, Guyot contended, these moral police protected the purveyors of vice and the destroyers of innocence. Not only prostitutes, but even the medical profession were subordinated to their new moral authority.[6]

Although instituted primarily for hygienic purposes, reglementation brought economic factors into play as well. In marriage, women and children ceased to be mere possessions and attained social status in relationship to society and the state, but prostitution reinforced a more direct relationship between sex and economics. It was this com-

bination of economics and sex, which reduced human relationships to mere economic exchange, that women reformers of the nineteenth century abhorred.[7]

The woman's movement, a religious movement in the
broadest sense, worked for the emancipation of women in
industrial society. Reglementation ran counter to their new
moralism in that it represented the legalization of female
slavery; it denied the sacredness and dignity of human
nature, physical and mental. Under police or military controls, licensed prostitution denied women personal liberties
and the rights of due process under law. Nor would women
accept the rationalization that prostitution had an
ameliorating influence by giving employment to women
who were suffering from the dislocating effects of industrialism. Women forced to the point of starvation were
not equals in contractual relationships. Even the temporary purchase of a "consenting" woman for trifling sums
of money made them subjects of trade and denied them
fundamental human freedoms. Women's leaders, as new
moralists, rejected both the hygienic and economic foundations of reglementation. In the final analysis, prostitution
was a moral issue, for from an exclusively economic point
of view, nothing was to prevent slavery from surviving.

THE AMERICAN COLONIAL EXPERIENCE

Anabaptists, who consituted the largest number of
religionists among the colonists, brought with them a
dynamic form of pietistic perfectionism that was a cornerstone of American civilization. Equally important in
mastering the wilderness was the inherent tension within
their religious thought: the conflict between perfect moral
order and perfect moral freedom. The fulfillment of their
dream of reformation depended upon their ability to recon-

cile this tension between obedience to moral law and the danger of curtailing freedoms of others through an overabundance of pietism.[8]

With the notable exceptions of sexual behavior in frontier communities and the South, the colonies held to the sexual asceticism of Protestantism. The Puritans were quick to establish those sexual norms by expelling Thomas Morton and destroying Merrymount. They wanted none of "Merry Olde England" in their New Jerusalem.[9]

Having established an ideal of government, Puritans strove to maintain Reformation ideals of sexual morality. The church became the major institution of moral control, administering a relatively lenient discipline upon delinquent religionists.[10] Despite this leniency, however, they were dedicated to churchways over folkways. In the administration of moral law, Puritans accepted imperfections and waywardness as understandable among the faithful, but they were quite capable of harsh persecution when deviations threatened the foundations of their moral order. Even in their leniency they reserved the right to judge personal purity and to require obedience to moral law. The tendency, in sexual matters, as D. H. Lawrence has noted, was to promote hypocrisy and to force sexual deviancy "underground." Ascetics who administered justice with cold dispassion, according to natural and divine law, felt the threats of both real and imagined sexual incontinence.[11]

As "worldly ascetics," they could not rest until they triumphed over sin and evil in the social realm. Their war against the "natural" within man generated another, irreconcilable tension between suppressed drives and prescribed social behavior.[12] Corporate Puritanism, mandating conformity, produced sexual longings and anxieties of considerable intensity. Daniel Defoe captured the quintessence of this intensity in his poetry:

Loose thoughts, at first, like subterranean Fires,
Burn inward, smothering, with unchast Desires.
But getting Vent, to Rage and Fury turn,
Burst in Volcanoes, and like Atna burn.
The Heat increases as the flames expire,
And turns the solid hills to liquid Fire.
So, Sensual Flames, when raging in the Soul,
First vitiate all the Parts, then fire the Whole;
Burn up the Bright, the Beautious, the Sublime,
And turn our lawful Pleasures into Crime.

The conflict between conformity and individualism keenly experienced by Defoe might be eased only through obedience to Christian law—the perfection of moral order. Defoe returned to the cultural ideal held by Puritans in old and new England. He prescribed Christian temperance, including suppression of unlawful sexual desires, plaguing his readers with the fear that even the marriage bed might become a bed of lust.[13] He expressed a common and underlying psychological state undoubtedly shared by his public. Christian asceticism made sexual self-control a requisite for personality development. In effect, Puritans were pansexualists, for whom sexual control was the key to all aspects of personality.

Among recorded sexual deviations in colonial New England church discipline cases, prostitution was infrequently cited. Prostitution, however, may have been practiced more by the unchurched. Although relevant statistics are rare, it may safely be concluded that prostitution was not a major problem in the colonial period of American history. Modern prostitution emerged with the industrial city. Although towns and cities played a significant role in colonial history out of proportion to their size or number, they were neither so large nor so numerous that municipal prostitution in the American colonies reached parity with that of Europe. Most certainly, reglementation was not a policy to be adopted.

Only Boston evinced prostitution in its commercial form, although the eleven cases of prostitution tried in the 1670-1680 decade out of a population considerably below twenty thousand may not justify the designation "commercial" vice. Philadelphia was troubled by prostitution on a lesser scale. The Society of Friends exercised close control over the moral behavior of its members, but was unable to control behavior outside the city limits, and prostitutes took refuge in the caves on the outskirts of the city. In this primitive setting, prostitution presented no immediate threat to the "civilized" status of the Quaker city. Nevertheless, these caves became so notorious that William Penn ordered them closed in 1685. Sexual deviation would find no refuge in the wilderness.

Prostitution grew in important urban centers in the seventeenth century but never reached the proportions of a system of commercialized vice. In the early eighteenth century it became a vexatious municipal concern, appearing with greater frequency and virulence. Even discounting imaginary charges of rampant immorality born of fantasies, evidence indicates prostitutes found lucrative employment in every major seaport. War conditions, accompanied by population dislocations, swelling urban centers, and willing soldiers and sailors, caused significant increases in reported cases of bastardy and adultery. Likewise, colonial armies had their camp followers. These new conditions, alien to austere colonial life, provoked a cultural reaction, as the case of Boston shows.

Boston's disrepute as a center of prostitution was greater than that of other colonial cities. As prostitution became more troublesome, Bostonians reacted with moral indignation and vigilance committees. In 1734 and 1737, mobs severely damaged two bawdy houses, forcing them to close. Since recruitments for brothels probably came from families of tradesmen and mechanics, their opposition was practical and personal as well as moral. Despite occasional mob action, however, prostitution flourished in a maturing colonial society.[14]

Colonialists tried to prevent the growth of prostitution as well as to suppress it. Philadelphians and Charlestonians fostered charitable institutions to assist the victims of vice, while Bostonians, with a stronger Puritan tradition, followed a different course. Boston mercantilists were practical men who celebrated work as a beneficent developer of character. Indeed, one mercantilist pamphleteer used this argument (that work diminished vice) in an appeal to the clergy.[15]

An enlarged population of unmarried women created a pool of potential recruits for the brothels. Boston merchants saw in economic development a device for eliminating a class of unemployed women and providing themselves with a new labor supply. Their program was successful. Early in the eighteenth century, enthusiasm for household manufacturing reached craze proportions. In 1721, Boston founded a spinning school to release the industrious energies of unoccupied women. To encourage gainful employment, the city conducted competitions in Boston Commons. Although the practice was abandoned after two or three years, other attempts to encourage industry were recorded in 1751, 1753, and 1754. More than three hundred spinsters took to the commons with their wheels at the zenith of the craze.

Commercialized vice did exist in the colonial period, but a cautious use of the term is advisable. Brothels, though they became fixed establishments, were still limited to major seaports. No evidence of an intercolonial trade or a municipal-wide organization in prostitution exists. Brothels, however, had become connected with taverns. To the reform mind, inclined to see sexual intemperance as the root of all vice, the excesses of drink and of the brothel became joined. However, the social evil, alarming as it may have been to colonialists, did not reach the magnitude of prostitution in London, Paris, or Berlin. The state intervened against the evil only through normal law enforcement practices. Further, the state remained relatively neutral in the colonies, whereas in Europe its functions expanded to cover regulating and licensing prostitution.

The dangers of prostitution had, by the nineteenth century, become clear for moralists. Early in the century Bostonians lamented the alarming proliferation of vice.[16] Though "Friends of the City," longing for a "city reformation," propagandized for moral revival, no urban revivalist came to rescue them. Boston had to wait for Charles G. Finney and the "Second Great Awakening." While Napoleon turned to reglementation, New Englanders affirmed their traditional cultural values.

The colonial pattern of response to prostitution—opposition—persisted into early nationhood, although hazy outlines of a newer pattern gradually emerged. Ministers occasionally referred to a particularly heinous crime, with the hope of shocking their congregants into a reaffirmation of traditional morality, but the customary policy was one of silence. Any discussion, religionists believed, might inflame passions and promote sin and vice. Ignorance and innocence were logical companions according to an Augustinian concept of human nature, which denied any natural goodness or rationality in man. These older techniques of combatting vice were doomed to failure, however, and religionists engaged limitedly in experimentation. Sunday School Societies, making their appearance after the American Revolution, disseminated pamphlets and established schools in the poorer sections of Boston. The Boston Society for the Moral and Religious Instruction of the Poor distributed religious information to encourage industry among the indigent. Through religio-economic tracts the society wanted to restrain the poor, protect property, and effect economies in poor relief. Though they did not specifically mention vice, it was implicitly related to ignorance and poverty. The societies reinforced traditional social values and reimposed traditional social controls. Simultaneously, they developed techniques for more efficient management of poor relief and for educating the unchurched in moral economy. According to one tract, religious instruction profited man in "this world and the next."[17]

Religionists also made traditional appeals for individual restraint in their battle against vice. Bible tract societies hoped to inspire a spirit of self-control in seamen, who, quite logically, were a ready clientele for bawdy houses. Evangelists organized a special seamen's tract society and sent delegations aboard ships to circularize literature and conduct prayer meetings. These new actions, it may be assumed, pointed toward a new consciousness of the growing dimensions of prostitution in the early nineteenth century. Unlike Europeans, who were turning to reglementation, American religionists restated traditional cultural ideals with great fervor and combatted sin and vice with great institutional efficiency.

THE ANTEBELLUM EXPERIENCE

In the early nineteenth century, the "Second Great Awakening" unleashed a tremendous wave of social reform. Nevertheless, attitudes about prostitution were amazingly similar to those of the previous century. Morality was not to be regulated by outside sources of authority enforcing law, but, rather, from an internalized morality that gave strength to the individual in his combat with temptations and vice. Christian temperance remained the formidable weapon in the arsenal of reform, and moral indignation the affective force to reimpose traditional moral standards. As Joseph R. Gusfield showed in his study of the temperance movement, moral indignation brought into play the quality of disinterested anger and upheld norms where apparently no personal advantage was at stake.[18]

SOCIAL REFORM AND PROSTITUTION

The first specialized antiprostitution group, organized in the mid-1820s, relied upon older explanations of the "fall" of woman. The American Society for the Prevention of Licentiousness and Vice and the Promotion of Morality imitated the organizational structure of the American Temperance Society—again illustrating the tacitly understood relation of prostitution and temperance. Continuing its dependency on the temperance movement, the new society borrowed temperance technique, style, and ideology. The two reforms, temperance and social purity, were the spearheads of a secularized American morality. Social purity and temperance movements, with their common institutional origins, related alcohol and prostitution as "twin evils." Temperance and social purity were twin forces to combat evil.

Unlike earlier sporadic efforts to save and care for "fallen women," evangelists, spurred by their fervent faith in the perfectibility of man, thought no case beyond the redemptive power of their evangelical skills. Even the prostitute, lowest of the low, might be redeemed. The Reverend John McDowall, touched by the plight of these forsaken women, journeyed, upon his graduation from

Princeton Theological Seminary, to the notorious Five Points in New York City, where he evangelized through the early 1830s. Combining his resources with those of William Goodell, editor of an antislavery newspaper, he published the *Female Advocate*, dedicated to the rescue of prostitutes. He had embarked on a collective evangelical campaign. Moved by the sincerity of McDowall, Arthur Tappan, a New York merchant interested in moral reforms, contributed the money that enabled McDowall to found the New York Magdalen Society. Tappan became its first president and McDowall its secretary.

McDowall campaigned aggressively with beneficial results. Preaching and publishing attracted attention to his pioneer efforts to rescue the "fallen woman." The society grew and won support within the religious and reform communities, including the New York Female Moral Reform Society, formed on May 12, 1834. Another organization, the American Society for Promoting the Observance of the Seventh Commandment, joined in the new enterprise. Additional societies dedicated to the same objectives were formed, but disappeared almost immediately.[19]

Undoubtedly, the American Moral Reform Association was the most important of the supporting organizations. With a board of directors composed overwhelmingly of clergymen, the association advocated a regenerative religious ideology. Through a publicity campaign, they awakened other clergymen to the "licentiousness of the age," and through repetition of essential religious ideals in their tracts, they reinforced traditional morality.

McDowallites welcomed feminine contributions and support. Although initially only allies in the reform, women eventually displaced the clergy as leaders. Operating through the New York Female Reform Society, which was directed by Mrs. Charles G. Finney, woman reform-

ers purchased McDowell's *Female Advocate*. The journal, now published as the *Advocate of Moral Reform*,
stimulated the rapid growth of the movement. By 1837, the
Female Moral Reform Society boasted 250 local groups.
Of these, 138 were located in New York, 25 in Massachusetts, 29 in Connecticut, 27 in Ohio, and the remainder
in Maine and Michigan.[20] In the course of reform
development, these women revealed their sympathy for the
moderate abolitionists active in New York City. In the
years before the Civil War, as general reform zeal waned
and as antislavery consumed more resources and energies,
the reform society returned to conservative educational activities. Many women then channeled their energies into
the maternal associations, which functioned as church auxiliary organizations and attempted to improve child rearing
and prepare children for admission into religious communities.

Repressive action against prostitutes, which ap-
proached vigilantism in its severity and was reminiscent of
the colonial pattern, reappeared and inhibited McDowall's
more positive efforts to rescue prostitutes. Members of the
Rochester branch of the American Female Reform Society
devoted themselves to the suppression of prostitution. They
ferreted out houses and reported them to the police. It is
quite possible that provincial patterns persisted in smaller
towns long after being abandoned in large cities.

The rapid collapse of McDowall's society saddened
the young minister. The publication, in 1832, of his
Magdalen Report of 1831, an account of prostitution in
New York City that was intended to gain adherents from
the general public, stirred up a hornet's nest. Community
leaders read the report with a cold disbelief that turned into
hostility directed against the young reformer. Most community leaders opposed the public discussion of prostitution, since they thought it swelled the ranks of whoredom.

McDowall's report was, to them, prurient literature. Public-spirited citizens took the case to the New York grand jury; the jury indicted McDowall and condemned his journal as a "public nuisance." Arthur Tappan withdrew from the Magdalen Society as a result of the public reaction. McDonnell continued his work with the Female Moral Reform Society. In 1836 his license as a Presbyterian minister was removed. Within the year McDowall, poverty-stricken, and having barely reached his thirty-fifth birthday, was dead.

POLICE AND PHYSICIANS SUPPORT REGLEMENTATION

Prostitution had supporters among the police and the medical professions. Since they dealt almost exclusively with crime and disease as sanitary problems, morality was of only tangential significance. For the police, reglementation seemed the best alternative to a policy of drift. Influenced by police and medical practices in Europe, American police argued that regulation protected the home from the evils of prostitution. Like the German burghers who had introduced municipal regulation in the Middle Ages, they expected prostitution to ensure marital purity.

Not only did the police support reglementation, they also worried over the reform movement. They wondered whether the growing interest in the dignity of woman would be damaged in attempts to end prostitution. Having accepted the idea of regulation to preserve domestic purity, the police were anxious to protect "pure" women who might be detrimentally influenced by reform activities. Given their premises, the police attitude was consistent.

No evidence exists to prove that the police enforced regulation before the Civil War. They did, however, pursue new policies in regard to prostitution. In their earliest dealings with prostitutes, Boston police discovered a satisfactory tactic in ejecting actresses of dubious reputation from the stage. Between 1850 and 1851, the police department assigned "special police" to this function. They directed their surveillance at only the lower class of prostitutes, while "palaces of gilded vice" catering to the "upper tenth" were scarcely noticed. The *Massachusetts Governor's Report* for 1866-1867 listed 351 houses that had been prosecuted in the previous three years.[21] As these straightforward and traditional techniques of suppression failed, however, the police resorted to regulation.

The New York Police Department requested a reglementation system in 1867, to be operated jointly by police and the Metropolitan Health Commissioners. The plan received some initial support. An editorial in the *Nation*, for instance, promoted the regulation system, even though such a system threatened traditional moral norms. The author offered an assortment of moral and hygienic arguments. Repeating the common view that only individual moral regeneration could eradicate prostitution, he conjectured that, in a utopian future,

> ages hence, centuries on centuries hence, when knowledge, refinement, culture, religion shall have produced an amount of respect for personal character, for the laws of health and happiness . . . for standards of purity undreamed of now, the roots of this hideous vice may die from lack of nourishment. Under present conditions, in the sixth decade of the nineteenth century, no efforts to eradicate the evil would stop the source of vice—lust.[22]

This attitude, an odd amalgam of perfectionism and presentism, optimism and pessimism, explained both the

existence and continuation of prostitution as a failure of individual morality. Prostitution was, according to such a
view, not really a social but an individual evil with social
consequences.

One brave soul, "Christian Commonsense," answered
the editorial. The letter writer, accepting the explanation of
prostitution's cause as lust, listed precautionary steps to
check the institution. Proper child rearing might prevent
the downfall of young men and women. Instructing boys in
the horrors of social diseases and providing physical and
mental exercises might divert them from the path of sin. As
in the past, early marriage was encouraged as a hygienic
device. Most important for "Christian Commonsense" was
extreme care in preserving female modesty.[23] This advice
would be repeated with frequency in subsequent discussions of prostitution.

The medical profession, which, like the police, was
more technically involved with venereal diseases, favored
regulation. Alarmed at the increasing incidence of
venereal disease, physicians saw in reglementation an opportunity for the practice of modern preventive
medicine.[24] If diseases such as syphilis were to be
eradicated, a new public attitude toward prostitution
seemed essential. If syphilis were to be "treated as other
diseases," prostitution ought to be accepted as permanent.
The editor of the *Buffalo Medical Journal* speculated in
1856 that prostitution might even be restored to its "old
Roman dignity."[25]

THE EXTENT OF PROSTITUTION

The interest of the police and the medical profession in
reglementation attests to the growth of the social evil. Although no real estimate of its actual extent can be made,
fragmentary statistics provide an indication of its growth.

As previously mentioned, the government prosecuted 351 houses in Massachusetts during a three-year span. Moreover, the public so accepted bawdy houses that, on the eve of the Civil War, gentlemen could purchase a guide to the seraglios in larger cities. The gentlemen's guide listed the better houses, giving addresses, benefits to be gained from particular establishments, and the names of favorite prostitutes. In addition, the guide listed houses of assignation—meeting places frequented by part-time prostitutes, many of whom desperately needed supplementary incomes. An abundance of houses catering to a wealthier clientele existed. For New York City, the place of imprint, the guide listed 106 houses; for Philadelphia, 57; for Baltimore, 15; for Washington, D.C., 7; for Boston, 6; and for Chicago, 5.[26] Probably the New York count was relatively accurate.

The gentlemen's guide was a new feature in American social life, but the publication of such handbooks had long been a European practice, having been introduced in the eighteenth century for the benefit of the aristocracy. Its use in the United States by a merchant aristocracy, and the informal legitimation of prostitution for the "upper tenth" was symptomatic of an unequal distribution of wealth and greater social stratification. Economic growth had resulted in random and irrational social development, creating a class of amoralists effectively free of moral sanctions, and thus endangering the traditional morality of Protestant religions. Indeed, with the extension of prostitution, the press reported on it openly and lightly.

Indignant reformers estimated the magnitude of the evil for themselves. Susan B. Anthony, a leading feminist and early crusader against prostitution, calculated, in the 1860s, that Chicago's five hundred brothels contained thousands of poor girls. She correctly associated the growth of the social evil with the conditions that nurtured it—in-

dustrialization and poverty. Dr. William Sanger compiled
the most accurate statistics for New York City in 1858. Using crude "pollster" techniques, Sanger surveyed 2,000
New York prostitutes, discovering that 1,204 were between the ages of eighteen and twenty-three. Within this
population at least 762 were native Americans and 1,038
were immigrants. The primary sources of recruitment were
American country and European immigrant girls recently
arrived in the city. Sanger estimated that in one year the
prostitute population of New York City had increased
about 20 percent, to 6,000, as a consequence of the 1857
depression. Although a highly compassionate man, Dr.
Sanger still proposed European reglementation as the best
remedy.[27]

REGLEMENTATION VERSUS ABOLITION

Sanger's support for regulation was indicative of a trend
toward reglementation among the medical profession and
police in the 1850s. By the end of the Civil War, police and
physicians were ready for actual implementation. Reformers, on the other hand, opposed prostitution and hinted at
an abolitionist policy. The reform view, however, was in
the minority. Indeed, limited efforts at eradication had
failed, and the interest of the reform community had
declined. Reformers were only weak opposition for the
reglementationists.
     At stake were two contending views of society, the
reglementationist's and the abolitionist's. Reformers had
accepted the feasibility of sinlessness and were continuing
in the pietistic-perfectionist traditions of Puritanism. In the
ferment of reform through the 1840s they seriously worked
toward an "applied Christianity," which, in its ultimate
meaning, would have meant the eradication of prostitution. Regulationists were more practical men, less moved

by the religious enthusiasm of the day. They wished to control the diseases attendant upon prostitution and placed limited emphasis on eventual eradication in the distant future. Both police and physicians perceived prostitution as either a concern for the sanitarian or the criminologist. Reformers perceived it as a moral and social concern.

After the Civil War, reformers gradually came to an understanding of the social and economic foundations of prostitution. From the beginning, temperance and purity ideologies shared similar premises. Social evils, originally sharing the same definition, came to be seen as deviations from social norms, normal being that "which is in conformity to the natural laws that govern the structural arrangements and functional activity of any being." Social evils, so the definition ran, impaired or threatened public health, hindered the advancement and diffusion of knowledge, and generally lowered the morality of society.[28] Among the social evils, sexual immorality was both socially debilitating and fundamentally demoralizing.

Among the many social evils of the nineteenth century, *the* social evil was prostitution. Eventually, the eradication of the brothel and prostitution became a reaffirmation of a Puritan ideal of society. In the process of secularization, reformers, dependent upon temperance and purity ideologies to give sociological unity to otherwise disparate religious groups, restated the Puritan view of society in social terms. During this process, reformers used a more symbolic definition of prostitution. The narrower and more technical definition, "sexual intercourse, except for propagation, is prostitution," was replaced by the more diffuse, "prostitution is the misuse of any power or function."[29] The symbolic definition placed prostitution within a broad social context that helped reformers understand that prostitution, by immediately affecting the family and marriage institutions, could alter the character of social organization. Reformers became more conscious of this relationship in the nineteenth century, developing a mature understanding of the social impact of the institution as they sought to rationalize and standardize social life. By the mid-nineteenth century, the dangers of the social evil for social organization were apparent, and reformers sounded an alarm bell. Changes in the man-woman relationship caused by changing attitudes toward women of the street were lamented and aroused in the reformer fears of declining morality. In the process of secularization, the symbolic definition gained primacy over the narrower, technical one. Henceforth, reformers considered prostitution to be more than an individual sin; it was, rather, a cause of the general corruption of social life.

ANTEBELLUM REFORM:
A NEW CONFIGURATION OF MORAL FORCES

For women reformers under the influences of abolitionism and transcendentalism, the struggle for emancipation extended beyond freeing themselves. They were, in the larger sense of the woman's movement, interested in elevating man to their higher spiritual standards. Through their efforts, they believed, mankind could reach a new and higher civilization, a "perfect equilibrium of the whole" harmonizing masculine and feminine forces in affairs of life. Women had, therefore, a special mission to lead men into this "higher stage of civilization." By reconstructing society according to principles of "Divine Law," they might attain the final objective of Christianity, the triumph of "Love over Lust." They were purifiers of American society.

Implicit in their new morality was a belief in the perfectibility of man. As long as religionists harbored traditional concepts of human nature, Americans would accept sin and evil as permanent and immutable, to be kept in check but not likely to be eradicated. Such a point of view severely inhibited social reform. The injection of perfectionist doctrine into antebellum reform represented an important step in the development of a dynamic ideology. William Lloyd Garrison, leader of the radical abolitionists, understood the pressing urgency of formulating dynamic social theories within the parameters of Christian morality. In 1841, Garrison published his "Declaration of Sentiments," a document imbued with the influence of John Humphrey Noyes' *Doctrine of Salvation From Sin* and articles in *The Perfectionist*.[30]

Nor was Garrison the only significant reform leader speculating on utopian themes and their importance to social reform. In 1841 Orestes Brownson in the *Boston Quarterly Review*, enquired into the causes of social evils and concluded that man should be perfected within society. Abandoning utopian communitarianism as he had experienced it as an Owenite, Brownson now contended that society would be perfected through the perfection of its individuals. Again, in 1841, Theodore Parker, a famed transcendentalist, underscored the importance of essential values in the "Transient and Permanent in Christianity." Boston reformers not only formulated an ideology of social reform but willingly threw themselves into the Brook Farm adventure under the leadership of George Ripley.[31]

These enthusiastic reformers did not await the formulation of social reform ideas. They were willing to act upon their sentiments, relying on the underlying values of Christianity and their own good intentions. As Joseph R. Gusfield has pointed out, by espousing temperance reforms (and, we may add, allied social and moral reforms), upper-class elements sharpened their feelings of difference from groups lower in society, buttressing a sense of status already, in point of fact, under change.[32] Reformers were

not passive onlookers, however. They wanted to move social change into more acceptable channels. Although
retreating from utopian communitarianism, they persistently held to a utopian vision of society founded upon a
new morality.

Reform had, in the ferment of the 1840s, entered into
a new phase of development. Reformers had enlisted in a
war against sin, conscious of their adversaries' obstinance
and expecting a long campaign. In preparation, they boldly
etched a reform design. Garrison, on the birth of a
grandson, contemplated with customary dry humor a
future of continuous moral conflict:

> Such a reinforcement for the Garrison is timely;
> and the adversary may take warning that there is
> to be warm work in the field of moral conflict in
> due time. For I trust the Newcomer will be
> spared to grow up in the spirit of reformers, and
> ready to do battle for unpopular right against
> unpopular wrong, and thus make the world all
> the better for their advent.[33]

Garrison envisioned a great reform machine for use in
righteous battle. Victory was not in sight and more troops,
militant Christians, were needed for the army. The great
abolitionist's unrealized dreams, however, were assumed
by the woman's movement. Feminists undertook the social
mission of transforming older institutions and constructing
new ones to humanize social life.

Women, guarding culture through the instruction of
children, had discovered in the redeemability of children
the potential salvation of the republic. Beginning in the
1830s, they had emphasized the importance of nurture for
social development. Indeed, Christian nurture, the internalization of desirable values, had promise as a tech-

nique of social perfectionism. Since aggregate character determined the national character, Christian nurture might lead to the Christianization of the nation. Through social character, they might control and determine the nature of society. Moreover, social character, cultivated through nonrational means, was a tribunal "from whose judgment there [was] virtually no appeal."[34]

Elizabeth Blackwell, pioneering medical and moral reformer, exemplified in her work the fusion of abolitionist and transcendentalist thought into the mainstream of the woman's movement. She advocated for women a "theology of action" to actualize their utopian vision. Artistically painting a picture of a readily attainable "Golden Age," she defined "the grand duty of life" as the releasing of the full potential in man's nature. She predicted the feasibility of sinlessness since man's evils were located in his heart and not in his flesh.[35]

As a venturesome conservative, Elizabeth Blackwell greatly influenced women physicians who came after her and the woman's movement that idolized her. Her formidable powers of mind exercised an influence quite independent of her charismatic qualities. In her activities, Blackwell carefully selected techniques to encourage social continuities. She rejected, for instance, a physiological explanation for the origins of sin—as she rejected materialistic science—but she also modified ascetic thinking. For her, the hardened body of the Spartan remained a worthy ideal. Her recruits, however, were for an army of reform, enlisted for social service. Like other women's leaders, Elizabeth Blackwell utilized familiar religious symbols and images to channel energies into reform activities.

Feminists of antebellum America were dedicated to the transvaluation of standards. They had accepted the purifying role of reconstructing American society ac-

cording to a model of greater equality. The woman's movement, with its quasi-religious characteristics, expressed this
objective in varying social forms that were apparently diffuse and inchoate but that, in actuality, shared common social functions and objectives. In their specific actions—sex
reform, antiprostitution activities, diet, and prison and
dress reforms—and in their newer views on child rearing,
they groped semiconsciously toward a purified society.[36]
Taken as a whole, these reforms constituted a new configuration of moral forces acting upon American society.

Lacking institutional channels through which to effect real social reform, women placed themselves in the service of reforms that might prove helpful to them in the long
run. Their involvement in popular health campaigns is a
case in point. A seemingly disinterested concern for public
health had latent social functions for the development
of the woman's movement. Through knowledge of physiology, women would be able to overcome misconcep-
tions and superstitions about the body that inihibited their
emancipation. By utilizing new child-rearing knowledge
women would be able to introduce new values into
American life on a grander scale. Furthermore, principles
of sound health, because they were dependent upon a temperance ideology, cut across denominational boundaries.
Popular medicine and religion met through shared values.
While medical science turned toward materialism, popular
health movements conserved traditional cultural values,
thus bridging the gap between religious ideals and a more
secularized world.

Dr. Sylvester Graham, water curist, diet reformer,
and inventor of the graham cracker, fused morality with
health in his popular health reforms. Dr. Graham broadcast
widely the popular thesis that health was a product of obedience to moral principle: "While we continually violate
the physiological laws of our nature, our systems will con-

tinue to be living volcanoes of bad feelings and bad passions, which however correct our abstract principles of morality may be, will continually break out in immoral actions."[37] Graham, like Defoe before him, emphasized the sexual metaphor, illustrating the intensity of religionists' feelings on sexual issues. Both voiced a typical ascetic fear of "passions and feelings." Drives were potentially dangerous, since they might lead to deviation from sanctioned moral norms. For Graham, the preservation of culture took precedence over the expression of physical drives. This was his sermon to America.

The gospel of moral physiology spread with astounding rapidity. By encouraging the formation of health societies in every American town, Graham reached the local community. Women, rallying to the banners of health and temperance reforms, proved the most ardent supporters of these societies. Later, they rallied with equal enthusiasm to the crusade against vice.

Elizabeth Blackwell also premised that health was a product of morality. Like Sylvester Graham, she preached that morality and physical fitness produced in man physical and moral perfection, but because she was less fanatical and more sophisticated than Graham, her secular language was more acceptable to the medical profession. She was able, therefore, to combat materialistic science and its denial of the moral aspect of health within the medical profession. As high priestess of a nascent social hygiene movement, Dr. Blackwell preached a religion of health.

Foremost woman physician of her time, Blackwell worked for a redefinition of women's reform roles. Within their homes, they had always been reformers, but Elizabeth Blackwell projected these traditional roles into general society. She encouraged women entering the medical profession, for instance, to become family physicians.[38] When writing about careers or roles in the home, Blackwell assigned two basic roles to women: first, through child rearing, to mold a free, independent individual; second, through reform activities, to remain alert to their responsibility for the preservation of the race.[39] She encouraged women to liberalize established institutions, while at the same time conserving their historical role as guardians of the home.

Dress reform was another objective possibly related to women's quest for social and physical health. Dress reform had, for the movement, moral, hygienic, and aesthetic aspects. The apparent eccentricities of reformers have obscured, unfortunately, their underlying motivations. Without a doubt, the bloomer costume appeared ludicrous to more conventional people, but its appearance started a movement for dress reform that affected the woman's movement throughout the century. It came to symbolize both the emancipation of women from fashion and a new achievement in rationality. Tight lacing, social critics charged, contributed to the decline of American morality by introducing French morality. Moreover, the corset represented "fashionable suicide" and bondage. Through dress reform, women protected puritan culture, rejected French morality, and created a more rational symbol for emancipated women. An immensely popular reform, women discovered in it a defense of American morality. In 1839, for example, the American Female Moral Reform Society denounced the love of fashion as disobedience to the laws of health and an obstacle to moral purity. Amelia Bloomer, anxious about such a decline in morality, publicized that message in *Lily*, a dress reform magazine written by women for women.[40] The impulse to standardize and rationalize dress contributed to a general reform aim: to channel social change within the limiting constraints of ascetic values.

In women's secular crusades to transform morality,

they invariably returned to child rearing as their most
popular and valuable technique. In a sense, they relied on
generational differences to realize their aims, for control
over the child permitted the inculcation of moral principles
to be carried into society and to transform it. Not only were
women able to form a new moral conscience, they could
prevent vicious behavior by imposing moral purity on children. They advocated, in short, both the creation of
morality and the repression of immoral impulses. As traditional guardians of the home, women now perceived their
roles in a new way. Their domestic role acquired greater
significance since they could transform character and thus
transform society.

Child rearing discussions were, moreover, an entering
wedge for expanding women's activities beyond the
household. The woman's movement had begun with an almost exclusive interest in child rearing and had gradually
expanded the range of its goals. This historical development merits a more detailed description.

Early in the nineteenth century, women formed
maternal associations, which, as auxiliaries to churches,
took up the task of investigating child rearing. Mrs. Edward Payson of Portland, Maine, formed such an association as early as 1815. Through prayers and responsible
work, these women dedicated themselves to rearing and
training children in the fear of God. Operating within
religious organizations, the associations had the limited object of preparing the child for admission into the church.

The reform proved popular. Mrs. Huntington, wife of
the Old South Church pastor, imitated Mrs. Payson's act,
and, almost simultaneously, the New York Maternal Association came into being. Other associations formed
rapidly—in the South and West as well as in the East. The
popularity of the enterprise now created organizational
problems only partially solved by the Reverend and Mrs.

Samuel Whittlesey of Utica, New York, when they, through the *Mother's Magazine*, coordinated the activities of the associations. The history of the associations was not one of unlimited success. Between 1845 and 1860, the movement declined in popularity, but it regained its vigor in 1860, with the formation of the Boston Union Maternal Association. By 1860, auxiliaries in the thousands were scattered over the nation.[41]

Originally, the maternal associations focused on more efficient techniques of child rearing but later the scope of their work expanded. Mrs. Charles G. Finney, wife of the famous evangelist, undertook a host of reform activities assumed by the movement. In response to her husband's sermons on the sacredness of motherhood, Mrs. Finney and other women met together in Mothers' Meetings. Under Mrs. Finney's direction the association moved, quite logically, to an interest in regeneration. Acting not only through maternal associations, Mrs. Finney, as directoress of the New York Female Reform Society, rescued "fallen women," and suppressed public licentiousness.

Female excursions into reform caused deep anxiety among traditionalists. The women's unbridled enthusiasm reawakened fears of antinomianism. Occasionally these fears were justified by actual events. As Mrs. Finney's female moral society retreated to more standard work in moral education, a splinter group renounced ascetic morality to follow John Humphrey Noyes into the Oneida community, one of the few instances of group marriage recorded in historical or ethnological literature. Two possible courses were open to modern man in escaping the limits imposed by ascetic religion: tabooed behavior could live an underground existence, or behavior previously condemned might be sanctified by a reformulation of religious doctrine. Oneida perfectionists had chosen the latter alternative. Traditionalists, however, encouraged repression.

On the surface, perfectionism seemed to be the theological error of the Oneida and Oberlin experiences. However, sexual discontents were a more fundamental cause of cultural deviations. As a result of the virulence of these discontents, upstate New York, "the burnt over district," became the spawning ground for polygamous Mormonism and the sexual associationism of the Oneida community. What followed in the wake of these changes was a tumultuous debate about sex, marriage, morals, and divorce in America. Oneida had become a symbol of free love and, hence, a threat to social organization. Whatever consensus had existed on sex ideas had been broken. Eventually liberalized divorce became the acceptable alternative to more fundamental changes in social structure, but not before a lengthy public examination of social institutions.

Within this fluid cultural situation the woman's movement advocated new morality and the purification of American society. Into this cultural milieu would be interjected a new interest in reglementation. The two movements, one for greater moral purity and the other for licensed prostitution were on a collision course. As was true of the temperance and prohibition movements after the Civil War, the moral purity movement would be reintroduced with greater urgency and deeper impact than had previously been the case. Reglementation went against the American moral grain. It substituted amorality for traditional morality, abandoned the prostitute, and, above all, stood in the path of the woman's movement's thrust toward emancipation.

NOTES

1. Emile Durkheim, "Moralité Sexuelle," *L'anée Sociologique* 7 (1904): 440; and August Bebel, *Woman in the Past, Present and Future*, trans. H. B. Adams Walther (London: William Reeves, n.d.), p. 32.

2. Benjamin Scott, *A State Iniquity: Its Rise, Extension and Overthrow* (London: Kegan Paul, Trench, Trübner & Co., Ltd., 1890), p. 4; and Benjamin Scott, *State Regulated Vice as it Existed Anciently in London* (London: Dyer Brothers, 1886), p. 8.

3. Vern L. Bullough, *The History of Prostitution* (New Hyde Park, N.Y.: University Books, 1964), pp. 115-16.

4. For a review of Christian thought on sex, see Bullough, *History of Prostitution*, pp. 127-30.

5. Philippe Ariès, *Centuries of Childhood: A Social History of Family Life* (New York: Alfred A. Knopf, 1962), p. 375.

6. Yves Guyot, *La Prostitution* (Paris: G. Charpentier, Editeur, 1882), pp. 42-3; and C. J. Lecour, *La Prostitution à Paris et à Londres* (Paris: P. Asselin, 1872), pp. 26-7.

7. For a general history of reglementation, see Bullough, *The History of Prostitution*, pp. 161-72; for a critique of prostitution as an economic institution, see Elizabeth Blackwell, *Purchase of Women: The Great Economic Blunder* (London: John Kensit, n.d.).

8. For a detailed analysis of this theme, see William G. McLoughlin, "Pietism and the American Character," *American Quarterly* 17 (1965): 163-86.

9. The Puritan case against Morton may be found in William Bradford, *Bradford's History of Plymouth Plantation*, ed. William T. Davis (New York: Charles Scribner's Sons, 1908).

10. Emil Oberholtzer, Jr., *Delinquent Saints: Disciplinary Action in the Early Congregational Churches*

of Massachusetts (New York: Columbia University Press, 1956).

11. Kai T. Erikson, *Wayward Puritans: A Study in the Sociology of Deviance* (New York: John Wiley and Sons, 1966), pp. 188-89; and David Herbert Lawrence, *Studies in Classic American Literature* (New York: Viking Press, 1964), pp. 13-31.

12. A reference to "worldly ascetics" immediately brings to mind Max Weber's contributions to the sociology of religion and the origins of capitalism. Although Weber may have incorrectly stated the relationship of religion to societal development, he still remains the starting point for much of the work in this field. While American historians have produced an abundant literature on Puritanism, they have tended to be overly dependent upon literature, sermons, and orations in defining what they mean by Puritan culture. If, on the other hand, they hope to deny the significance of Puritanism as a determining force in American history, they have relied upon actual behavior as a foil for cultural ideals. This is an unfortunate bifurcation, since there is an obvious connection between cultural ideals and actual behavior. By studying puritanical behavior over large spans of time, patterns of interrelationship are made clearer. For an analysis of the Puritan image through historical time that may demonstrate, perhaps unintentionally, the intersecting of mythical with historical thought, see James Robert Vitelli, "The Resurrection of the Puritan Image" (Ph.D. diss., University of Pennsylvania, 1955).

13. Daniel Defoe, *A Treatise Concerning the Use and Abuse of the Marriage Bed* (London: T. Warner, 1727), pp. 45-8. Almost two centuries later, Benjamin O. Flower, a latter-day Puritan, echoed Defoe's fears. Like Defoe, Flower worried over the marriage bed's being prostituted and, also like Defoe, he urged Christian temperance to prevent demoralization. Benjamin O. Flower, "Some Causes

of Present Day Immorality and Suggestions as to Practical
Remedies," *The National Purity Congress: Its Papers, Ad-
dresses and Portraits*, ed. Aaron M. Powell (New York:
Caulen Press, 1896), p. 306.

14. Carl Bridenbaugh, *Cities in Revolt* (New York:
Alfred A. Knopf, 1955), pp. 121-22, 317. The "upper
tenth," as colonial society matured, acquired the cultural
traits of an aristocracy. Attitudes toward prostitution were
to a degree symptomatic of social stratification.

15. Amicus Republicae, *Trade and Commerce In-
culcated, in a Discourse, Showing the Necessity of a Well-
Governed Trade, in Order to a Flourishing Common-
wealth*, in Stuart Bruchey, *The Colonial Merchant:
Sources and Readings* (New York: Harcourt, Brace and
World, 1966), p. 36.

16. For the reaction of Boston's clergy to urban
revivalism, see Edwin Gaustad, *The Great Awakening in
New England* (Gloucester, Mass.: Peter Smith, 1965), pp.
80-101.

17. *Third Annual Report of the Boston Society for the
Moral and Religious Instruction of the Poor* (n.p.: November 8, 18?), p. 3.

18. Timothy L. Smith, *Revivalism and Social Reform*
(New York, 1957); and Joseph R. Gusfield, *Symbolic
Crusade: Status Politics and the American Temperance
Movement* (Urbana: University of Illinois Press, 1963),
pp. 111-38. Elizabeth Blackwell urged women to rely on
moral indignation as they rejected established medical
theory. "Whatever revolts our moral sense as earnest
women is not in accordance with steady progress, it can not
be permanently true." Women would serve the medical profession by searching out what revolted their sense of right
and wrong. Elizabeth Blackwell, *The Influence of Women
in the Profession of Medicine* (London: George Bell &
Son, 1889), pp. 18-21.

19. Lewis Tappan, *The Life of Arthur Tappan* (New
York: Hurd and Houghton, 1871), pp. 112-19; Josiah W.
Leeds, "Arthur Tappan and the Cause of Social Purity,"

Christian Statesman, June 10, 1886, pp. 5-6; Robert Fletcher, *A History of Oberlin College*, 2 vols. (Oberlin, Ohio: Oberlin College, 1943); Bertram Wyatt-Brown, *Lewis Tappan and the Evangelical War Against Slavery* (Cleveland: The Press of Case Western Reserve University, 1969), pp. 65-66, 70; and Carroll Smith Rosenberg, "Beauty, the Beast and the Militant Woman: A Case Study in Sex Roles and Social Stress in Jacksonian America," *American Quarterly* 22 (1971): 562-84.

20. Fletcher, *A History of Oberlin College*, 1: 298.

21. Roger Lane, *Policing the City: Boston, 1822-1885* (Cambridge: Harvard University Press, 1967), pp. 64-5, 114-15, 138.

22. *Communication from the Metropolitan Board of Police and Board of Health in Answer to a Resolution in Relation to Prostitution in the City of New York, February 9, 1867* (Albany: Van Benthuysen Sons, Legal Printers, 1867); and "the Social Evil and Its Remedy," *Nation*, February 21, 1867, p. 153.

23. "Letter to the Editor," *Nation*, March 14, 1867, p. 220.

24. For studies showing changes in preventive medicine, see Charles Rosenberg, *The Cholera Years: The United States in 1832, 1849, and 1866* (Chicago: University of Chicago Press, 1962); and Richard Shryock, *The Development of Modern Medicine; An Interpretation of the Social and Scientific Factors Involved* (Philadelphia: University of Pennsylvania Press, 1936).

25. Untitled article, *Buffalo Medical Journal*, April 1856, p. 680, Library of Congress, Toner Collection.

26. *Directory to the Seraglios in New York, Philadelphia, Boston, and all Principal Cities in the Union*, edited and compiled by a free Loveyer (New York: n.p., 1859).

27. Ida Hasted Harper, *The Life and Work of Susan B. Anthony* (Indianapolis: Hollenbeck Press, 1898), p. 1012; and William Sanger, *The History of Prostitution* (New York: Harper and Brothers, 1858), pp. 452, 456, 575, 670.

28. Frederick Howard Wines, "Social Evils and Their Causes," *The Charities Review* 6 (May 1897): 193, 196-7.

29. "Sexual Reformation," *Alpha*, July 1, 1879, p. 10; and "Editorial," *Family Culture* 1 (May 1896): 10.

30. Walter M. Merrill, *Wind Against Tide: A Biography of William Lloyd Garrison* (Cambridge: Harvard University Press, 1963), p. 181.

31. "Social Evils and Their Remedy," *Boston Quarterly Review* 4 (July 1841): 277; Henry Steele Commager, *Theodore Parker* (Boston: Little, Brown & Company, 1936), p. 74; and Katherine Burton, *Paradise Planters: The Story of Brook Farm* (London: Longmans, Green and Co., 1939), p. 40.

32. Gusfield, *Symbolic Crusade*, pp. 29, 111-38.

33. Garrison to Samuel J. May, Jr., June 15, 1875, Samuel J. May Papers, Boston Public Library.

34. Elizabeth Blackwell, *Medicine as a Profession for Women* (New York: New York Infirmary for Women, 1860), p. 5.

35. Elizabeth Blackwell, *The Laws of Life* (New York: S. P. Putnam, 1852), pp. 14, 18-19, 28.

36. Women's rights leaders performed an important role as a modernizing elite. In the process of secularization they upheld commonly shared values and orientations that were critical for the development of a mass-consensual society. They were contributing to the formation of new cultural and social symbols that served as a social bond in the emergence of modern America.

37. *The Graham Journal of Health and Longevity* 2 (July 7, 1838): 212, 221.

38. Blackwell, *Medicine as a Profession for Women*, p. 16.

39. Elizabeth Blackwell, *The Human Element in Sex: Being a Medical Enquiry into the Relation of Sexual Physiology and Christian Morality*, 2nd ed. (London: J. and A. Churchill, 1884), p. 18.

40. "Women the Hope of our Cause," *The Graham Journal of Health and Longevity* 3 (November 9, 1839): 369; and Paul Fatout, "Amelia Bloomer and Bloomerism," *New York Historical Quarterly* 36 (1952): 362-3.

41. Mary Louise Butler, "Early History of Maternal Associations," *The Chatauquan* 31 (May 1900): 138-42.

2

Repulsing the Regulationists

WOMEN'S ASSUMPTION OF A LEADERSHIP ROLE

Women had been the principal combatants against
prostitution and continued their opposition after the Civil
War. Freed to undertake new reforms after the war, radical
feminists reintroduced the idea of women's suffrage as a
serious proposition. Ignoring conservative objections,
Susan B. Anthony, Elizabeth Cady Stanton, and the ec-
centric Francis Train interjected "votes for women" into
the Kansas campaign for the ratification of the Fifteenth
Amendment. These suffragists devoted their energies
primarily to politics but did participate in other reforms. In
fact, new abolitionists praised them, crediting them with
the introduction of social purity interest into moral reform.
This interest originated from other sources as well. Julia
Ward Howe, a moderate reformer, considered social purity
of paramount importance to reform. She read an address
on the subject before the American Association for the Advancement of Women shortly after the war. As president of
the newly constituted organization, Howe informed her au-

dience of the overwhelming significance of social purity reform for the future of the woman's movement.[1]

It was Susan B. Anthony, however, who took to the lecture circuit to alert the public to the dangers of legalized prostitution. Learning of New York police support for an 1867 regulation bill, she confronted Judge Charles J. Folger, the bill's author. Folger tried devaluing her criticisms, and, in keeping with his belief that discussion of the social evil was not permissible for women, wanted to deny Miss Anthony the right to speak on the topic. Undaunted, Miss Anthony warned Folger she would carry the issue to the women of the state if he persisted in his support of reglementation. The bill was not presented to the state legislature.

In December 1871, regulationists introduced another scheme, the Holland Social Evil Bill. Again, Susan B. Anthony prevented passage. Public opinion, she discovered, was a tremendous force in changing the minds of legislators. Convening a public women's meeting, she read the bill, section by section, editorializing as she read. Public morality was on her side, although the public press doubted the propriety of women participating in public discussions of the evil. Despite such journalistic reservations, she successfully defeated the Holland Social Evil Bill.

Dissatisfied with being on the defensive, Miss Anthony took the initiative from the regulationists. Although apprehensive about public presentations on social purity, she overcame her inhibitions to deliver a speech at the Chicago Grand Opera House on March 14, 1872. She was well received. Bronson Alcott, Parker Pillsbury, and A. J. Grover, luminaries of abolitionism, came forward to congratulate her. Encouraged and no longer fearful, Miss Anthony toured Wisconsin, Illinois, Iowa, Kansas, and Missouri, addressing capacity crowds. Her press was not always favorable. Rural editors, firmly convinced of the ef-

ficacy of silence as the best way of preserving moral purity,
contended Anthony encouraged licentiousness. The urban
press, however, was more realistic about conditions in the
city and supported her.

Anthony's campaign was timely, for a profusion of
social evil bills recommending reglementation were being
introduced into state legislatures. In New York alone,
reformers defeated regulation bills in 1868, 1871 (the
legislature approved the bill but the governor vetoed it),
and 1875 (a special legislative committee recommended a
system of license). The most shocking proposal, from the
perspective of purity reform, came in 1877, when the Committee of Public Charities and Corrections of New York
City, a body of reformers, recommended regulation. Antiregulationists wondered what fellow reformers saw in the
illusionary benefits of regulation.

THE POLARIZATION OF THOUGHT AND ACTION

ST. LOUIS

American moralists, shocked by the social evil bills, were
stunned by developments in St. Louis, the infamous
"Whiskey Ring" headquarters in the Gilded Age. The St.
Louis City Council had, in 1870, legislated regulated
prostitution by using a loophole in a state law. In one major American city, regulation was no longer an abstraction
or a figment of the reformer's imagination.

St. Louis regulationists were doubtlessly influenced
by European experiments. For years, European cities had
established municipally regulated prostitution districts under police control and medical supervision. Paris, Berlin,
and Stockholm used the system. Spanish, Bavarian, and
Austrian cities had experimented with it.[2] Physicians

traveling abroad came in contact with regulation; medical literature from abroad praised the plan; and European medical experts diffused information on the subject as they traveled in this country. Moreover, St. Louis, which had a large German-American population, had a strong anti-temperance tradition.

The system had local variations but Paris served as a model. (Later in the century Berlin, rather than Paris, became the model reglementarian city.) Regulationists cited Paris for its efficiency. Le Bureau des Moeurs, under the Prefect of Police, M. Lecour, administered a department of police and physicians who, in turn, supervised Parisian prostitutes. Upon inspection, the police issued weekly health certificates. The prostitute could not work without a license. If a prostitute was diseased, physicians committed her to La Maison de St. Lazare, a combined house of detention and correction and a hospital and infirmary.

Reglementation was not easily accepted in the United States. In responding to criticisms, St. Louis regulationists claimed first, that the government had no policy without reglementation and second, that St. Louis had a de facto licensing system even before legislation. Arguing for medical and police control of prostitutes, they contrasted regulation in European cities with nonregulation in London. The lack of policy in London, according to St. Louis regulationists, was the major source of uncontrolled crime and disease.[3]

In the course of the St. Louis debate, two purity leaders provided leadership for the antiregulationists. Coming from different antebellum reform movements, they represented the two major intellectual sources of opposition. William Greenleaf Eliot, pastor of the Church of the Messiah (St. Louis) and formerly the editor of the *Western Messenger*, a leading western transcendental journal, had demonstrated unflagging interest in temperance and purity work. Clinton Fisk, a former abolitionist active in the Freedman's Bureau, allied himself closely to Eliot. He, too, was a temperance reformer.[4] The appearance of two leaders—one an abolitionist, the other a transcendentalist, but both temperance men—reflected the antebellum antecedents of purity reform.

Religionists and women rallied to support Eliot's and Fisk's opposition to the St. Louis law, awakening politicians to the significance of the issue. Politicians quickly responded to the public outcry of indignation. A joint session of the Missouri legislature assembled to review the St. Louis "iniquity." Lieutenant Governor Charles P. Johnson, in an extraordinary address, brimming with invective, condemned the St. Louis Social Evil Law, admonished the St. Louis politicians who had enacted it, and urged the legislature to correct the error.[5] After four years of legalized prostitution, the Constitutional Convention, meeting shortly after the uproar, removed the right of St. Louis to act on regulation without state approval. Antiregulationists had turned what seemed to be defeat into victory; they had argued for the uniqueness of American morals, contending that the regulationists' "Parisian morals" went against the American cultural grain. Apparently many supported their views, for public opinion was decisive in St. Louis and Missouri in turning the tide in the antiregulationists' favor.[6]

St. Louis regulationists refused to accept defeat. They were as sincere in their beliefs as the antiregulationists were in theirs. Considering their clash with Eliot and Fisk only a temporary reversal, the regulationist exerted pressure on the state legislature for another social evil law. When Eliot heard of their plans, he took immediate action. Learning that Police Commissioner Lewis Dorsheimer planned to introduce a new bill in the Assembly, Eliot

turned again to public disclosure as a technique for constraining regulationists and initiated a newspaper debate.
When faced with public allegations, the police commissioner denied involvement.[7] Perhaps Eliot was wrong in
fixing responsibility on Dorsheimer, but, despite protesta-
tions and denials, the St. Louis Grand Jury, in June 1877,
did recommend regulation.

Strictly defined, Eliot and Fisk were antiregulationists. They were neither new abolitionists nor purity
reformers. As antiregulationists, they wanted only the
restoration of traditional morality. In the course of debate,
however, perceptible attitudinal changes came about—
they moved toward an abolitionist policy.

Since regulationists argued for their program on social hygiene grounds, Eliot, in order to offset sanitarian
claims, formulated a positive program of medical control.
He intended, through the implementation of his plan, to
check the social evil. As he reexamined the problem, Eliot
returned to earlier reform ideas. Like the Reverend
McDowall before him, Eliot assumed the rescue of "fallen
women" could be accomplished through regeneration;
thus, he advocated converting the Social Evil Hospital and
House of Industry into a home for "fallen women."[8]
Eliot planned a revival campaign to reform prostitutes.
Revivalism in the late nineteenth century, however, was
most unrealistic; the theological language of regeneration
seemed increasingly inconsonant with a secular society.
(In one instance, prostitutes and their clients jeered an
evangelical minister preaching in the streets.)

As an antiregulationist leader, Eliot gained a national
reputation for his reform activity and his social theory. As
purity reform became a movement, the St. Louis battle
became legendary. Reformers relièd upon Eliot's pamphlets as skirmishes with regulationists proliferated. Purity
reformers quoted him, circularized his pamphlets to the

public, and judiciously distributed them among public administrators and politicians. Eliot lent ministerial authority
to his pamphlets, but he did not have the scientific
authority of public health physicians. Antiregulationists
were vulnerable on this score.

Antiregulationists did, however, have supporters in
the medical professions. Edmund Andrews, author of
"Prostitution and its Sanitary Management," came close,
in his writings, to an abolitionist policy. Andrews recommended that police compile secret lists of prostitutes but
not have the right to enforce registration of prostitutes. Andrews, despairing of man's basic licentiousness, thought
prostitution had to be tolerated but without giving official
sanction to the institution.[9] Although not reflecting an
abolitionist point of view, Andrews' pamphlet served as a
tactical weapon against regulationists.

Antiregulationists had no clear social policies on
prostitution through the 1860s and into the 1870s. They
did evolve positions and programs, however. In Europe
and the United States a lively public debate raged between
regulationists and abolitionists. Arguments varied with
time and place, but the salient points in the following summary generally expressed the viewpoint of each side.

Regulationists advanced their plan of medical control
with the general claim that it contributed to the preservation of public health. Although regulationists, in the abstract, anticipated an end to prostitution and brothels,
they urged "realism" in managing the present problem.
According to their view of physiology, sexual intercourse
was necessary for mental and physical health. Given man's
nature and the laws of health, therefore, prostitution was
a social requisite. Cesare Lombroso, the famed criminologist, even contended that it diminished the crime rate.[10]
Regulation, entailing police and medical supervision, was

in the best interests of society and the prostitute, giving protection to both.

The abolitionists rejoined: prostitution was not a social requisite, since chastity and health were consonant. There was no physiological need for sexual intercourse. Furthermore, since policy involved social and moral considerations as well, the matter was not purely "scientific." Consider, they pleaded, the plight of the fallen woman. She deserved redemption and regeneration, not a pariah status to satisfy the animal propensities of man. Finally, the new abolitionists countered the regulationists on sanitary grounds, claiming that regulation actually increased disease rather than diminished it, because issuance of health certificates lulled youths into a false security detrimental to their own and society's well-being. Instead of sanctioning sin and evil, the community's moral force should oppose prostitution.

CHICAGO

The ideological clashes between abolitionists and reglementationists were repeated in city after city. The enactment of regulation in St. Louis encouraged the reglementationists in other cities to put forward their plans. In Chicago, a coalition of women and ministers defeated an 1870 effort to legislate municipal regulation. Dissatisfied with merely holding the line against reglementation, Chicago antiregulationists challenged both regulationists and traditional reformers. Antiregulationists organized a Society for the Promotion of Social Purity. The first of its type, it promised, in name at least, to go beyond defense. Although a significant institutional innovation, the organization failed to fulfill its promise. The society defined a positive reform of social purity, but it moved only haltingly and in-

completely in the direction of preventive reform. Nevertheless, the Chicago Society for the Promotion of Social
Purity was a significant precursor of future organizational
innovations coming from antiregulationist agitation.

Led by a Unitarian minister, the Reverend Robert
Collier, the society inquired into the social functions of
purity reform. No longer concerned only with the preservation of social equilibrium by controlling prostitution, the
society infused its objectives with millenial aspirations. Social purity was an instrument to elevate youth to a new
moral level through the suppression of "habits of sensuality."[11] Although the society devised no plan for social transformation, it called for a "Holy War," in which
every social agency would be used to raise a race of men
and women who dared to be Christians.[12] Unlike earlier
transcendentalists, who, to legitimize their views, had appealed to higher law, these reformers were more realistic.
They wanted to actualize moral law by internalizing it.
Thus, they envisioned an organic society and an organic
law. In the process of defeating prostitution, they were
changing the social functions of moral law.[13]

Fragmentary evidence makes it impossible to trace
the organizational development of the Social Purity Society. Either the organization changed completely, with
new leadership, or another Social Purity Society also existed. It is safe to conclude, however, that the Chicago
agitation was popular, since the antiregulationists collected
thousands of signatures on their petitions. The Chicago incident also produced Elizabeth Gay as a future leader of
purity reform. Elizabeth Gay, Sidney Howard Gay's wife
and a noted reformer in her own right, participated in antiregulationist activities in 1870-1871 and 1873-1874. She
later moved to Staten Island and resumed activity in the
movement as secretary to the National Purity Alliance in
1895. Her career in purity reform began in 1876. In 1906

she was still a member of the National Purity Alliance Executive Board.

WASHINGTON AND PHILADELPHIA

When, in 1871, reglementationists lobbied for an act in Washington, D.C., former antislavery crusaders were especially dismayed. The District of Columbia had symbolic importance for them, for they feared that, just as the abolition of slavery in the District of Columbia had established a national example, the enactment of reglementation in the District would act as a false symbol for other states and municipalities. The District House of Delegates shared the antiregulationists' view and met in special session when it considered the bill.[14]

An aroused womanhood, uncertain of the delegates' political judgment, strived to make its opposition indelibly clear. Calling a mass meeting in Lincoln Hall for September 22, 1871, women's club members publicized their vehement objections. They shocked Washington's newsmen, to whom public discussion of prostitution seemed unthinkable. Only the *Morning Chronicle* reported the meeting.

Women speakers at the mass meeting rejected the idea that prostitution was attributable to the individual moral lapses of women. Rather, they blamed the double standard of morality and asserted that only the elimination of the double standard could make the eradication of prostitution possible. As women reformers, they committed themselves to raising men to a level of greater purity. As in Chicago, "race regeneration" emerged as the dominant theme.[15] It remained a recurring theme in women's rights literature.

Both Washington and · Chicago antiregulationists started with a belief in the perfectibility of man. Although both groups devoted themselves to the antiregulationist cause, they failed, utopian rhetoric notwithstanding, to advance programmatically beyond the immediate situation. Washington antiregulationists encouraged the study of physiology, the practice of early marriage, and the liberalization of marriage and divorce laws. One sage went as far as to commend compulsory marriage to replace imprisonment for certain sex offenses.[16]

Regulationists had the political initiative, however, and pushed their organized drive for legislation despite reform counteractivity. In Pennsylvania, Dr. A. L. Cressler presented a bill to the 1874 legislature that basically recapitulated earlier plans. In making his case, Cressler explained the causes of prostitution as a consequence of individual choice.[17] For him, prostitution was an economic institution, involving reciprocal exchange, and, as such, not fundamentally a moral issue.

As in every situation of this type, moralists came forward to voice their opinions, but Pennsylvania antiregulationists differed from those in other localities. The Moral Education Society of Philadelphia, an organization of women physicians and women's rights leaders with a primary interest in child-rearing theories, led the antiregulationist forces. Among the moral educationists were Dr. Harriet French, Mr. and Mrs. Enoch Lewis, and a Doctor-Morton. Unlike members of antiregulationist societies, these highly educated individuals were independent of direct clerical influence and control. Liberated from religious doctrine and dogma, they nevertheless retained ideas of "essential" Christianity. Accordingly, they experimented with social techniques intended to actualize Christianity. As in the case of other moral educationists before them, the Philadelphians moved quite easily from one reform to the other; therefore, it was natural to turn from child rearing to antiregulation.

Pennsylvania's moral educationists also differed from

other societies in their political style. They did not call mass meetings but quietly turned to lobbying techniques. When Dr. Harriet French, president of the Moral Education Society, discovered the regulation bill when reading an account of legislative business, she committed the organization to action without hesitation. The society's first act was to republish Eliot's pamphlets and mail copies to every Pennsylvania legislator.

Regulationists also relied upon lobbying activities. Dr. Samuel Gross, a leading regulationist, supported the Pennsylvania bill. As a physician of national reputation, he had an advantage over the Moral Education Society. In order to offset Gross's national reputation, French collected the signatures of fifty-three physicians on a petition against regulation. Lacking mass support, the Moral Education Society determined to create an illusion of state-wide advocacy for their viewpoint, and they urged sympathizers throughout the state to petition the legislature. The society defeated the bill.

Moral educationists did not withdraw from antiregulation agitation after that momentary victory. Given an opportunity, two years later, to change medical opinion on the subject, French campaigned to win the medical profession to abolitionism. As the 1876 centennial drew near, and plans for an international medical congress at the centennial were discussed, the Moral Education Society prepared a pamphlet, "Forewarned, Forearmed," as an antidote to any regulationist literature distributed to delegates. Looking back on the congress, moral educationists believed their pamphlet prevented the issue from being deliberated on the convention floor.

Philadelphians also sounded an alarm heard outside their state. Moral educationists alerted their sisters in Boston and New York to the reglementationist danger. Boston antiregulationists, more than eager to act, were de-

nied their opportunity. No bill materialized. A New York
Women's Social Educational Society, however, received
deserved credit for its 1876 defeat of regulation.[18]

In the late 1860s and early 1870s many states and
municipalities considered legalizing prostitution. Where
women were well organized or had ready access to politicians, they repulsed the reglementationists easily. The
Holland Bill received widespread attention in San Francisco and throughout California. Newspapers gave their
endorsement, but women's groups remained adamant in
their rejection of legalizing vice. The California Women's
Suffrage Club not only argued that the bill was an ineffective device to control disease but also urged legislators
to devise a better method for the "purification of our
social system."[19] Other cities and states—Washington,
Chicago, Baltimore, Cincinnati, Pittsburgh, San Francisco,
St. Louis, New York, and Pennsylvania—repulsed the
reglementationists, some more than once. The national
debate over regulation extended over a number of decades.
Reglementation was not easy to defeat. Its advocates persisted in advancing their cause.

THE IDEOLOGICAL TRANSFORMATION TO SOCIAL PURITY

The frequency of ideological exchanges over reglementation led many reformers into an expanded interest in social
purity. Although antiregulationists fell back upon antebellum precedents for the management of prostitution—revivalism and a policy of regeneration—they were
dissatisfied with the results. Moreover, reglementation
policies proved more virulent than reformers had expected.
Because the exchanges were protracted over a number of

years, antiregulationists were able to accommodate themselves to the development of preventive medicine and evolve new policies that moved them from antiregulation to new abolitionism. In the process of ideological transformation the antiregulationists located their best allies within the woman's movement.

Feminist leaders clearly understood the significance of social purity concepts. The attainment of social purity and the eradication of prostitution became consuming interests, which diverted women from other reforms and profoundly influenced their social ideas. The process of transformation was one dominated by specific events that elicited specific responses. Women's involvement in antiregulation campaigns was direct and immediate. Their reaction to regulationist ideas was so immediate and emotional as to be almost an involuntary cultural response as well as a politically motivated one. In the process of active participation, purity reform, at first lacking clear contours, rapidly took shape, with the woman's and purity movements converging ideologically in a common drive for social transformation. Lacking a well-defined program, antiregulationists instinctively perceived prostitution as an aspect of social impurity. Prostitution, as an issue, was subsumed by the larger concern for social purification, and the feminist leadership willingly participated in its suppression. Without comprehending the full meaning of social purification, reformers rejected prostitution as antithetical to their cultural values. Thus the emergence of the social purity movement was highly pragmatic, being molded by the force of events and emotions. The reformers had no chart to consult and no compass to guide them in their journey toward a moral society. While they had cultural consensus on women's opposition to legalized prostitution, purity reformers were uncertain of their direction as the reform

developed. Their only certain guide was their cultural
ideal. The symbol of social purity, a reminder of their
Puritan heritage, was their north star.

Women also agreed on the long-range importance of
child rearing to the reform. Hoping to eradicate prostitution by eliminating the moral double standard, women saw
in proper child rearing the most effective technique for
reaching this object. Like earlier education societies, women
reformers had only a vague notion of how to proceed with
child rearing reforms, but their broad appeal offset other
limitations. Feminists found it relatively easy to mobilize
women under the new standard and define specifics as
needed. The social purity movement's very open-endedness
and grand utopian attributes allowed it the latitude to
develop and refine theories of child rearing. As a master
symbol of social purification, it proved highly adequate for
the redefinition of concepts of child rearing and women's
social roles as well.

As in the case of antebellum purity reforms, the new
antiregulation movement was decentralized and localistic.
As such, it acted in response to immediate and limited problems. This indigenous American social purity movement
(a similar movement came into being in England), ac-
tivated in its first phase through antiregulation activity,
lacked the national leadership to provide coordination and
lend authority. English events at this time gave focus to the
American movement, giving it perspective as it became
related to European movements and developments. In this
way the antiregulation movement became the new abolitionism and in the process renewed contacts with the International Abolitionist Federation. As an indigenous
movement in the decade after the Civil War, the antiregulationist impulse contained the potential for becoming both a social purity movement and the new abolitionism. Although the three reform movements, antiregula-

tionism, new abolitionism and social purity, remained identifiable after their merger into a single movement, over time the purity movement gained more importance; antiregulationism gave way to new abolitionism; and, in turn, the social purity movement subsumed new abolitionism.

The catalyst causing the first shift in emphasis came from England. Josephine Butler had engaged in antiregulationist activities in England and on the Continent almost a decade before such activity began in the United States. Anglo-American reform communications were close, and American reformers received her pamphlets—such as "The Constitution Violated"—enthusiastically. According to Butler, the Contagious Diseases Act (an English variant of reglementation) would deprive women of their basic civil liberties and constitutional rights. In practice, she contended, accused women denied trial by jury might be forced into prostitution through the arbitrary decision of a justice of the peace. William Greenleaf Eliot of St. Louis had read this pamphlet during his ideological exchanges and had submitted a copy to the court to lend weight to his argument against the authority of the city to implement regulation.

Josephine Butler had been on the Continent in 1869 to win the ballot for women and improve their educational opportunities. At that time a prominent European feminist warned Butler that legalized prostitution was a special obstacle Continental women had to overturn. On her return to England, Butler learned the Contagious Diseases Acts had been passed and English women might share that obstacle. Medical and military men, influenced by practices on the Continent, had introduced the dreaded system into England. Between 1864 and 1869, Parliament passed, with minimal publicity, a series of contagious diseases acts. The Admiralty championed the Act of 1864, the Contagious

Diseases (Animal) Act. To the abolitionists, however, the act had little to do with animals and much to do with introducing regulation into England. The act, drafted for the protection of military personnel, divided England into fourteen military districts for the administration of reglementation.[20]

An aroused womanhood, commanded by Harriet Martineau, Florence Nightingale, and Josephine Butler, was not acquiescent. Butler brought the fight directly to Parliament, carrying the "Woman's Protest" of 1870, a manifesto signed by two thousand prominent English women. The unleashed zeal of a wronged womanhood was uncontainable. After repulsing reglementation in England, Butler and her sympathizers invaded Continental regulationist strongholds.

In March 1875, Butler contributed to the formation of the British, Continental, and General Federation for the Abolition of State Regulated Prostitution. The delegates elected James Stanfield president, Henry J. Wilson, honorable treasurer, and Butler, honorable secretary. At that moment, new abolitionism was born. European in origin, its major arena was on the Continent where new abolitionism contended with Continental regulationists for supremacy over social policies on prostitution. Compared with Continental regulation, St. Louis deviations and American struggles were pale shadows of the major ideological contests. Within a short time the comparison would be reversed, for, unlike the antiregulationist movement, the social purity movement in American was much fiercer in the pursuit of its goals than its European counterpart.

THE CONTRIBUTION OF OLD ABOLITIONISM

English reformers heard of the work of American antiregulationists. Hoping to mobilize supporters for the American cause, the International Abolitionist Federation selected Henry Wilson and the Reverend J. P. Gledstone for a mission to the United States. The two men were well supplied with detailed lists of supporters from the antislavery cause and the new cause as well. The 1876 mission was timely, for American abolitionists had lost the unity and drive gained in the antislavery crusade. Debates over the future of abolitionism in the United States revealed a strong interest in sustaining reform activity, although division over which reforms to take up. A group of old abolitionists moved into a campaign to repulse the new moral contagion. They were ready recruits, and Wilson and Gledstone were eager recruiters. In their short visit to the United States the Gledstone-Wilson mission enlisted many antislavery enthusiasts into a crusade against white slavery.

The old abolitionists, prepared intellectually by reports from England, were predisposed to favor the new movement. Former leaders of the antislavery cause did much to legitimize it. William Lloyd Garrison with his confidante and close supporter, Samuel J. May, had lent his name to petitions supporting new abolitionists in England. Garrison immediately recognized in the new reform "the old ring of uncompromising warfare against sin."[21] Aaron Macy Powell, an editor of the *Anti-Slavery Standard*, also aware of new abolitionism, was a faithful subscriber to the *Sentinel*, the British social purity journal.[22] He readily supported the English mission. In later years, as Josephine Butler reviewed the achievements of Gledstone and Wilson during their visit, she expressed

amazement at the magnetic attraction new abolitionism
had for former antislavery crusaders.[23]

Mrs. Butler's observation was sound; former abolitionists did indeed rally to the new standard. Abby Hopper
Gibbons and Aaron Macy Powell, both of New York, had
been abolitionists, as had Elizabeth Gay.[24] Louisa May
Alcott, noted novelist and daughter of Bronson Alcott,
pledged her support, as did Abby K. Foster. Charlotte Joy
Mann, Rebecca Collins, John Greenleaf Whittier, and
Mrs. Ralph Waldo Emerson, the abolitionist old guard,
responded heartily to the new call.[25] The abolitionist imprint was brilliantly indelible. In fact, a survey of 106
purity leaders prominent in 1895 yields thirty-five
leaders over the age of fifty-five, which indicates that they
could also have been active in the antislavery crusade. Of
that number, twenty-eight had been members of the antislavery party, three probably had been members, and
four probably had not.[26]

Abby Hopper Gibbons and Aaron Macy Powell
belonged to the Garrisonian faction interested in new
reforms. In making the transition to new abolitionism, they
deliberately used antislavery symbols to attract a following
and divert former colleagues into antiregulation activity.[27] Both Mrs. Gibbons and Powell understood the
potential in abolitionism for the reconstruction of
American society. For them, new abolitionism provided
new cohesion for a disintegrating movement.

Abolitionists were not the only ones utilizing antiregulation for larger purposes. Feminists interested in
moral education also recognized its value as a political
force in a struggle for "right generation." *Alpha*, the national journal of the Moral Education Societies, also applauded the Gledstone-Wilson mission and, independently
of Gibbons and Powell, called "old antislavery veterans"
into the agitation.[28] An abolitionist psychology per-

vaded these separate groups of antiregulationists. The abolitionists' perception of a larger social goal was an underlying source of unity, as was their need for a common goal. New abolitionism, therefore, was not merely a new political tactic. New abolitionists understood their moral basis for political action and probably appealed to a social type who urgently needed action to maintain his identity—the essential religionist committed to the Christianization of society. Elizabeth B. Chace had just such a character. At the age of eighty-five, she groped toward a larger understanding of the abolitionist crusade: "It is too late to become an Abolitionist now. But in the process of overthrowing one great wrong, there is always laid bare some other great wrong, which requires the same self-sacrificing spirit."[29] Mrs. Chace, despite her advanced years, was a purity worker.

Both abolitionists and new abolitionists sought a perfect moral system. They agreed that morality, eternal and unchanging, could be, and had to be, manifested through conduct in society. This was, in fact, the measure of perfectionism. They wanted from people a characterological response, an instinctively moral behavior measured against eternal principles. Intellectual imperatives for behavior were less critical than characterological imperatives.[30] This ideal type, this "same self-sacrificing spirit," was common to old and new abolitionists. The moral perfectionist, when challenged, slid into the "old anti-slavery method of *instantly renewing the warfare*. . . ."[31] He permitted no compromise, for in compromising one was touched with "pitch, smirched by the half and half way."[32] On a group level, character resistance was a force for social change, the "dynamic of human progress."[33] The struggle against vice, the abolitionists hoped, would be its own reward. They hoped it would be not merely a duty but a pleasure. They attributed to social character the "whole of life; its purpose,

its objects, its intentions, its methods, its results, its enjoy-
ments, its happiness, its usefulness."[34] Their understanding of morality even pervaded their view of history, making
of it a "cumulative character of moral force," an accretion,
that is, of moral capital, invested in public opinions,
memories, books, and institutions to cement the social
bond.[35]

In searching for "perfect purity," reformers feared
"casual metamorphosis"; they desired, rather, change that
reflected the unfolding of their principles, assuming new
forms but conserving essential values. In achieving social
perfection, holiness too would be attained. The two were,
for them, synonymous.[36] The past gave unity to the
historical process. It composed its essential nature. Change
meant vital expansion and growth; the replacement of ar-
chaic social forms with newer ones; an evolution of concrete forms that did not violate that essential past. New
abolitionists saw in character the locus of a new social
religion and the dynamic for social change. For them, the
plan of Providence was to develop character; its method
was to mold it by the subtle influence of social conditions.[37] As a social religion of daily life, it was a vehicle to
hasten the millenium and to assist in the growth of
humanity. Above all, social character led to ultimate salvation through action.

As former abolitionists and moral educationists explored this new dynamic of social character, they soaringly
anticipated a new civilization. They placed their hope in
the child, the potential redeemer of the republic, believing
that he could be taught the proper "relations of life and its
holiest sanctities in the light of health, of growth, of
usefulness, of character, so that the thought of vice shall
become instinctively repellant and abhorrent."[38] These
emotions constituted character resistance. Through
character the child could overcome temptations; through

character a new ideal of physiology might be realized; but most importantly, through character, youth would pass the ultimate test in its ability to resist the brothel's temptations. Character, an internalized morality, was a new pillar for society, invisible but invincible.

New abolitionists also appropriated the abolitionist reform style. They borrowed it in order to perpetuate an historical legacy. When the New York Committee for the Abolition of Regulated Vice closed its parlor meetings, members often sang "Battle Hymn of the Republic." The new abolitionists, increasingly popular in the 1880s, experimented with techniques for arousing mass support. Continuing their effort to abolish slavery, new abolitionists now crusaded against white slavery, thus emphasizing continuity with old abolitionism. To them any trade in bodies was slavery.

William Lloyd Garrison and Wendell Phillips were held up as culture heroes meriting emulation by the young. The hero, by abolitionist definition, was capable of sustaining precious principle under stress.[39] Character, molded under adversity, prepared the reformer for social sainthood. Heroism, as a consequence, was no sudden or spontaneous act, but a result of careful preparation. Attention to small detail, even drudgery, was a blessing, for it forged character and produced the Garrisons, Phillips, and Whittiers of the movement.[40]

During their visit, Gledstone and Wilson understood the importance of abolitionist psychology and believed their cause needed a symbolic act, a "laying on of hands," to attain legitimacy. The British abolitionists appealed to Garrison, the titular head of the old guard, to perform this ritual. He complied, officiating at a public meeting called to welcome the British delegates to Boston. Later, in a pamphlet, he opposed the licensing of sin, for ". . . if one sin can be licensed, why not another?"[41]

The landing of the delegation in New York City was most opportune, for Abby Hopper Gibbons and Aaron Macy Powell were actively engaged in an antiregulationist newspaper campaign. They had directed public attention to the issue, and, under these circumstances, Gibbons and Powell were inestimably valuable to the Englishmen. The mission, in turn, proved equally valuable for the New Yorkers, enabling them to organize the New York Committee for the Suppression of Legalized Vice, an informal, voluntary, and provisional committee.

The New Yorkers, continuing to assist the delegates, accompanied them on tour, making appropriate introductions along the way. Every city had a reform committee eager to help. In Washington, Dr. Caroline Winslow, President of the Moral Education Society and editor of *Alpha*, hosted a YMCA conference on social purity, contributing to the appearance of another municipal vigilance committee. After a Boston meeting, called by Garrison and chaired by Wendell Phillips, antiregulationists established a vigilance committee with fifty members. Lucy Stone and Mary Livermore, leading New England feminists, were counted among the members. After a similar session in Philadelphia, Joseph May, Unitarian minister and son of Samuel J. May, and Mr. and Mrs. Enoch Lewis organized yet another vigilance committee.[42] As a benefit of the tour, the mission had stimulated the organizations of local committees in every major northeastern city visited.

The New Yorkers gave other important assistance. Powell also helped disseminate new abolitionist information. As a vice-president of the National Temperance Union, he scheduled the Englishmen for an address to an International Temperance Convention convened in Philadelphia. Powell, deeply involved in purity and temperance reform movements, strengthened the invisible bond between the two allied reforms.

In assessing the significance of the English mission, it may be concluded that the International Abolitionist Society had accomplished its object. Americans were alerted to the regulationist threat. English abolitionists had placed Americans on guard against what seemed to be a momentary crisis. They were wrong in their estimate. Neither they nor their American supporters anticipated the long-run effects of their reform upon social development in the United States.

NOTES

1. Anna Garlin Spencer, "Mrs. Howe on Social Purity," *Woman's Journal*, July 20, 1889, p. 225.

2. *Compulsory Medication of Prostitutes by the State—Republished from the Westminster Review, July 1876, by the New York Committee for the Prevention of Licensed Vice* (New York: n.d.), p. 8.

3. William Barrett, *Prostitution in Its Relation to Public Health* (St. Louis: Office of the Health Officer, May 29, 1873).

4. Perry Miller, ed., *The Transcendentalists: An Anthology* (Cambridge: Harvard University Press, 1950), p. 164; Charlotte G. Eliot, *William Greenleaf Eliot, Minister, Educator, Philanthropist* (Boston: Houghton Mifflin, 1904), p. 298; and "Clinton B. Fisk, Obituary," *Philanthropist*, August 1890, p. 5.

5. *The Social Evil Speech of Lt. Governor Charles P. Johnson on the Bill to Abolish the So-Called Social Evil Law of the City of St. Louis, Delivered in the Senate of Missouri, February 19, 1874* (n.p.: 1874).

6. For more information on reglementation in St. Louis, see *The Missouri Democrat*, July 6, 1870, p. 4; July 7, 1870, p. 4; September 1, 1870, p. 4; and September 3, 1870, p. 4.

7. "Letter to the Editor," *St. Louis Globe Democrat*, January 30, 1877; see also *St. Louis Globe Democrat*, January 14, 1876, p. 4.; January 21, 1876, p. 3; and May 20, 1876, p. 3.

8. "Draft of a letter to Mayor Powers," William G. Eliot Diary, February 15, 1875, p. 126, Washington University, St. Louis. "Eliot to the Editor," *St. Louis Times*, November 21, 1874, *Eliot Diary*, p. 61.

9. Edmund Andrews, *Prostitution and Its Sanitary Management* (St. Louis: n.p., 1871), pp. 21-23.

10. "Sexualité et Capitalisme avec une histoire de la Prostitution," *Grapouillet* 54 (October 1961): 63.

11. *Prospectus: Society for the Promotion of Social Purity* (Chicago: November 8, 1870), in Frances Willard Papers, National Woman's Christian Temperance Union, Evanston, Illinois.

12. Robert Laird Collier, *The Social Evil: An Address* (Chicago: Rand, McNally and Company, 1871), p. 8.

13. For a thorough analysis of the change in the function of law, see Franz Neumann, *The Democratic and the Authoritarian State* (Glencoe, Illinois: Free Press, 1957), pp. 22-68.

14. *Legislative Assembly, Special Session, House of Delegates, Bill No. 94 in the House of Delegates, District of Columbia, December 18, 1871*, Toner Collection, Library of Congress.

15. *The Social Evil: Remarks of Mr. Riddle to the Mass Meeting of the Woman's Club, at Lincoln Hall, September 22, 1871* (Washington, D.C.: 1871), p. 3.

16. John A. Jones, *The Social Evil* (Washington, D.C.: 1871), p. 6.

17. *An Inquiry into the Extent of the Social Evil and the Proposed Remedy: Speech delivered by the Honorable A. L. Cressler in the House of Representatives, March 18, 1874*, p. 14.

18. Henry J. Wilson and James Gledstone, *Report of a Visit to the United States* (Sheffield, 1876), pp. 3-4; and

Aaron M. Powell, *State Regulation of Vice: Regulation Efforts in America* (New York: Wood and Holbrook, 1878), p. 54.

19. "The Social Evil," *San Francisco Chronicle*, July 6, 1871, p. 2; "The Supervisors," *San Francisco Chronicle*, October 17, 1871, p. 3.

20. A. S. G. Butler, *Portrait of Josephine Butler* (London: Faber and Faber Ltd., 1953), p. 64; and Josephine Butler, *Personal Reminiscences of a Great Crusade* (London: Horace Marshall and Sons, 1896), pp. 7-8.

21. Garrison to Samuel J. May, July 23, 1875, William Lloyd Garrison Papers, Boston Public Library; and Anna Rice Powell to Elizabeth Gay, January 3, 1878, Sidney Howard Gay Papers, Columbia University.

22. Aaron Macy Powell was an ardent Garrisonian abolitionist. Leaving the Albany Normal School after one year, he devoted himself to abolition, temperance, prison, peace, and purity reforms. A Quaker, Powell was an editor of the *Standard*, later the *National Standard*. Secretary of the American Anti-Slavery Society, 1866-1870, he next devoted himself to temperance reform, serving as an assistant secretary of the National Temperance Society from 1873 to 1894. He was editor of the *National Temperance Advocate* and the *Philanthropist*. In 1894 he resigned his position in the Temperance Society to devote himself to purity reform as president of the American Purity Alliance.

23. *Woman's Journal*, October 20, 1894, p. 330.

24. Abigail Hopper Gibbons was the daughter of Isaac T. Hopper, noted Quaker abolitionist and reformer. President of the Women's Prison Association of New York and the New York Committee for the Prevention of the State Regulation of Vice, she has been called the "Elizabeth Fry of America."

25. Louisa May Alcott to Aaron M. Powell, May 5, 1876, in *Philanthropist*, May 1894, p. 5; Abby K. Foster to Aaron M. Powell, October 9, 1876, Aaron Macy Powell

Papers, Swarthmore College; and *Philanthropist*, March 1893, p. 2.

26. For further information about the purity elite, see Appendix A.

27. Oliver Johnson to Samuel J. May, March 13, 1865, Samuel J. May Papers, Boston Public Library; Aaron M. Powell to Antoinette Brown Blackwell, October 21, 1868, Blackwell Family Papers, Radcliffe College; and *Proceedings of the Sixth Annual Meeting of the Free Religious Association Held in Boston, May 29 and 30, 1873* (Boston: Cochrane and Sampson, 1873), pp. 43-50.

28. *Alpha*, May 1, 1876, pp. 6-7.

29. *Philanthropist*, July 1891, p. 5.

30. "Editorial," *Journal of the American Medical Association* 1 (July 1883): 57; and Elizabeth Blackwell, *The Influence of Women in the Profession of Medicine* (London: George Bell and Sons, 1889), pp. 19-20.

31. Samuel J. May to Elizabeth Gay, December 9, 1890, Sidney Howard Gay Papers, Columbia University.

32. Anna Rice Powell to Elizabeth Gay, January 3, 1898, and Samuel J. May to Elizabeth Gay, January 7, 1898, Sidney Howard Gay Papers, Columbia University.

33. Julia Ward Howe, "Ralph Waldo Emerson as I Knew Him," *The Critic* 43 (May 1903): 411-13.

34. Julia Ward Howe, "Education," November 1881, Julia Ward Howe Scrapbook, Radcliffe College, p. 140.

35. Julia Ward Howe, "Optimism and Pessimism as Efficient Social Forces," (n.p., n.d.), Julia Ward Howe Papers, Library of Congress.

36. Elizabeth Powell Bond, "Spiritual Growth," November 28, 1871, Elizabeth Powell Bond Papers, Swarthmore College, p. 27; and Joseph May, *The Beauty of Holiness: A Sermon* (Philadelphia: First Unitarian Church, n.d.).

37. Joseph May, *The Unity of Spirit: A Sermon* (Philadelphia, First Unitarian Church, n.d.), pp. 5-8; and *Influence, Not Constraint, the Method of Providence: A*

Sermon (Philadelphia: First Unitarian Church, n.d.), p. 15.

38. Antoinette Brown Blackwell, "Comments," *Philanthropist*, March 1887, p. 7.

39. Elizabeth Powell Bond, "The Youth of Some Eminent Americans," Elizabeth Powell Bond Papers, Swarthmore College; and Joseph Flint, *His Perpetual Adoration* (Boston: Arena Publishing Company, 1895). Flint's novel details the temptations of a Civil War hero who finds the inner strength to resist an immoral southern belle.

40. William C. Gannett, *Blessed Be Drudgery* (Boston: Unity Short Tracts No. 13, n.d.). In writing about social character, I have been influenced by Wilhelm Reich's writings. I have not, however, written a psychoanalytic history.

41. William Lloyd Garrison, *On State Regulation of Vice* (New York Public Library, Miscellaneous Pamphlets).

42. Wilson and Gledstone, *Report of a Visit*, p. 23.

3

The Emergence of the
Social Purity
Alliance, 1877-1885

Abolitionists first reacted to reglementation without benefit of a clearly articulated ideology. An emergency situation had precipitated the formation of vigilance committees along the Eastern seaboard, but no one had anticipated a continuing function for the committees once reglementation was repulsed. The defeat of the regulationists took longer than expected, however, and, as the years passed, new abolitionists acquired a better understanding of their reform enterprise. But consciousness came slowly. Initially, abolitionists and moral educationists varied in their mode of combatting prostitution. While new abolitionists emphasized the remedial aspects of purity reform—rescuing the "fallen woman" and closing brothels—moral education societies emphasized prevention through education and child rearing. What united the two reforms were common objectives, not coincidental opposition in emergency situations. Although, as reform took on new functions, separate agencies developed for specific activities, moral educationists and new abolitionists remained unified by shared objectives and common values. William Greenleaf Eliot showed, through his work, how common interests coincided. In gaining a national reputation for his crusade against legalized vice in St. Louis, he also acquired a reputation as a writer on the subject of "right generation."[1] Eliot appreciated the interdependence of remedial and preventive aspects of anti-prostitution reform pursued by vigilance committees and moral education societies.

MORAL EDUCATION SOCIETIES AND THE SOCIAL PURITY MOVEMENT

Moral education societies were separate agencies that came into existence shortly after the Civil War. As a continuation of antebellum purity efforts, they were lineal heirs to both early feminist and popular health reformers' interest in child rearing. Horace Bushnell had established an intellectual precedent for child rearing literature with the publication of "Christian Nurture"; the full burden of the reform, however, fell upon feminists. The woman's movement (with the assistance of women physicians) followed his lead and assumed responsibility for popularizing child rearing reforms. Quite logically, their interest in child rearing kept pace with the general growth of the nineteenth-century woman's movement. Moral educationists, assessing their reform role in the 1870s, concluded that they had departed radically from the church's ordinary call for regeneration by substituting a more dynamic view of child rearing. This dynamism, foreshadowing applied evolutionary theory in the child study movement, rejected evangelical ideas of child salvation. For moral educationists, the evangelical interest in bringing the child to Christ was insufficient for preserving social order in modern urban society.[2] They believed new child rearing theories necessary, and took a special interest in their development.

By giving new meaning to women's traditional roles the reformers revitalized their cause. Moral education societies appeared in Boston, New York, Philadelphia, and Washington, D.C., in the early 1870s. Like so many other developments within the woman's movement, the early history of the movement was deceptively simple. The Boston Moral Science Committee decided, in 1870, to launch an educational program. They started by searching for the principles of right generation but then moved into an action program. Not wishing to deny the benefits of their findings to other women, they commissioned Lucinda Chandler to spread their message. Chandler carried news of the reform to Philadelphia and New York in 1872. Her pleas for enlightened motherhood fell on receptive ears. Women had a special mission. In fact, the pulpit clamor for regeneration would be unnecessary, she contended, if mothers only generated their own children properly.[3] Women, responsive to this message, turned to organizing moral education societies.

Women physicians, though limited in numbers, followed Elizabeth Blackwell's example of dedication to moral education and came to dominate the societies. Like Dr. Blackwell, they were part of a transcendental revolt against materialist science. In defending human values, they commingled religious and scientific thought in their child rearing theories. For instance, Caroline Winslow, editor of *Alpha*, the societies' journal, expressed a transcendentalist aspiration similar to Blackwell's. By striving for the preservation of innocence, she hoped to direct the forces of body and brain into proper channels under the guidance of enlightened reason and extend a "baby's freshness throughout life."[4] This secular innocence, protected by a positive and attractive morality, would guarantee a better life for mankind.

For moral educationists, sexual morality was the key to innocence and, moreover, the root of all morality. Sex theorists relied upon Elizabeth Blackwell's *The Moral Education of the Young* as an inspirational source. Blackwell had stated the aim of the book as the preservation of innocence. An authoritative volume in its field, the book commanded the respect of American moral educationists were dependent upon the temperance movement Publishers, apparently, did not share this admiration. Unobjectionable as *The Moral Education of the Young* may seem today, Blackwell had much difficulty in finding a publisher. Refused by seventeen English publishers, Blackwell finally printed the book at her own expense. Its reception was not highly favorable—it elicited excited opposition from critics.[5]

The entry of women physicians into the leadership positions in antiregulation and moral education movements eased the task of unification. In the final analysis, moral educationists provided the ideological justification for fighting legalized prostitution. In turn, moral educationists were dependant upon the temperance movement for their ideology. Temperance reformers, for example, wanted to eliminate a need for reform by educating people to a "taste for higher things." In defining their function as the rescuing of "sexual drunkards," moral educationists betrayed their dependence on temperance thought. Temperance, social purity, and moral education, although separated institutionally, were partners in secularization and worked toward the same goals.

Moral education committees, also serving as vigilance committees, devoted themselves primarily to family reform. They were social educationists engaged in long-range work. Mrs. Abby Morton Diaz, a member of the Boston Moral Education Society and later president of the Woman's Educational and Industrial Unions, stated the moral educationists' aspirations in a speech, "The Develop-

ment of Character In Our Schools, or, What Shall We, The
People, Do To Be Saved?" delivered in 1880.[6] National
salvation required standardizing and rationalizing social
behavior. A major concern of moral educationists,
therefore, was the development of public school curricula.

Although only a few women belonged to the moral
education societies, the societies exercised a great influence
on allied reforms. *Alpha*, published monthly and never ex-
ceeding a circulation of 1,500, got much of its financial
support from Dr. Caroline Winslow. It had a very select
and elite audience, however, for candid discussion of sex
subjects was difficult, even within reform ranks. At times
Alpha shocked and embarrassed its highly select group of
readers. This audience, in fact, constituted an American
reform leadership. Hence, *Alpha*'s primary function was to
mold and develop attitudes toward sex reform among,
primarily, leaders of the woman's movement. These
women, in their turn, addressed a larger, perhaps even
mass, audience. By 1889, Winslow could no longer bear
the physical and financial strain of publication. *Alpha*
ceased publication, but not before it had made its mark on
the woman's movement. Upon its demise, a Reverend Mr.
J. B. Caldwell undertook the publication of *Christian Life*,
patterned after *Alpha* and subsequently the official organ
of the International Purity Federation.

Although these highly educated moral educationists
were few and their societies failed to win a large national
audience, they exercised a steady influence upon reform,
particularly in the most populated urban areas. Interest in
moral education societies spread westward: by 1885, a
moral education society had been organized in Chicago,
and Dr. Alice Stockham had carried the moral education
gospel to San Francisco and laid the groundwork for a society in California. A National Conference for Moral Education scheduled for 1885, however, never materialized.

After the financial collapse of *Alpha*, the moral education societies were gradually absorbed into the social purity movement as vigilance committees and moral education societies merged.

A LEADERSHIP IN SEARCH OF A FOLLOWING

During the first phases of antiregulation agitation, Caroline Winslow gave coordination and direction to various local campaigns and tried to consolidate the movement nationally. The American Committee for the Prevention of Legalizing Prostitution met in 1877 for its first—and probably last—session in the Washington Young Women's Christian Association parlors. Dr. Winslow presided as chairman and, momentarily, as national leader. Despite Dr. Winslow's many qualifications—she was a pioneer in moral education, she was an acknowledged leader of women physicians, and she had been invited, with Dr. Susan Edson and Aaron Macy Powell, as a delegate to the 1877 International Congress for the Abolition of Government Regulation of Prostitution in Geneva—Aaron Macy Powell and Abby Hopper Gibbons assumed the mantle of national leadership.

Powell, accompanied by Julia Ward Howe, Elizabeth Blackwell, and Caroline Winslow, did attend the 1877 Geneva Congress, which was accurately described as "a general uprising of the moral and religious world."[7] Powell, who was identified with the antislavery crusade, renewed European friendships and reinforced his association with the American antiregulation movement in European minds. He maintained his contacts with European reform leaders, reporting on American antiregulationist actions and using the New York Committee as a clearinghouse for the international reform movement. Within the United States, he was also widely identified with new abolitionism. Indeed, Powell published the first book on the new abolitionism given national distribution.[8] In 1879, he strengthened his claims to leadership by publishing the *American Bulletin*, a monthly report on American antiregulationist and social purity activities that was relied upon by European abolitionists. Later, in 1885, he expanded the *Bulletin* into the *Philanthropist*, the official American social purity journal.

Powell's New York location was an advantage in his quest for national leadership. New York, the largest American city, possessed the preconditions required for a well-developed reform community. The size of the reform community allowed specialization and still permitted easy communications among the reformers. The city served as a laboratory for municipal reforms. Powell exploited the institutional maturity of New York reform and systematically explored both the social functions of purity reform within general reform movements and the larger relationships among them. The New York Committee at regular meetings examined the significance of prostitution in American life, devising techniques to repress or, hopefully, eradicate it. The Committee was ably led by Abby Hopper Gibbons with the assistance of Aaron and Anna Powell. Seeing themselves as "a sort of inner circle . . . the heart of other meetings,"[9] the individual members of the New York Committee returned to other reform agencies to disseminate social purity ideas and programs throughout the institutional structure of the woman's movement. Although the committee attributed its success to the force of moral ideas, its practical ability to mobilize religious and reform agencies in a concerted attack on prostitution was a decisive factor in those agencies' accomplishments.

In its first ten years, the New York Committee, a provisional ad hoc agency, showed remarkable flexibility. Entry into new aspects of the reform constantly surprised its members, but they became accustomed to a seemingly endless proliferation of new activities and revelled in the seeming boundlessness of the movement. Purity reform, now almost uncontainable, grew far beyond the immediate comprehension of even its leaders.[10] Yet as exciting as the new movement was for the members of the committee in the 1870s, its extension into the woman's movement proceeded at a disappointingly slow pace during the decade.

The New York Committee was the "inner circle" of the reform movement and had special ties with the New York reform community, but new abolitionism relied upon the woman's movement for its national achievements. In 1876, the Woman's Christian Temperance Union gave stalwart support to the struggle against prostitution by initiating rescue work. This quite traditional activity led to more adventurous experiments as purity reform developed within the WCTU. In 1883, the WCTU, reinforcing its commitments, instituted a new department for the suppression of prostitution. The work, however, repelled most members of the WCTU and the department failed to grow. Only a concentration on preventive reform attracted women.[11] The introduction of child rearing instruction through the mothers' meetings transformed antiregulation into a positive and attractive reform and allowed social purity to gain wide support within the organization. Mothers' meetings, therefore, were vehicles for the wide dissemination of moral education theory. Public discussion of child rearing cast social purity in a new mold and breathed new life into the movement.

Moral indignation unleashed women in the first antiprostitution campaign. Later, the same moral indignation became a major force in urban reconstruction. Changing social mores triggered the moral outrage of educationists and new abolitionists and stiffened their resolve as new moralists. Elizabeth Blackwell, watching Americans returning home after sojourning in indolence and luxury, prescribed a modern Savonarola to "stir them up in New York," as a remedy for urban conditions.[12] Her sister Antoinette Brown Blackwell, America's first ordained woman minister, had an even stronger remedy in mind for New York. After the Boston fire of 1871, she reflected upon the punishment of a vengeful God on the city: "Poor Boston! One feels like mourning that the crooked city will now be compelled to straighten her paths. Will it be New York's turn next to get purified so by fire, I wonder!"[13] Frances Willard, president of the WCTU, in assessing social change in the United States, diagnosed a fundamental moral crisis in the nation. She resolved, with moral indignation comparable to the Blackwell sisters', that traditional morality would be preserved in the delicate period of transition from the old to a new social order.[14]

New abolitionists believed the nation basically sound in its morality but occasionally lax in its behavior. They intended to conserve an innately sound morality through their vigilance committees. Comfortable in this belief, the New York Committee abandoned mass public appeals in favor of lobbying. Only when public opinion seemed critical for the defeat of a social evil bill did new abolitionists return to newspaper exchanges to excite public support.

Abby Hopper Gibbons—president of the New York Women's Prison Association, a Quaker humanitarian reformer, and an early lobbyist—spearheaded the purity drive at the Albany legislature and gained a reputation as a woman lobbyist for reform causes. Francis P. Weisenburger correctly stressed the early entry of prison reformers into more general social reforms.[15] His observation is sound when applied to either Gibbons or Powell. Judiciously distributing new abolitionist literature, Gibbons influenced legislative opinion on purity subjects. When regulationists made inroads into legislative opinion, the New York Committee produced the St. Louis literature to raise the specter of rampant sexual immorality.

In the early reform years, Powell and Gibbons divided the political territory. Gibbons covered the New York capitol and Powell guarded New York City's morals. In 1878 rumors of possible municipal regulation reached the New York Committee. It countered the threat by circulating Josephine Butler's *The Constitution Violated* among members of the city government as a statement of principle. Powell even made a personal visit to Mayor Ely to hold the mayor in line against regulation.[16]

Lobbying had its limitations. The ethnic heterogeneity of New York City precluded any cultural consensus on prostitution. Because historical experiences with the social evil varied, ethnic groups also varied in their current estimates of the institution. The New York Committee wanted to mold a consensus among these disparate groups. They believed that social conditions mandated a public education campaign, but they lacked the resources necessary for direct assaults. Since mass campaigns were not feasible, the committee decided to influence newspaper coverage of the subject, a technique that ultimately would have a salutory and diffused effect. They directed their campaign at newspaper editors, mailing pertinent representational literature to them. Editors of medical journals received special attention and were occasionally visited in an effort to persuade them. New abolitionists appreciated the authority of the medical profession on sex issues. In earlier campaigns, the New York Committee, lacking antiprostitution arguments appropriate to the American experience, had relied upon British pamphlets to influence the New York medical community.

New York and other Eastern reformers had come to

rely on lobbying. The refinement and institutionalization of these operational modes were indices of their sophistication in changing a modern social system. These advances were regional. Western reformers were unaware of these procedural innovations and still relied on mass appeals, managed by coalitions of ministers and feminists.

THE CAMPAIGN TO CHANGE MEDICAL OPINION

The medical profession was slow in absorbing the meaning of the social purity message, even when reformers brought extraordinary pressures to bear. Decidedly unsympathetic to abolitionism, physicians were open to sanitarian and regulationist viewpoints. True, a few isolated physicians were abolitionists, but they had not, as yet, coalesced into a pressure group within medical associations. Because physicians lacked their own abolitionist political factions, the New York Committee filled a vacuum by propagandizing within important medical societies and journals. Trends in medical thought were with the abolitionists. As European practice shifted towards abolition, the debates at international conventions and articles in important journals prepared American medical men for the New York Committee's ideas.

In 1874, the American Medical Association was predominantly regulationist. Dr. J. Marion Sims, its president and the father of American gynecology, officially sanctioned regulation at the 1874 Detroit Convention. Doctors Samuel D. Gross, a noted Philadelphia surgeon, and Albert Gihon, medical director of the United States Navy, abetted by a favorable policy statement from the Committee on State Medicine, attempted to win the profession to reglementation. As chairman of the Committee on the Prevention of Venereal Diseases, M. H. Henry favored a national board of physicians to coordinate American reglementationist activities with the international movement.[17] New abolitionists apparently found it easier to influence local medical societies than to effect policy changes in the American Medical Association.

New abolitionists, clearly on the defensive, launched a three-pronged campaign to change medical opinion—in medical journals (an ideological conflict), at the American Public Health Association Conventions (an institutional power struggle), and within legislative halls (power *loci* in the legislative process).

Powell assumed the responsibility for educating the medical profession to the new morality. Never doubting his competency in the field, he commenced his campaign by placing an article in the leading public health journal, *Sanitarian*. He wisely selected an article by the respected British abolitionist and statistician J. Birbeck Nevins, timing its placement to ensure publication prior to the 1880 American Public Health Association Convention. Not to be caught short, the regulationists immediately countered with an article by Albert Gihon.[18] With medical and public health journals now open to them, the new abolitionists had finally gained a forum. An earlier attempt to gain access to scientific and medical professions had failed. In 1876, new abolitionists had tried publicizing the issue of social evil in *Popular Science*, but the editor, E. L. Youmans, had cavalierly rejected their article with the comment that public discussion only compounded the problem.[19] Access to the *Sanitarian* was, therefore, a triumph. New abolitionists were now assured of a hearing before medical and public health organizations.

Acceptance of new abolitionist articles also reflected the profession's loss of confidence in regulation. Doctor Castiglioni and M. LeCour of Rome and Paris respectively, leading regulationists, had publicly expressed second

thoughts on reglementation. American medical journals
not only noted this change but also reported that European
venereal disease rates had not diminished as a consequence
of medical supervision. In the past, both regulationists and
abolitionists had considered prostitution as socio-moral
and medical problems. The difference in their positions
was one of emphasis: abolitionists focused on the socio-
moral aspects of the problem; regulationists on the medical
aspects. The object of each policy was the protection of the
family. As medical journals reevaluated the social data,
they concluded that regulation, rather than protecting the
family, further endangered its viability as a social institution. Regulationists were evidently developing an appreciation for the social dimensions of prostitution.

A moment of equipoise had been reached in the
ideological struggle. Abolitionists continued their relent-
less attack on the recalcitrants and gradually forced
the regulationists into a defensive posture. The medical
public became apprised of these changes when, in 1882,
the antagonists engaged in another ideological foray in the
Maryland Medical Journal. Gihon, as chairman of the
AMA Section On State Medicine (1882), wrote an article
defending regulation.[20] As might be expected, he triggered an exchange and provided abolitionists with another
opportunity to publicize their views.

An abolitionist hit away at the weak point in Gihon's
position. Citing changing attitudes of European physicians,
the critic reminded his readers that the infamous Parisian
police des moeurs, the administrators of Parisian reglementation, had been abolished as a conspicuous failure. He further criticized—with justification—the medical techniques
used for diagnosing venereal diseases.[21] Emphasizing
the inadequacy of medical diagnostic technique, he cast
suspicion upon reglementationists' statistical claims of a
declining venereal disease rate. The last regulationist arti-

cle in the exchange dealt with the core disagreement in social medicine. Eschewing statistical argumentation, the
"expert" lashed out at the abolitionists in a fit of bad
humor. He insisted science and morality were separate enti-
ties not to be confused or mixed. In the final analysis, he
stated, the profession had to make a choice. Was medical
opinion to be formed by the profession or were Josephine
Butler, J. Birbeck Nevins, Wendell Phillips, and the
Reverend Frederick Wines, moralists all, to determine the
course of the profession?[22]

Abolitionists were not cowed by these arguments. On
the contrary, they sensed the vulnerability of regulationists
and tried to debunk the illusion of scientific authority.
First, they charged that the "medical evidence" used to defend Gihon's position had been solicited from a brothel
keeper. According to the principles of evidence, at least
abolitionist principles, evidence so gathered was inadmissi-
ble. Second, they reminded readers of the *Maryland
Medical Journal*, with telling effect, that eleven of eighteen
speakers on prostitution at the London International
Medical Congress had opposed reglementation.[23]

Gihon knew that the debate had taken a bad turn.
Staggered, but unwilling to capitulate, he searched for a
compromise. Knowing the importance of the principle of
equality to abolitionists, Gihon experimented with
strategies designed to satisfy both abolitionists and regulationists. He proposed equality within regulation: compulsory medical inspection would be applied to men and
women.[24] Woman's rights leaders were not persuaded.
They also opposed compulsion.

Abolitionists had won in the medical journals. A final
regulationist article appearing in 1886 was little more than
a coda to the exchange. The frustrated author resorted to
exhortation and tirade; cloaking himself with the authority
of science, he attacked abolitionists as "moralists."[25]

After 1882, the journals reflected the changed attitudes of the medical profession. Perhaps the most dramatic change came in the publications of the New York Academy of Medicine. With the abandonment of police and medical control and the absence of social policy, the profession gradually became receptive to new ideas. What they sought was a philosophy of social medicine in harmony with social mores. They needed a program acceptable to the public if they were to avoid further setbacks. (It was conceded that public opinion and woman's rights leaders had prevented the implementation of regulation.) Therefore, sections of the medical profession inevitably had to contend with social reform in their search for the causes of prostitution.[26] Abolitionists and the medical profession were reaching an ideological accommodation; physicians recognized moral forces as important in social medicine, while abolitionists acknowledged the right, indeed the duty, of the medical profession to participate in social reform.

Position papers presented at the Academy of Medicine now struck an abolitionist note. One paper, "The Social Evil; its Cause and Cure," might easily have been written by a feminist.[27] A major paper, presented in 1886, moved the Academy even closer to abolitionism. Its author outlined a program for the final elimination of prostitution, involving the emancipation and elevation of women, proper education on the sanctity of marriage, social ostracism for moral transgressors, consideration of the moral aspects of prostitution, and undertaking a public campaign to develop a new man-woman relationship. In accord with traditional concepts of social control, the author advanced culture—theater, art, literature, and other sublimations—as an outlet for sexual energies.[28] Consciously or unconsciously, the author advocated the temperance and purity program for the moral uplift of the American people.

AMERICAN PUBLIC HEALTH ASSOCIATION

Abolitionists, as they labored to change medical opinion, also acted on a second front—within the American Public Health Association. As in the case of the AMA, reglementationist thought initially dominated discussions of prostitution at the APHA conventions. Since important institutional power was at stake, abolitionists had to reverse the situation. They relied upon the same cultural factors that had turned the tide against regulation among the public within these conventions. Again, the abolitionists had to contend with the same leaders of the opposition. Albert Gihon, perennial nemesis of new abolitionists, introduced in 1879 a typical regulation plan, appending to it a humanitarian appeal for the protection of the innocent and helpless of the community. The convention took no action, but referred the proposal to an investigating committee with instructions to report to the next convention.[29]

The committee reported at the 1880 New Orleans convention. With his plan continually attacked before the convention, Gihon defended the report against "pseudomoralists" who had challenged him. Gihon, a military social hygienist, cited military statistics to justify regulation and prove its efficacy. Active in both the AMA and the APHA, he had merely expanded and amplified the plan presented to the 1877 meetings of the AMA. Gihon's tactic was easily understood: implementation of any plan depended upon public health personnel. To win the American Medical Association to reglementation was essential, but winning the American Public Health Association was critical. A regulationist victory at New Orleans could have resulted in the national implementation of regulation. Aware of this new threat, abolitionists became apprehensive. Lacking delegate strength to defeat the proposal, they adopted a delaying tactic. They managed to have the report postponed to the next convention.[30]

As the date for the Savannah meetings drew near, new abolitionists feverishly prepared for the anticipated final round. Redoubling their efforts, they used every technique available to them. Powell provided literature for every delegate at the convention, placed articles in the *Sanitarian* to publicize the abolitionist program, and caucused with Dr. E. M. Hunt of the New York Board of Health in order to mobilize the strength of abolitionist delegates at the convention.[31] Powell's efforts were, nonetheless, insufficient, but not disastrously so.

At Savannah, Gihon reported extensively and proudly on the committee's work over the previous year. Having completed its inquiry, the committee had adopted the stratagem of lobbying state legislatures for contagious diseases acts. New abolitionists, familiar with these actions, did not share Gihon's enthusiasm. Although victory had eluded him before, Gihon imagined it now within his grasp. He was again disappointed. Abolitionists had mobilized enough strength to deny him victory, but not enough to defeat him. Another stalemate resulted. The convention tabled the committee report, convinced that it would not be heard again. As in the case of the medical profession, public health officials now lacked a social policy on prostitution, which severely limited their public appeal and the range of action to be taken against venereal diseases. Neither abolitionists nor regulationists, as a result, had won a final victory.

Regulationists, convinced of the correctness of their course, did not capitulate. Denied the right to report as a committee, they were able to use a parliamentary device to reintroduce the report by having it presented by the association's legal advisor.[32] It was a futile gesture, for new abolitionists dominated the association by then. One committee member, the Reverend Frederick Wines, philanthropist and vigorous defender of the family, submitted a minority abolitionist report, defending the family as a social institution and stressing the adverse effects of regulation on marriage and public morals.[33] Like the medical profession, public health officials were being influenced by abolitionist theories and were compromising with social reform forces.

STATE AND NATIONAL POLITICS

The third arena in the new abolitionist counter-campaign was within the sphere of state politics. As in the instances just explored, regulationists started with the initiative and new abolitionists had to counteract them. Gihon, Sims, and Gross, familiar regulationist activists, devoted their energies to securing national and state contagious diseases acts. In 1876 Sims had lobbied for the New York Social Evil Bill. In the same year, Gross had supported a contagious diseases bill before the Pennsylvania legislature. Finally, Gihon, with the esteem gained as a leader in two medical associations, undertook a political effort, almost a crusade, to secure contagious diseases legislation in the various states. Vigilance committees, individual reformers, and moral education societies, functioning as sentinels for the abolitionists, reported these political moves to Aaron Powell in New York.

Abolitionists, remembering the British experience with contagious diseases acts, were more than a little anxious. Though they had repulsed reglementation every time, they nevertheless feared that it might be implemented circuitously. Concerned and lacking faith in the medical profession, new abolitionists reasoned that any board of health with broad powers might provide an opening wedge for regulationists. Moreover, if politicians converted boards of

health into administrative units, de facto regulation might
follow. Antiprostitution forces, enjoying a constituency of
newly politicized women, had no fear of the legislative
process. They were proven and seasoned political cam-
paigners. They were less certain, however, of administrative
processes, since they had no control over them and since
administrators could formalize policies without benefit of
legislation. The thought was anathema and more than fan-
tasy. Dr. Gross, complaining that legislation of contagious
diseases acts attracted too much public attention, fueled
their anxieties.[34] If regulationists could implement their
program silently through administrative processes alone,
they might, away from public scrutiny, achieve their end.
New abolitionists, without benefit of an outraged public,
could not control the regulationists.

When Congress received a bill to create a national
board of health in 1878, purity reformers believed their
worst apprehensions had been justified. Dr. Caroline
Winslow, sounding an alarm, warned other reformers that
Congress had just passed a "contagious diseases act."
Winslow remained optimistic, however, expecting a
presidential veto. New abolitionists, while they agreed with
her analysis of the situation, did not waste time. They
mobilized for a new battle. Cooperating with Dr. Winslow,
the New York Committee hurled another jeremiad at the
New York Academy of Medicine. If the president signed
the bill, the New York Committee warned, public morality
would sink to a new low, injustice would be legislated, and
women would be practically enslaved. Although their jeremiad aroused the New York Academy, new abolitionists
failed to prevent Rutherford B. Hayes from signing the National Quarantine Bill. The worst was not over, for, to their
consternation, President Hayes appointed Gihon to the National Board of Health. Hayes made their defeat even
harder to accept.[35]

Defeated for the moment, vigilance committees returned to watchful waiting, intent on preventing any further expansion of the board's powers. In 1882, Congress
did consider expanding the board's powers. Purity reformers interpreted this move as another attempt to legislate a
contagious diseases act. Supported by Senator George
Hoar (R-Mass.), Abby Hopper Gibbons came to Washington, D.C., to counter the threat. With assistance from
the Moral Education Society, she alerted the Senate to the
bill's implications. Their combined effort was sufficient to
defeat the bill and temporarily contain the power of the
National Board of Health. Ignoring essential medical functions performed by the board in matters other than
prostitution, new abolitionists had attributed to it quasi-
demonic powers and almost destroyed it. The House of Representatives voted to abolish the board when it next requested enlarged powers in 1886. Only the Senate's failure
to concur prevented the board's destruction, but its request
for expanded powers was not granted.[36]

The persistence of regulationists was only outmatched
by the firmer resistance of new abolitionists. Having failed
to win national legislation, regulationists returned for
another sally upon the state legislatures. Choosing New
York as a prime target, the regulationists had another bill
submitted to legislature. The patterned response of the new
abolitionists followed with almost boring consistency. They
defeated the bill.[37] A rash of bills submitted to other state
legislatures met a similar fate.

VOLUNTARY REGULATION

Since regulationists could not secure state legislation, they
turned to utilizing the mechanism of voluntary associations. Accordingly, they formed the New York Society
for the Prevention of Contagious Diseases. Relying on

voluntaristic principles, a concession to believers in *laissez-faire*, they gave the society authority to issue health certificates to prostitutes and to provide a maternity home for them. Purity leaders, recognizing the political hazards of condoning the association, urged the legislature to deny it a charter. The legislature did not grant the charter.[38]

Regulationists, as religiously committed to their own plan as the vigilance committees were to theirs, displayed great tenacity in their campaign for public health. Failure to gain legislative support did not cause them to abandon their objective. They tried, as in previous situations, to be flexible, but they were no match for the new abolitionists. Regulationists could not muster large-scale public support, while new abolitionists, who were more attuned to American cultural ideals, had located a large and responsive audience.

The New York plan for voluntaristic regulation signalled a new departure for reglementationists. The new schemes were a greater threat to purity reformers, since regulationists believed de facto regulation could succeed without state endorsement. De facto regulation might assume two forms, either a system of voluntarism or one of police compliance. Both had to be defeated. While they had been on the defensive, new abolitionists had demanded a neutral state; now they urged state intervention against de facto regulation. They called for an aggressively moral state to counteract immoral social voluntarism and to actualize the new morality. Their idea of the moral state, a complement of the welfare state, was comprehensive: they envisioned not only the defeat of reglementation, but an opposition to vice in all its forms.

Aileen S. Kraditor, in analyzing two types of suffragist arguments, has suggested that this new concern for public morality was of pivotal importance. As the state ceased being a "night watchman," merely restraining men's interference with one another's rights, and became more of a social welfare agency, women's suffrage was advocated not only *as* a reform but as a *means* to reform as well.[39]

Regulationists had been opposed and defeated. The larger enemy, prostitution itself, remained as a visible denial of the goals of the woman's movement. Experience and inquiry forced reformers to decide, by 1885, that commercialized vice with international dimensions existed in the United States. The New York Committee was convinced that a syndicate supplied girls for New York brothels. Humans were being sold for immoral and illegal purposes in the white slave traffic. Although a white slave traffic did exist, reformers were sometimes misled by their imaginations. Once they claimed a "railroad magnate" planned to license Colorado prostitution in every town with a population of more than five thousand.[40] Although their contention was never substantiated, some western states did license prostitution in keeping with a high-license policy in regulating saloons and licensing gambling. Invariably prostitution, gambling, and liquor came to be associated with each other. New abolitionists saw in this association a political alliance between the saloon and the brothel, the "twin evil." Only reform organization might counterbalance and eventually eliminate organized vice in the United States.[41] If American society was to be purified, new abolitionism, too narrow in its appeal and too literal in its ideology, had to be transformed into a social purity crusade.

THE SOCIAL PURITY CAMPAIGN

PROSTITUTION AND PRISON REFORM

Antiregulationism had, from the start, been merely one aspect of the new abolitionist movement. Reformers had made numerous efforts to eliminate the brothel and to save

the "fallen woman." As religionists, they never lost sight of
their most significant remedial goal—the redemption of
prostitutes. The prostitute, an unfortunate and unprotected
woman, deserved not only protection but also salvation.
New abolitionists kept foremost in their thoughts the
biblical stricture against casting the first stone. Discontented with revivalist techniques for restoring reformed
prostitutes to the community, purity reformers experimented with new social techniques.

Between 1876 and 1885, new abolitionist attitudes
toward prostitutes underwent a transformation. Having
defined prostitution as an improper use of function, or as
sexual intemperance, they considered its primary cause to
be disobedience to the laws of God and hygiene. Rejecting
the older theological view of a "fall from grace," they explained sexual incontinence as either delinquency or
criminality.

Modern prostitution had reached mass proportions,
and combatting the institution demanded new departures
in rescue work. Prison reformers were forced, in their ex-
plorations into social etiology, to relate specific social pa-
thologies to more general causes. In the process, they also
analyzed the causes of prostitution. Criminologists, relying
on new findings, searched for techniques for the redemption of the prostitute.

Undoubtedly these new perceptions were partially attributable to Abby Hopper Gibbons' and Aaron Macy
Powell's activities in New York prison reform. Although
they combined a concern for the reformation of criminals
with a desire to protect society, reformation took precedence. In the 1870s, new abolitionists were attracted to
prison reform. Gibbons was the leading spirit behind
organizing the Isaac T. Hopper Home, sponsored by the
Woman's Prison Association of New York. The Hopper
Home served as a halfway house for women as they left

prison. Despairing of the treatment of women prisoners and of the almost insurmountable obstacles placed in the way of rehabilitation, prison reformers provided a sheltered environment for women where they could live and adjust to life outside the prison. The emphasis in this home was upon vocational education and character building to prevent the return of women to criminality. Later, the home was used as a model for the first women's reformatory in New York State. Since other states emulated New York experiments in prison reform, the Hopper Home had national significance for setting standards for the rehabilitation of prostitutes.[42]

Prison reformers, as early participants in preventive social work, did not rely exclusively on individual casework. As new abolitionists learned from their experiences as prison reformers, they paid more attention to the circumstances and situations that promoted and encouraged immorality. Appalled by prison inadequacies, prison reformers thought the prisons themselves were a major source of impurity. To their astonishment, reformers learned prisons actually fostered criminality, and, under certain circumstances, permitted illicit sexuality. Most appalling to them was the fact that prisoners were not even segregated by sex; in practice, prostitutes might even continue their trade within prisons. Women prisoners not convicted as prostitutes were placed in the cells with those who were. Moreover, they charged, policemen abused the women prisoners.

Prison reformers proposed fundamental corrections for these offensive practices in municipal prisons. In order to protect women—prostitutes and non-prostitutes—they recommended that police matrons replace male guards and that criminals be segregated according to sex, age, and degree of criminality. Discontented with merely technical or piecemeal changes, reformers demanded a totally new reformation system. Prisons or penitentiaries were no longer adequate institutions in a civilized society. Only the substitution of reformatories for older institutions was in the new reformist "spirit of the age."

From a contemporary perspective, a request for police matrons was a simple remedy for common abuses, but women reformers hailed it as a significant improvement in the status of women prisoners. Police matron reform signified, additionally, the emergence of a new profession for women, one appropriate to their civilizing role in urban society.[43] The police matron, as a new professional, devoted herself entirely to the reformation of women criminals. Her femininity gave her an edge over males engaged in the same work, allowing easier rapport with women prisoners. As a woman, she appreciated the unique problems of women prisoners.

Police matron work included diverse elements of modern social work. She interviewed prisoners to advise courts on appropriate sentencing, distributed clothing to the destitute, recommended country homes when criminals might benefit from sheltered, rural life, and performed as a probation officer, corresponding with or visiting probationary girls. Police matrons, in keeping with the remedial nature of their job, used the case method of social work. Although attempting to comprehend the social causes of prostitution, prison reformers still emphasized individual treatment. In many ways plans for reforming prostitutes in the Hopper Home contained the essentials of a larger plan for the reformation of criminals. Purity reformers in prison reform shared common values and assumptions with other prison reformers not necessarily involved in purity work; they tended, however, to be more radical in their plans for liberalizing American society.

The campaign for police matrons, like other specific reforms, provided a vehicle for popularizing the social purity movement. Widely publicized and readily accepted by national reform leaders, police matron reform, by 1886, had managed tremendous successes. In that year, the National Conference of Charities and Corrections listened to an appeal for the hiring of police matrons. Archbishop Ireland of Chicago, a member of the audience, declared it among the most important topics discussed, while President Rutherford B. Hayes, responding to another presentation before the National Prison Congress, requested wide distribution of a paper on the subject.[44]

Prison and purity reformers had a better reception from other reformers than from legislators. Gibbons, already canvassing Albany legislators for the antiregulation agitation, also energetically lobbied in favor of police matrons in 1882. Although he sent more than one hundred letters in favor of a police matron bill, Gibbons did not stir a lethargic New York legislature. The bill died in committee.[45]

Elsewhere, however, women reformers could report limited legislative victories. As the woman's movement took over the police matron idea, the campaign became national in scope. Women's groups accounted for many municipal gains. In 1884, the Women's Educational and Industrial Union underwrote the salary of a police matron for Buffalo. The New Century Club of Philadelphia persuaded Mayor Stokely to appoint a police matron in 1885. Moral education societies, incorporating the project, secured legislation in Washington, D.C., in 1888.[46]

THE PROTECTION OF WOMEN IN AN URBAN SOCIETY

The reform of prostitutes was a critical but limited enterprise for purity reformers. They preferred taking the offensive in their fight against prostitution. In demanding forceful legislation to suppress the white slave traffic, feminists became more familiar with intellectual trends among criminologists. Moreover, focusing attention upon the white slave traffic also highlighted the lack of civil liberties for young women, especially in regard to age of consent. Ellice Hopkins, the English purity reformer, called attention to age of consent in her 1883 pamphlet *Social Wreckage*. Surveying the effects of pauperism and poverty on women in Liverpool, Miss Hopkins promoted preventive social work to rescue the young from the vice trade. Ideas on preventive reforms had been voiced even earlier in Europe, but Hopkins' writings bridged the gap between English and American reform. Shortly after Miss Hopkins' views had been introduced into the United States, purity leaders began to popularize the ideas through their writing. As early as 1885, *Union Signal*, the journal of the WCTU, reproduced them for its reading public.[47]

"Age of consent" was the age at which a girl could legally consent to "carnal relations with the other sex." Age of consent covered the broad field of rape, seduction, abduction for immoral purposes, and procuring. Social developments had made existing legislation anachronistic, however. For instance, Americans, especially those of the "middling sort," were deferring the age of matrimony. Early marriage was no longer considered important for social hygiene. Simultaneously, urbanization loosened the moral restraints common to small towns of a pre-industrialized era. Many states fixed the age of consent at what, under modern conditions, were absurdly and shockingly low ages. Delaware, for instance, fixed the age at seven. Although Delaware had the dubious distinction of having the lowest legislated age, many other states were not far behind, fixing the age at about ten years. Women reformers recognized in low age of consent laws a persistent threat to family purity and a bar to woman's social and spiritual advancement. Furthermore, the extremely low age permitted the recruitment of scarcely adolescent girls into the brothels. Women's rights leaders smarted from a fundamental sexual injustice that resulted in higher sentences for stealing a woman's purse than for stealing her "honor." Even more painful for them was the realization that existing laws permitted girls to sell their virtue, but denied them the right to sell their dolls or pocket handkerchiefs.[48] While concerned with women's legal disabilities, purity reformers kept sight of their main objective, the realization of a new morality, and dealt with age of consent in the larger context.

Age of consent was an issue with which women could identify in a time of rapid urbanization. The city not only provided more opportunities for women in business, commerce, and industry, it also provided expanded dangers and temptations. Since urbanization destroyed the close kinship ties of a pre-industrial era, and the urban culture lacked the restraints of the small town, reformers developed agencies for single women to serve as a substitute for family environments. For years, the Young Women's Christian Associations had been "homes away from home." A major social function of the YWCA and similar agencies was the preservation of individual purity. Girls' friendly societies and legal aid societies performed similar social functions by assisting women. Churches, as they became aware of the protection young women needed in the city, also undertook activities for their benefit.

Purity reformers devoted much energy to expanding protection for working women, but the distinction between protection and social control was always tenuous. Interested in more than lodgings for women, purity workers aimed at finding substitutes for the low entertainments and corrupting influences of the urban life. Their motivation was directly related to their concern with prostitution. As great numbers entered a discriminatory labor market, low wages and limited job opportunities made prostitution a major problem. Mrs. E. S. Turner of Philadelphia's New Century Club confided to prominent Philadelphians, probably in the mid-1880s, that 110,000 Philadelphia working women had to be taught the "dignity of labor" and learn to have pride rather than shame in their new position as workers. Only by providing substitute homes could the debilitating influences of "insidious dancing classes," cheap theaters, variety shows, and concerts be negated. The alternative was, as Turner saw it, a slow erosion of morality.[49] Turner and other purity reformers were not anti-city, but wanted to construct a social environment to conserve morality. Innocence, a fragile quality, needed nurturing. Only through preventive social reforms could the republic be saved.

No longer satisfied with proclaiming the importance of cultural values, purity reformers now were institutionalizing them. Institutions, built to perpetuate the new morality, transmitted values into the social sphere and selectively serviced those urbanites most requiring moral support. In the process, reformers were working for a greater socio-cultural integration.

Motivations varied among purity reformers who advocated combination of women as a method of self-protection. Emily Blackwell thought working women possessed social characteristics and self-images that inhibited them from entering the labor market. Social combination allowed women to develop new social roles. Combination further contributed to woman's emancipation by encouraging real opportunities for the emergence of new leadership. Moreover, associationism forced society to reevaluate the importance of women and allowed women to find a suitable self-image. As long as women remained self-effacing, they would be "second-class citizens." Ultimately, self-help programs raised women in men's esteem.[50] Turner and Blackwell both recommended the formation of women's groups, but for different reasons: the former wished to preserve and protect innocence; the latter, to elevate the status of woman by improving her self-consciousness.

Although women came to reform from varying motivations, they eventually unified in the common cause of purification. Boston's moral educationists illustrated this point quite well. In 1873, a small band of Boston women met on Sunday afternoons to read essays and exchange thoughts about vital contemporary issues. In 1877, under the leadership of Dr. Harriet Clisby, the association went from discussion to social action, providing vocational training and placement services for women. In this way, moral educationists reorganized themselves into the Women's Educational and Industrial Union. Originally located in Boston, the WEIU underwent geographical and functional expansion. When Abby Morton Diaz assumed the presidency in 1881, the association was regional in scope.[51] It quickly identified with social purity reform.

Mrs. E. S. Turner's association, another case in point, paralleled, but was independent of, the New England-based group. Moved by her 1883 pamphlet warning citizens of urban dangers for working women, the New Century Club of Philadelphia authorized the formation of an auxiliary, the New Century Guild of Working Women. Functionally, the Guild was a settlement house. It was designed to serve all working women, not just to service a neighborhood or ethnic group. With that larger view of social work, the New Century Guild enjoyed a unique status among Philadelphia neighborhood and working girls' guilds, assuming a leadership role and coordinating settlement house and working girls' guild activities in Philadelphia.[52]

Another local endeavor to improve the conditions of

working women originated in New York City. Inspired by
Mrs. E. S. Turner and Ellice Hopkins, Grace Hoadley
Dodge, of the famous New York merchant family, em-
barked on another local project for New Yorkers.
Cooperating with Virginia Potter, daughter of New York's
Bishop Potter, Dodge inquired into the potentialities of
preventive social work for preserving morality. To broadcast the results of her inquiry, she contributed "Preventive
Work: or, The Care of Our Girls" to reform literature, a
pamphlet that did little more than paraphrase Ellice
Hopkins' ideas. Like Turner and Blackwell, Dodge wanted
to inspire collective moral action among working girls; she
stated her reform objective as the preservation of
morality.[53] Dodge, perhaps more than most purity
leaders, appreciated the relationship of preventive social
work to purity reform, and she clearly understood her special reform role of preventing the growth of prostitution.
She consulted Aaron Powell and gained his support for her
preventive reform. As the New York Committee invited
new members and directed the organization of Social
Purity Alliances in 1885, she made her contribution by attending meetings to report on the growth of her new Working Girls' society. Although she was frequently too busy to
attend executive meetings regularly, she always kept communications open with other national leaders.[54]

Dodge deliberately introduced purity reform thought
into the Working Girls' Society. Circulating purity
literature sent by the New York Committee, she prepared,
as an outgrowth of her moral concerns, "A Bundle of Letters to Busy Girls." First delivered as a series of talks
before the society, she later published the letters as a
book.[55] The letters, by modern norms, were quite conventional, but in the 1880s they represented a major step
forward in sex education. Through her talks and in her
publications, Dodge assisted in the destruction of the

"conspiracy of silence," which, by ignoring sexuality, mystified it. The Working Girls' Society, a substitute for the family, taught sex education as a matter of course. It was a "training school for the home."

Paying attention to institutional values was only one technique for purifying the city. If purity values were to be actualized in an urban environment, urban society had to become more "homelike." Drawing a line of defense at the doorway and concentrating on the purification within the family alone might lead to failure. Not only did women carry the germs of the city into their homes because their skirts dragged along the city streets, but they and other family members came in contact with "moral germs" as well. Moralists could respond to new urban conditions in two ways: by prohibiting specific behavioral deviations, or by constructing social environments that eliminated the potential for that behavior. Working girls' guilds were designed for the new social environment. Censorship, a remedial reform, performed the latter function in social transformation; by purifying the social environment, it supposedly improved social behavior. In a period of fundamental social change, censorship groups could clearly be expected to arise.[56] And they did.

Although Anthony Comstock was America's best-known censorship advocate in the late nineteenth century, Josiah and Deborah Leeds of Philadelphia deserve greater attention for their careers as public censors. Comstock and the Leeds were allied within the purity movement, but the Leeds were, in many ways, more resourceful and inventive than Comstock. Acting as a liaison between the purity movement and the WCTU, they were more interested in defining acceptable social behavior than in suppressing prurient and obscene literature.

Eager to prevent "germs of licentiousness" from contaminating the national morality, Leeds began his long career as a censor with a campaign to suppress undesirable billboard advertising during the 1876 Centennial held in Philadelphia.[57] This small start launched a career that included the prohibition of objectionable theatrical performances, ballet, social dancing, "pornographic magazines." (the *Police Gazette* above all), and "indecent art." More essential-minded than Comstock, Leeds examined the nature of his reforms, searching for a larger social meaning. In his analysis of the causes of impurity, Leeds believed he had located the key to the maintenance of purity in personal habits. His conclusions led him to write a pamphlet on "Simplicity of Attire in Relation to Social Purity" in 1886. The pamphlet, quite timely, reinforced the reform ideology. As soon as Frances Willard, president of the WCTU, read the tract, she acknowledged its importance to the purity cause. After enthusiastically congratulating the author, Miss Willard had the pamphlet republished as a WCTU tract.

PREVENTIVE REFORM, THE WHITE CROSS, AND THE DEVELOPMENT OF A MASS MOVEMENT

Before 1885, antiregulationist and new abolitionist involvements accentuated the defensive, remedial quality of the purity movement. Although the complementary actions of working women's guilds, moral education, prison and censorship societies expanded the scope of new abolitionism, remedial and preventive aspects of these reforms frequently operated against each other. As social purity thought developed, however, it rejected the static concepts of society and older religious theories that described human nature as immutable, determined, and unchangeable. Purity reformers, therefore, departed from traditional modes of conserving morality. In practical day-by-day reforms, they gradually emphasized the actualization of the new morality and preventive reforms over the remedial. Making this shift required a more systematic analysis of social causation and a clearer concept of social organization. The integration of complementary reforms depended upon the purity reformers' intellectual thoroughness in making the larger connections among the reforms explicit.

English purity reform, perhaps more intellectually sophisticated, continued to exert its influence on American thought, materially speeding the transformation of new abolitionism into purity reform. The Anglo-American nature of the movement was illustrated in the case of Benjamin DeCosta, a New York Episcopalian minister. On a visit to England, DeCosta met and conferred with English reformers, among them Eunice Hopkins, Josephine Butler, and William T. Stead, editor of the *Pall Mall Gazette*. Purity reform inspired DeCosta, and he resolved to make a contribution to it. On his return to the United States, he almost immediately established the White Cross Army, which was patterned after the Church of England's society.

The Church of England had initiated the White Cross Society to promote social purity and to assist young men in their resistance to illicit sexual relations by giving sex education within the church. In some ways the Society performed the functions of girls' friendly societies, providing a safe refuge in the city; in other ways it performed functions similar to those of the youth temperance societies. Organized at a meeting chaired by Bishop Aucland on February 15, 1883, it shortly gained status as a church organization, with the Bishop of Durham as its president. Within days after it became a church organization, the Church of England made the society a diocesan institution and extended its branches to the British Empire. Enthusiastic Episcopalians resolved, at the Lambeth Con-

ference of Bishops in 1888, that the clergy and laity had
a solemn duty to support and promote social purity
work.[58] With the sanction of English churchmen, Benjamin DeCosta formed a New York branch at the parish of
St. John the Evangelist in 1885. As a result of his actions,
he moved easily into the inner circle of purity reformers.[59]

American Episcopalians copied the English organiza-
tion plan, and, to guarantee rapid national acceptance,
secured a committee of bishops to supervise their work.
The bishops of New York, Chicago, Baltimore, Minnesota,
Pittsburgh, Boston, and Illinois sat on the committee.
Local churches sanctioned purity work quite readily. On
May 26, 1886, the Chicago diocese commended White
Cross work. In the fall, the Episcopalian General Convention, meeting in Chicago, appointed a committee on social
purity. Forty-six bishops at the convention also signed a
petition endorsing the single standard of morality.[60]

The general public received the White Cross Society
favorably. Journalists telegraphed news of its organizational meeting to every city. Powell reported in the *Philanthropist* that the "best classes" supported the White Cross
Society, making "White Cross" a household word.[61]

Not to be left behind in championing progressive
reforms, the WCTU added White Cross and, subsequently,
White Shield, the female equivalent of the society, to its
lengthening list of purity activities. Frances Willard, frequently a leader in popularizing reform, undertook a major propagandist role. Intent upon getting the message to
the largest audience possible, Miss Willard prepared a cir-
cular to publicize White Cross Societies, which was sent to
WCTU locals, clergymen, teachers, physicians, and
editors. Newspapers across the nation reprinted the story of
the White Cross.[62] To further publicize her view, Willard
toured the nation as a White Cross speaker. She addressed

"immense audiences" in Chicago, New York, Philadelphia, Boston, Baltimore, and other large cities. When, in 1887, the American Social Science Association invited her to address its convention, the Association legitimated and, therefore, assisted the movement.[63] With wide public acceptance, new abolitionism, now augmented by the White Cross movement, had forged a new image as the purity crusade. In broadening its ideological appeal, purity reform had become a mass movement. The new abolitionists had found their public.

The Church of England's reform was not suitable, in its original institutional form, for denominational America. Within a year, purity reformers had seen these limits and broken with the English plan of organization. Episcopalians, of course, persisted in using the original institutional format. Otherwise, reformers recommended that White Cross Societies be grafted on to existing religious and reform societies. In this way, purity reform cut across denominational boundaries. White Cross, adapted to American institutional structures, received the same support from reformers as the purity movement.

A further innovation accommodated the White Cross idea to American society. If, indeed, reform was to assist in the abolition of the double moral standard, reformers also had to pledge themselves to a single moral standard. The WCTU organized the White Shield Society for this purpose, and although it was never as popular as the White Cross, it did give some ideological symmetry to the movement.[64]

White Cross is known to have been a relatively popular society, but an accurate assessment of its membership is impossible. The societies were highly decentralized and lacked institutional records, and they never bothered to compile a membership tabulation. Only fragmentary estimates are extant. One purity reformer estimated tens of thousands enrolled in the society in 1886, its first year.[65] Although the figure cannot be substantiated, it gives some indication of rapid growth. The assistance of the YMCA gives another indication of popularity. YMCA secretaries initially refused to affiliate with the White Cross Society, but after reconsideration, the New England YMCAs systematically included purity reform as an adjunct of their work. A single meeting of the White Cross Society held at the New York YMCA attracted 1,000 members. The New York "Y" reported membership growth of 700 in one year. The Philadelphia YMCA reported 250 members in its fledgling White Cross Society. Benjamin DeCosta, reporting to the society's 1887 convention, boasted of branches in every state and territory. Indeed, the society's work had grown so large that he recommended hiring an administrative assistant to keep the society going.[66]

The White Cross Society, as a mass movement, was a tremendous boost to the woman's movement. Through its appeal to young men it educated both young men and women to the new ideal man-woman relationship. When young men or women pledged themselves to a "pure life," they committed themselves to the objectives of the woman's movement. The White Cross Society, like the woman's movement, further spiritualized sexuality. The society tacitly agreed that women's moral standards were higher than men's. Purification, the common goal of the reform movements under discussion, implied the sanctification of womanhood.

Because of its relationship to other reformers, the White Cross Society efficiently mobilized the churches behind purity reform. In the process, it transformed clerical opinion and enlisted the clergy in the fight for social reforms. Like civil service advocates or temperance reformers, purity reformers learned the importance of the social gospel to reach ends. The social gospel, however, was only one technique utilized. Practical reform took precedence over theology, and social education, to which the social gospel contributed, was the over-riding interest of social purists. Moral exhortation, symptomatic of the clergymen's resistance to change, faded into the background.[67] Clergymen allied with the purity movement were applied sociologists.

White Cross Societies aided in the development of urban social control. Young people who otherwise might have been victims of urban temptations found mutual strength and support through group activities and identity.[68] Although White Cross Societies at first only gave limited support to the purity movement, they became willing instruments for social purification upon acknowledging the real nature of their mission—to achieve the general moral elevation of society. As a significant educative agency, White Cross Societies showed purity reformers the importance of social education and underscored the need for sex education, preferably within the family, but from members of the medical and clerical professions, if necessary.

Although many religious denominations supported purity reforms, none came close to the full commitment of the Society of Friends. The Quakers, like the Episcopalians, came to the movement early. In fact, many purity reform leaders, including Gibbons and Powell, were Quakers.[69] Hannah A. Plummer, in describing the social functions of the society's Philanthropic Labor Union, articulated the view that Quaker reform agencies were an instrument for the purification of the social order.[70] The society was commited ideologically and institutionally to purity reform. In 1884, the society formed a committee on corrupt literature within its Yearly Meeting. In 1885, the Western Yearly Meeting endorsed purity reform. By 1886, almost every Monthly Meeting included purity reform on its list of concerns.[71] The urge for purification united both ardent religionists, still affiliated with churches, and secularists, who, breaking with organized religion, were attracted by the cultural themes of the purity cause. Josiah W. Leeds, the public censor, played a formidable role among the denominations. In 1882, Leeds and Anthony Comstock seemed alone in their struggle against "impure" literature. Three years later, Leeds boasted of his inroads into organized religion. Many churchmen, through the actions of individual reformers, became ardent friends and supporters of reform.[72]

The participation of religious denominations in purity reform broadened the popular base of the movement. For example, the Reverend A. H. Lewis, Seventh-Day Baptist leader, published *The Light of Home*, which he sent to more than one hundred thousand homes.[73] *The Light of Home* advocated the implementation of social purity through family reform. Not only did purity leaders speak through their own publications, but they now had popularizers within religious denominations.

The WCTU, however, remained the most important agency for extending the base of the reform movement, since it transcended denominational barriers and was unstinting in its efforts. Once purity reform eclipsed new abolitionism, it reached departmental status within the WCTU, and attracted these women at a rate unprecedented by any other reform in WCTU history.[74]

Early in the purity movement's development, Frances Willard, the president of the WCTU, considered herself the national leader of purity reform. She invited Aaron and Anna Powell to serve as national superintendents of the WCTU's department of social purity, organized in 1885. They were afraid, however, that the New York Committee might be overshadowed, and they refused. After the

Powells rejected her offer, Willard offered Dr. and Mrs.
James H. Kellogg of Battle Creek, Michigan, the superintendency.[75] The Kelloggs were eminently qualified.
Besides being a purity reformer, J. H. Kellogg was a leading hydropathist. (Abolitionists, old and new, had
displayed sympathy for the "water cure" in medicine.)[76]
When the WCTU formed a department for the suppression
of impure literature, Willard managed to place Josiah W.
Leeds and his wife, Deborah, in the superintendency.[77]
The use of husband-wife teams in these departments symbolized the equality of sexes and the single moral standard
upheld by the WCTU.

Although the WCTU popularized purity reform
through the implementation of numerous programs, the
relationship between the WCTU and the New York Committee was clearly defined from the start. When Mary T.
Burt of the New York WCTU began attending New York
Committee meetings, she deferred to them as leaders and
pledged to follow wherever the committee led. Frances
Willard, through her leadership of the WCTU, heralded a
"New Society," a new Christian theocracy in government,
or a "common religion" with women serving through
philanthropic work. Willard was a key figure in purity
reform, but, nevertheless, only one ally, albeit an important one, in this major reform drive.[78] The New York
Committee maintained its leadership initiative.

NEW COALITIONS FOR SOCIAL PURITY

After ten years, the provisional committees organized to
defeat reglementation remained active. As the nucleus of
later reform organization, committee membership changed
only slightly in the transformation to purity reform. The

provisional committees had, however, outlived their
usefulness and required institutional modification. Purity
reformers, both abolitionists and moral educationists, acknowledged the critical importance of reorganization.
Moral educationists, like other reformers, sensed a social
breakthrough, an imminent acceptance of reform by the
general public. On the brink of tremendous expansion, the
work of the committees seemed limitless, multiplying their
functions beyond the immediate comprehension of either
of the Powells.[79] Compared to its English counterpart,
however, American purity reform was in an early phase of
institutional development.

The English had experienced similar growth pains,
and, in 1883, had reorganized into the Social Purity
Alliance. English purity reformers at that time had urged
Americans to emulate them.[80] The Social Purity
Alliance combined men's and women's groups into one
organization, ending sexual segregation in purity reform.
The reconstruction of reform and society would proceed
on the basis of equality between the sexes. Reformers, having combined moral education societies and vigilance committees into a common organization for sex reform, now
addressed themselves to actualizing equality in general society by breaking down sexual segregation.

The American social purists followed the English
lead. On a municipal level, local moral education societies,
always complementing new abolitionism, searched for new
reform coalitions. In Washington, former members of the
moral education society cooperated with the Washington
White Cross Society and the Washington WCTU in 1885,
to form a Social Purity Alliance. Washington churches,
sympathetic to the new reform organization, sent delegates
to the alliance convention. In Philadelphia, religious
leaders and former moral education society members
cooperated in establishing a Social Purity Alliance in

1887.[81] They elected the Reverend William McVickar president. Social purity alliances, institutionally reflecting the new reform *gestalt*, combined moral education, anti-prostitution, suppression of impure literature, mothers' meetings, and a host of other reforms under one broad reform umbrella.

Consistently interested in urban social problems, purity reformers made limited excursions into politics in the 1880s. Elizabeth Blackwell, contemplating the political ramifications of purity reform, longed for a "moral municipal league."[82] Social purity alliances, although not yet operating as moral municipal leagues, were moving in the direction of Blackwell's ideal. Temperance reform, coincidentally, paralleled this trend. In Philadelphia, for instance, the temperance movement did enter municipal politics. Representatives from religious, philanthropic, and charitable societies organized the Citizens' Representative Committee, as an offshoot of the Law and Order Society, the enforcement arm of the temperance movement. Like the Law and Order Society, which enforced temperance laws, the Citizens' Representative Committee acted as a moral watchdog, zealous for the enforcement of vice laws. As the Moral Committee of One Hundred, its popular name, it tried to purify municipal morality, just as the Committee of One Hundred, a businessmen's political reform group, tried to purify municipal politics.[83] Philadelphia reformers, on reconsideration, rejected the representational principle, however, and the Moral Committee went out of existence. Nevertheless, within a decade the social purity alliances would move into municipal politics once again.

While purity reformers were alerted to the need for coordination and cooperation among their various agencies, religious groups were undergoing a corresponding awakening. The Interdenominational Congress met to

discuss problems of the cities in 1885. The Evangelical
Alliance, a more important forum, conducted a General
Christian Conference in Washington, D.C., on December
7-9, 1887, exploring "National Perils and Opportunities."
During its sessions the delegates discussed the social evil
thoroughly. A clear correspondence of interest existed between purity reform and the Evangelical Alliance in their
common interest in family protection. The "national
peril," from the Evangelical Alliance perspective, was the
danger to the family, the social foundation of society.[84]
The New York Convention of Women's Suffrage Associations in 1885 also feared the consequences of family
disintegration.[85] Among religionists, social purists, and
feminists a pervasive sense of imminent danger existed. At
its base was a fear for the stability of social structure.

Purity reformers believed leadership to "control the
moral atmosphere" was essential in order to eliminate vices
that were causing the degradation of the community.[86]
Suspicious of church leadership, these leaders believed
every institution, including the churches, had been cor-
rupted. Antoinette Brown Blackwell, anticipating an
American Reformation leading to the purification of society, charged that the young men of the churches could
not be relied upon to live pure lives. If Blackwell's memory
served her well, DeCosta physically recoiled at the statement, the remark cutting through him "like a dagger."
DeCosta, so Blackwell reported, knew the truth of the
claim.[87]

Religious and reform leaders seemed poised for a major urban reform offensive in the latter 1880s. The new social purity alliances, conscious of the importance of
municipal moral reform, were organizationally better
equipped than previous reform institutions. Moreover,
Gibbons and Powell had emerged as uncontested national
leaders. Purity reform had broadened its popular support

and acquired denominational support as well, and Powell converted his newsletter, the *American Bulletin*, into the *Philanthropist*, a national purity journal. In addition, the woman's movement's acceptance of purity reform coincided with a national and international reawakening of moralists and religionists. Purity reform trends were propitiously conducive to a new departure. Conscious of entering a new phase of activity, Powell redirected the movement toward more positive and preventive reforms.

NOTES

1. William Greenleaf Eliot, *Early Religious Education Considered as the Divinely Appointed Way to Regenerate Life* (Boston: Crosby, Nichols and Company, 1855). See also standard works on child rearing: Bernard Wishy, *The Child and the Republic: The Dawn of Modern American Child Nurture* (Philadelphia: University of Pennsylvania Press, 1968); Philip Ariès, *Centuries of Childhood* (New York: Knopf, 1962).

2. Purity reformers consistently repeated anti-evangelical statements in their writings. Working closely with moral educationists, they placed their hopes with education and child rearing.

3. C. L. Lewis to Elizabeth Gay, September 8, 1876, Sidney Howard Gay Papers, Columbia University; and Mrs. Bernard Whitman, "The Moral Education Association," *The Chautauquan* 16 (October 1892): 86-87.

4. *Alpha*, April 1, 1885, p. 4; and "Religion of the Body," May 1, 1885, pp. 11-12.

5. Elizabeth Blackwell, "Women's Entrance into Medicine," *Nation* 62 (May 7, 1896): 364-65.

6. "Boston Moral Education Society," *Alpha*, January 1, 1880, p. 6.

7. "Editorial," *Alpha*, December 1, 1877, p. 6.

8. Aaron M. Powell, *State Regulation of Vice: Regulation Efforts in America* (New York: Wood and Holbrook, 1878).

9. "Purity Alliance Conference," *Woman's Journal*, December 14, 1895, p. 393.

10. Abby Hopper Gibbons to Anna Rice Powell, February 24, 1886, in *Life of Abby Hopper Gibbons*, ed. S. H. Emerson (New York: G. P. Putnam and Sons, 1896), 2, 246; and Anna Rice Powell to Elizabeth Gay,

October 19, 1886, Sidney Howard Gay Papers, Columbia University.

11. "Mother's Department," *Alpha*, June 1, 1886, p. 11; *Minutes of the National Woman's Christian Temperance Union at the Seventh Annual Meeting in Boston, October 27-30, 1880* (New York: National Temperance Society and Publishing House, 1880), p. 15; and *Minutes of the National Woman's Christian Temperance Union at the Eleventh Annual Meeting, St. Louis, October 22-25, 1884* (Chicago: WTPA, 1884), p. xviii. For the history of the WCTU, see Norton Mezvinsky, "The White Ribbon Reform, 1874-1920" (Ph.D. diss., University of Wisconsin, 1959).

12. Elizabeth Blackwell to Barbara Smith, November 10, 1883, Elizabeth Blackwell Papers, Columbia University.

13. Antoinette Brown Blackwell to Miss Booth, November 12, 1872, Alma Lutz Collection, Radcliffe College.

14. Frances Willard, "Presidential Address to the WCTU," in *Woman's Journal*, November 10, 1888, pp. 355-63.

15. Francis P. Weisenburger, *Ordeal of Faith: The Crisis of Church-Going America, 1865-1900* (New York: Philosophical Library, 1959, pp. 128-29.

16. Anna Rice Powell to Elizabeth Gay, February 22, and April 25, 1878, Sidney Howard Gay Papers, Columbia University.

17. Powell, *State Regulation*, p. 88; Henry J. Wilson and James Gledstone, *Report of a Visit to the United States* (Sheffield, 1876), p. 5; and M. H. Henry, "The Discussion of the Prevention of Syphilis with Reference to the Regulation of Prostitution, at the Third International Medical Congress, Held at Vienna, August 1873—With Additional Remarks," *American Journal of Syphilography and Dermatology* 5 (1874): 23.

18. Anna Rice Powell to Elizabeth Gay, April 23 and

July 8, 1880, Sidney Howard Gay Papers, Columbia University.

19. Anna Rice Powell to Elizabeth Gay, November 6, 1876, Sidney Howard Gay Papers, Columbia University.

20. Albert Gihon, "The Contagious Diseases Act of Great Britain," *Maryland Medical Journal* 8 (March 1882): 518.

21. Richard H. Thomas, "Reply to Gihon," *Maryland Medical Journal* 9 (May 1882): 31.

22. George H. Rohe, "State Regulation of Prostitution: Evidence in Its Favor," *Maryland Medical Journal* 9 (June 1882): 83.

23. "R. H. Thomas to Editor," *Maryland Medical Journal* 9 (July 1882): 121, 122.

24. Albert Gihon, "The Prevention of Venereal Disease by Legislation," *The Sanitarian* 10 (June 1882): 341.

25. R. Harvey Reed, "Who is Responsible?" *The Sanitarian* 27 (May 1886): 411-21.

26. Fred R. Sturgis, "The Regulation and Repression of Prostitution," *Boston Medical and Surgical Journal* 108 (1883): 299-301.

27. Charles H. Kitchell, *The Social Evil: Its Cause and Cure; Read before the Society of Medical Jurisprudence and State Medicine at the Academy of Medicine, New York, May 13, 1886* (New York: Press of Beeker and Gerry, 1886).

28. William M. Laury, *Social Ethics* (New York: Society of Medical Jurisprudence and State Medicine, 1886).

29. Albert Gihon, "On the Protection of the Innocent and Helpless Members of the Community From Venereal Diseases and Their Consequences," *Public Health: Reports and Papers, Volume V, 1879* (Boston: Houghton Mifflin and Company, 1880), pp. 55-65.

30. "Report of the Committee on the Prevention of Venereal Disease," *Public Health: Reports and Papers, Volume VI, 1880* (Boston: Houghton Mifflin and Company, 1881), pp. 402, 413-14, 423.

31. Aaron M. Powell to Elizabeth Gay, November 13 and 23, 1881, Sidney Howard Gay Papers, Columbia University.

32. Frank Wolfe, "Report of the Legal Advisor," *Public Health: Reports and Papers, Volume X, 1884* (Concord: Republican Press Association, 1885), p. 329.

33. Frederick Wines, "Minority Report," *Public Health: Reports and Papers, Volume X, 1884*, pp. 334-36. For an analysis of Wines' work in divorce reform, see William L. O'Neill, *Divorce in the Progressive Era* (New Haven, 1967).

34. J. Birbeck Nevins, ed., *An Address to the Members of the American Legal and Medical Professions from the British, Continental and General Federation for the Abolition of State Regulation of Prostitution and the National Medical Association (Great Britain and Ireland) for the Abolition of State Regulated Prostitution* (London, 1877), p. 4.

35. Anna Rice Powell to Elizabeth Gay, August 25, 1878, Sidney Howard Gay Papers, Columbia University; *Contagious Diseases Act for the United States: Address to the New York Academy of Medicine* (New York: New York Committee for the Suppression of State Regulated Vice, June 1878), p. 3; Aaron M. Powell to Elizabeth Gay, May 1, 1878, Sidney Howard Gay Papers, Columbia University; and "Address to British Continental and General Federation in Congress," *Alpha,* November 1, 1880, pp. 1-2.

36. *Alpha*, May 1, 1886, p. 13.

37. *Philanthropist*, May 1886, p. 4.

38. *Philanthropist*, August 1886, pp. 4-5; "A Dangerous Bill," *Philanthropist*, April 1886, p. 4, and July 1886, p. 1.

39. Aileen S. Kraditor, *The Ideas of the Woman Suffrage Movement, 1890-1920* (New York: Columbia University Press, 1965), p. 66.

40. *Philanthropist*, February 1889, pp. 2, 5.

41. Aaron Macy Powell, "Social Purity," *Proceedings of Friends' Union for Philanthropic Labor, 1888*, p. 84.

42. *52d Annual Report of the Women's Prison Association, 1896* (New York: G. P. Putnam's Sons Printer, 1897), p. 7. For a history of New York's penitentiaries, see W. David Lewis, *From Newgate to Dannemora: The Rise of the Penitentiary in New York, 1796-1848* (New York: Cornell University Press, 1965).

43. Frances Willard, "A Day Among the Chicago Philanthropists," *The Chautauquan* 8 (March 1887): 348-49.

44. *Proceedings of the National Conference of Charities and Corrections at the 13th Annual Session Held in St. Paul, Minnesota, July 15-22, 1886* (Boston: George H. Ellis, 1886), p. 419; and J. K. Barney, "Police Matrons," *Lend a Hand* 2 (1897): 472.

45. Abby H. Gibbons to Anna Rice Powell, March 12 and April 26, 1889, in Emerson, *Life of Abby Hopper Gibbons*, 1: 270-71.

46. Frederick J. Shepard, "The Women's Educational and Industrial Union of Buffalo," *Publication of the Buffalo Historical Society* 22 (1918): 150; *New Century Club History* (Philadelphia, 1899), p. 56; and *Philanthropist*, August 1888, p. 1.

47. "Ellice Hopkin's 'Social Wreckage,' " *Chautauquan* 4 (October 1883): 40-42; and Aaron M. Powell to Elizabeth Gay, December 14, 1885, Sidney Howard Gay Papers, Columbia University.

48. Helen Campbell, "The Age of Consent: A Symposium" *Arena* 12 (April 1895): 285-86; and *White Cross* 1 (n.d.): 6, Benjamin DeCosta Papers, New York Historical Society.

49. E. S. Turner, *Confidential* (Philadelphia, n.d.), Historical Society of Pennsylvania.

50. Emily Blackwell, "Need of Combination Among Women for Self-Protection," *Philanthropist*, May 1887, p. 2.

51. *The Women's Educational and Industrial Union, Boston, Massachusetts, 1892-93* (Boston: L. Boreta and Company, 1893), pp. 14, 17.

52. *Executive Board Minutes of the New Century Guild, May 8, 1891*, New Century Guild, Philadelphia, pp. 184-85.

53. Frances Willard to Anna Rice Powell, June 4, 1886, Frances Willard Papers, Radcliffe College. (Ellice Hopkins also directly influenced the activities of Frances E. Willard in social purity work.) Grace H. Dodge, "Preventive Work; or, The Care of Our Girls," October 4, 1883, Grace H. Dodge Papers, National YWCA; "Work among Working Girls," *Christian Union*, November 1, 1883, p. 361. Grace Dodge understood that the protection of morality meant an aggressive extension of it into new areas.

54. Grace H. Dodge, "Talk at Friends' Conference," January 23, 1891, contained in Scrapbook, p. 71, Grace H. Dodge Papers, Teachers' College, Columbia University; Anna Rice Powell to Elizabeth Gay, February 26, 1885, Sidney Howard Gay Papers, Columbia University.

55. Grace H. Dodge, *A Bundle of Letters to Busy Girls on Practical Matters* (New York: Funk and Wagnalls, 1887).

56. Thomas C. Cochran, "The Historians Use of Social Role," in *Generalization in the Writing of History*, ed. Louis Gottschalk (Chicago: University of Chicago Press, 1963), p. 107.

57. Josiah W. Leeds, "Philadelphia's Duty to Her Centennial Guests," *Christian Neighbor*, April 12, 1875, in Josiah W. Leeds Scrapbook, Josiah W. Leeds Papers, Haverford College.

58. Benjamin F. DeCosta, *The White Cross: Its Origins and Progress* (Chicago: Sanitary Publishing Company, 1887), p. 3; and Herbert Everitt to Benjamin F. DeCosta, January 23, 1891, Benjamin DeCosta Papers, New York Historical Society.

59. *The White Cross* I, no. 1 (n.d.): 4, Benjamin DeCosta Papers, New York Historical Society. As new purity reforms were developed, their originators became members of the purity elite.

60. *The White Cross*, I, no. 1 (n.d.): 5, Benjamin DeCosta Papers, New York Historical Society.

61. "DeCosta's White Cross Movement," *Philanthropist*, January 1886, p. 1.

62. *Plan for Work for 1886, Department of Social Purity, NWCTU to Local Unions, Clergymen, Teachers, Physicians and Editors* (n.p., 1886), and White Cross Scrapbook, Frances E. Willard Papers, Evanston, Illinois.

63. *Minutes of the National Woman's Christian Temperance Union, Fourteenth Annual Meeting, Nashville, Tennessee, November 16-21, 1887* (Chicago: WPTA, 1888), pp. clxix-xi.

64. "Kate Bushnell Report," *Philanthropist*, January 1890, p. 3.

65. Elizabeth Powell Bond, "The Movement for Social Purity," Elizabeth Powell Bond Papers, Swarthmore College, p. 32.

66. "Third Anniversary of YMCA, N.Y. White Cross Society," *Philanthropist*, April 1888, p. 1; *Philanthropist*, April 1886, p. 4; August 1887, p. 6; and "Third Anniversary of White Cross Society," *Philanthropist*, April 1887, p. 3.

67. "Seventh Anniversary of White Cross Society," *Philanthropist*, March 1891, p. 6.

68. "Night Life of Young Men," *White Cross*, 1, no. 1 (n.d.).

69. See Appendix A for the purity elite's denominational affiliations.

70. Hannah A. Plummer, "What Relationship should the Society of Friends Hold Regarding Humanitarian Reform?" *Proceedings of Friends Union for Philanthropic Labor, 1882* (Richmond, Ind.: Telegram Printing Co., 1882), pp. 14-15.

71. *Proceedings of Friends Union for Philanthropic Labor, 1884* (Richmond, Ind.: Book Job Printing Company, 1884); *Philanthropist*, October 1888, p. 8; *Proceedings of Friends Union for Philanthropic Labor, Fourth Conference, 1886* (Richmond, Ind.: Telegram Printing Co., 1887), pp. 65-66.

72. "Men, Measures and Morals," *Christian Nation* (N.Y.), May 13, 1885, p. 290.

73. *Light of Home* 2 (January 1887).

74. Frances E. Willard, *Glimpses of Fifty Years* (Chicago: Woman's Temperance Publishing Company, 1889), p. 428.

75. Anna Rice Powell to Elizabeth Gay, December 18, 1885, Sidney Howard Gay Papers, Columbia University. Kellogg's activities covered many reforms. He operated a sanitarium at Battle Creek, Michigan, was a leading temperance advocate, and invented breakfast cereals. See Gerald Carson, *Cornflake Crusade* (New York: Rinehart and Company, 1957).

76. L. G. Stephenson, "Science Down the Drain," *Bulletin of the History of Medicine* 29 (January-February 1955): 1-26.

77. H. W. Smith to Deborah Leeds, October 17, 1887, and Mary Woodbridge to Deborah Leeds, November 24, 1887, Josiah W. Leeds Papers, Haverford College.

78. *Philanthropist*, March 1887, p. 8, Frances E. Willard, "Society and Society Women, A New Definition," *Social Review*, July 28, 1894, and *Social Purity, The Latest and Greatest Crusade* (New York: Funk and Wagnalls, 1886), pp. 21-2.

79. Abby H. Gibbons to Anna Rice Powell, February 24, 1886, in Emerson, *Life of Abby Hopper Gibbons*, 2: 246; and Anna Rice Powell to Elizabeth Gay, October 19, 1886, Sidney Howard Gay Papers, Columbia University.

80. "Society for the Promotion of Social Purity," *Alpha*, August 1883, p. 9.

81. *Alpha*, April 1, 1886, p. 11; February 1, 1887, p.

8; October 1, 1886, p. 10; and "A Social Purity Alliance in Philadelphia," *Philanthropist*, July 1886, p. 4.

82. Elizabeth Blackwell to Barbara Smith, April 12, 188?, Elizabeth Blackwell Papers, Columbia University.

83. *Philadelphia Times*, April 12, 1885.

84. Samuel Dike, *Perils to the Family: An Address before the Evangelical Alliance Conference* (Washington, D.C., December 8, 1887).

85. Women's societies focused upon the family and defined their reform activities in relation to this institution.

86. *The New York World*, February 16, 1885.

87. Anna Rice Powell to Elizabeth Gay, March 3, 1887, Sidney Howard Gay Papers, Columbia University.

4

Becoming a National Movement, 1885-1895

Between 1885 and 1895 the movement against licensed prostitution changed from a defensive action against reglementation policy into an aggressive advocacy of abolitionism. Purity reformers continued with remedial activities for changing medical thought and rehabilitating the prostitute and branched into a more general movement for the purification of society. In their latter activities they adopted the principle of prevention popular in medicine and public health. In so doing they became social hygienists.

The process of transformation, like any fundamental change, was highly complex. To lend clarity to an otherwise inchoate process, this chapter is divided arbitrarily into two parts. The first section will be devoted to continuing remedial activities and the second to the meaning of social purity for an urban society. The actual process, however, was not so cleanly divided. Purity reformers incrementally redirected their movement into a more concerted drive for social purification. Frequently, remedial activities led social purists into preventive reforms.

CONTINUING REMEDIAL ACTIVITIES

A NATIONAL CAMPAIGN AGAINST PROSTITUTION

The development of social purity alliances, despite rapid public acceptance in the mid-1880s, was retarded by conservative sexual attitudes held by Americans. Purity reformers were convinced that a "conspiracy of silence" obstructed them. Despite significant victories, they lamented newspaper editorial policies on sex—the old policy of enforcing silence to preserve innocence. Nor were educators more receptive to the new ideals. As long as they refused to review their policies, educators denied purity reform access to the vital communication channels of public education. Purity reformers needed patience, for policies were gradually being liberalized. By 1885, newspapermen were less reticent about the subject. Public campaigns against brothels and prostitution were frequent, and newspapermen reported them more often. Yet purity reformers wanted something dramatic to signal the end to the "conspiracy of silence." Until such a dramatization, popular journals and magazines excluded purity propaganda. England provided the man and the event to force journalists abruptly into fundamental reevaluation of their policies.

William T. Stead, noted English reformer and journalist, rarely allowed social custom to slow his ceaseless efforts to purify society. Encouraged by Josephine Butler and Benjamin Scott, Chamberlain of London, to break the "conspiracy of silence" by exciting public opinion, Stead was determined, through the *Pall Mall Gazette*, to destroy prostitution, the brothel, and the white slave traffic. Forewarning the faint of heart to read no farther, Stead presented, in 1885, the first modern exposé of the vice trade. Indeed, "The Maiden Tribute of Modern Babylon" disturbed his readers, causing them to hold mass demonstrations in Hyde Park and, consequentially, to pressure Parliament into modifying the criminal law. Not everyone, however, came to the support of purity reform, for public discussion resulted in negative responses as well. The police were especially resentful—they charged Stead with commission of a criminal act.

In staging the exposé, Stead had enlisted the aid of Rebecca Jarrett, a known brothelkeeper, to purchase Eliza Armstrong from her parents, ostensibly for a brothel. The Armstrongs seemed, at that time, quite willing to sell their young daughter, apparently not an uncommon transaction. After Stead publicized the arrangement in the "Maiden Tribute," and after newspapers excited adverse public opinion, the Armstrongs displayed public remorse. Socially ostracized, they regretted their initial decision and registered a complaint against Stead with the police. They charged Stead with "abduction," although they knew their child was safe in a Salvation Army matron's custody in Paris. The police knew the facts of the case, but they smarted under the exposé and willingly harassed Stead. They arrested the journalist on an abduction charge and the court adjudged Stead guilty on a legal technicality, sentencing him to three months in prison.[1]

His arrest, trial, and imprisonment were a *cause célèbre* in England. It provided the dramatic act reformers required to stir the public conscience, and purity reformers on both sides of the Atlantic willingly exploited the incident. American reformers were the most interested spectators. They attentively followed the details of the Stead trial, expecting, with perfect justification, that advantages in the form of public sympathy would accrue to them. They were not mistaken. The new crusade for the protection of womanhood that followed met with unbridled enthusiasm from religious reformers. Many religionists perceived the new reform as the turning of militant womanhood against impurities on an international scale.

Stead, however, did not receive universal praise even within purity ranks. Contending that he stirred "animal propensities" that led to vice, more traditional-minded reformers opposed his actions. Americans perceived Stead's entrance into American reform as an unwarranted intrusion. Even reformers who initially had favored his actions feared detrimental effects for American reform and reconsidered their earlier endorsements. Benjamin De-Costa, after such reconsideration, deplored Stead's methods. Sensational journalism, DeCosta believed, encouraged public outcries for repression. The spirit of purity reform, in contradistinction, was reformative.[2] This tension between reform and repression became more acute as the purity movement gained in popularity.

Other social purists, on the other hand, applauded Stead, minimizing his detrimental effect. In a moment of rhapsodic flight, Aaron Powell even proclaimed Stead the "John Brown" of the white slaves, a man to be commended for his motives, but criticized for his methods.[3]

Powell immediately grasped the importance of the *Pall Mall* exposé. Interested in exploitation, he accepted a public relations role for himself. If the public formed a positive image of Stead, purity work would be greatly advanced. If they did not, the Stead incident might become a decided liability. Not a man to allow pure chance to determine events, Powell distributed an historical sketch of the reformer and his work to newspaper publishers and editors.

The tactic proved rewarding. Although New York newspapers had originally reported the Stead incident unfavorably, after further consideration they reversed themselves. Powell played a substantial role in this change.

When the *New York Tribune*, which had a reputation for reform, reported the Stead incident negatively, Powell contacted Whitelaw Reid, the editor, to acquaint him with Stead's status among English reformers. *Tribune* coverage, as a consequence, became more favorable, but Powell was not comforted by the *Post* or *Nation* reportage. Within two years, however, New York papers came to agree with Powell's evaluation and actually praised Stead for the *Pall Mall Gazette* exposé![4]

Stead's reputation became almost legendary among nineteenth-century reformers. As late as 1900, newspapers remembered him appreciatively for his earlier activities.[5] Stead returned the praise showered upon him in kind. He reinforced purity reform by praising its American proponents; he proclaimed Frances Willard the "Uncrowned Queen of American Democracy." Frances Willard was equally gracious. This mutual admiration between Stead and American women reformers lasted for a number of years.

Stead acted as a catalytic agent in accelerating public acceptance of purity reform. His exposés unleashed a storm of moral indignation directed at urban conditions generally and at prostitution specifically. The public accepted Stead's message and came to abhor the white slave trade.

William T. Stead may be credited with breaking the "conspiracy of silence," and clearing away obstructions to the popularization of the development of social purity ideology. Silence, once considered the ideal method for combatting prostitution, was henceforth condemned as criminal.[6]

THE AMERICAN DISCOVERY OF WHITE SLAVE TRAFFIC

Americans had learned of an English white slave traffic,

but comforted themselves with the false belief that no
American traffic existed. A romanticized concept of
American life persisted in the face of blatant social realities. Having departed from European history, the United
States, it was commonly believed, had escaped the degradation and moral decline rampant in Western Europe. Purity
reformers wanted to awaken citizens to the moral contamination within the nation. To accomplish this end, they
required an American exposé of the white slave traffic.
The WCTU uncovered an incident with a potential for exciting the public imagination. In an article, "Another
Maiden Tribute," they revealed a white slave trade in the
Wisconsin and Michigan lumber camps.[7]

Remembering the impact of Harriet Beecher Stowe's
Uncle Tom's Cabin on the American public, they reported
in the abolitionist rhetorical style. The theme was one of
deceived innocence. In 1887, a young girl searching for
employment had replied to a cunning advertisement. Her
captors had spirited her into a compound for prostitutes in
upper Michigan. Guarded in a virtual prison and used to
satisfy the lusts of lumbermen from surrounding camps, she
and other unfortunates had little chance for escape. Vicious
dogs were kept to discourage such attempts and to track
girls who tried. Despite the tremendous odds against her,
the impulse for freedom stirred the young captive, like
slaves before her, to escape. Hunted and harried by a dog
pack, the young woman fled into the swamps in an unsuccessful try for freedom. Her captors eventually returned
her to the compound where they punished her severely
and returned her to a degraded life.

The exposé failed to spark the emotion of moral indignation. The plea for the suppression of prostitution and
an investigation of the Michigan vice camps went
unheeded. Discouraged but resolute, purity reformers tried
again. Placing another article in the *Union Signal*, they

called upon the WCTU to institute a campaign against vice dens.[8] The Evangelical Department took up the call by conducting revivals in Michigan lumber camps.

Dr. Kate Bushnell, a WCTU missionary, conducted the investigation of Michigan dens in a manner that encouraged comparison with William T. Stead. As in the Armstrong case, an incredulous public rejected her findings. Her white slavery reports in the *New York World* bordered on the unbelievable and, to lend credibility, Frances Willard came to Bushnell's assistance. Gaining corroborative evidence from Judge C. B. Grant, who possessed a national reputation for vice suppression in his judicial district, she buttressed her assistant's report. Grant substantiated the accuracy of Dr. Bushnell's report, but criticized her for hyperbole.[9]

On the second try, new abolitionists stirred a public outcry of moral indignation. As reformers had hoped, Michigan women acted to suppress the white slave traffic. At a mass meeting in Detroit's Grand Opera House, the WCTU demanded that the governor use his executive powers to suppress the dens. To encourage this action and to enlist more supporters, they convened similar meetings throughout the state.

Journalists, dissatisfied with Dr. Bushnell's disturbing report, wanted further substantiation. They duplicated her investigations and, in the end, accepted her findings. Despite abundant evidence, Governor Rush of Wisconsin discounted the reports as "exaggerated." State legislators, however, were more responsive to the alarm of their constituents. After it had conducted its own investigations, the Wisconsin legislature invited Dr. Bushnell to address the body.

The nativistic WCTU reports on the lumber camps blamed immigrants for bringing the institution with them. Kate Bushnell, extending her investigations into the camps

throughout Wisconsin and Michigan, interviewed 577
degraded women in sixty dens. She concluded that den
operators were foreigners or men of foreign extraction.[10]
Prostitution, inimical to a puritanical culture, was explained as an impure intrusion.

Investigation uncovered another disturbing fact:
reglementation, in fact, existed. Communities were using
contagious diseases laws, following the example of the
British. Ashland, Wisconsin, for instance, provided
medical inspection and health certificates for prostitutes in
the camps. Even more disturbing than isolated instances of
regulation was the realization that commercialized vice
seemed to be an accepted feature of American life.

The Wisconsin exposé heightened interest in the
subject of commercialized vice and intensified anxieties
about the social health of local communities. Commercialized vice was not a small-town or rural phenomenon; it
appeared in cities as well. An investigation of Newark,
New Jersey, revealed a system comparable to that uncovered in Wisconsin. Staid Bostonians were shocked to
discover the system in their city. To their consternation, a
Boston madam had introduced self-regulation by combining the better houses into a "landladies union."

England's political reaction to the Stead incident had
come rapidly. In England a National Crime Commission
had reinvestigated the Armstrong case and corroborated
Stead's findings. Parliament then moved quickly and
decisively to modify age of consent legislation. American
reaction to Stead's revelations was, by comparison, slow,
with public opinion only fully created after the lumber
camp investigations. American purity reformers, hoping to
emulate the English response, called for the formation of a
national vice commission in 1890.[11] Congress never
responded to the call, despite renewed appeals. Therefore,
the cities were left to solve their own vice problems, and

they did respond. As a result of public disclosures, almost every major American city formed municipal vice commissions.[12]

THE FIGHT FOR AGE OF CONSENT LEGISLATION

Given the complexity of a federal system of government and since commercial prostitution tended to be located in the northeastern industrial states, purity reformers failed to win a majority of congressmen to their cause. Congressmen from rural districts lacked a feeling of immediacy and urgency.

Purity reformers did, however, gain support for reform through mass political action. Age of consent legislation served admirably for purity reform as a vehicle into mass politics. Action to win "legal protection for purity" was an excellent educational technique since it reminded Americans of their traditional social missions. Moreover, legislating age of consent enlisted law on the side of civilizing forces and represented the "culmination of centuries of effort in the rise from barbarism." Law, as an educative force, was usable for worthy social goals. Legal change resulted in two benefits for purity reform. First, it raised the age of consent, and second, it categorized illicit sexual behavior as a crime, with law deterring and constraining evil.[13] A successful age of consent campaign might reestablish norms of behavior, counter immorality, and reorient people in socially desirable directions.[14]

Aaron Macy Powell and Emily Blackwell seized upon the interest in age of consent to initiate a public campaign. Anticipating favorable public reaction, they temporarily abandoned lobbying since it seemed insufficient for the purposes of social education. The petition campaign, an old standby, seemed better suited. After consulting Chief

Justice Davis, New York Supreme Court, they drew up a petition to enlist mass support. With Frances Willard pledging WCTU support, the campaign's success was, from the beginning, virtually guaranteed. Seeking maximum utilization of limited resources, the WCTU pressured for federal legislation covering the District of Columbia and the territories. The legislation would establish a new national ideal, and would impel, it was expected, the various states to enact their versions of the Federal law.[15] William Channing Gannett, the Baptist leader aligned with purity reformers, urged ministers to participate in the petition drive. Gannett interpreted his ministerial role as a "higher criticism" of social institutions, which would serve to actualize the "sociologic dream of Jesus."[16]

Iowa, an early center of agitation, testifies to the campaign's effectiveness. H. E. Jarvis of Birmingham, who led the purity drive in that state, sent age of consent articles to every major newspaper editor in the state, and, through newspaper coverage, startled thousands of women from complacency. Although the Iowa legislature did not enact an age of consent bill, the woman's movement still benefited from a larger constituency and audience.

The national campaign proved even more successful than the state campaigns. With considerable assistance from the Knights of Labor, the WCTU collected a petition over two hundred feet long and half a yard wide. More than half the signatures on it had been contributed by the Knights.[17] Religious and philanthropic organizations sent more than twenty-five additional petitions to Congress. As a result, in 1887 Congress passed legislation raising the age of consent from ten to sixteen years for the District of Columbia and the territories.[18] Purity reformers did not win a complete victory, however, for they had expected the age of consent to be set at twenty-one. When Congress passed the Broderick Act raising the limit to twenty-one years in 1899, purity reformers realized their ideal.

Purity reformers maintained political pressure on state legislatures. Over a decade they made substantial gains, but not without renewed efforts. Their age of consent campaigns peaked three times, in 1886, 1893, and 1895. In each instance the American public was better educated to the objectives of the movement. This highly diffuse effort, cutting across national and state political boundaries, defies coherent description. One may gain, however, a sense of its scope and popularity by referring to the legislative scorecards in Table 1.

TABLE 1

Age of Consent

	1886 Age	1889 Age	1893 Age	1895 Age
Alabama	10	10	10	10
Arizona Territory	n.a.	14	18	18
Arkansas	n.a.	18	14	16
California	n.a.	10	10	14
Colorado	10	10	10	18
Connecticut	10	14	14	16
Delaware	7	n.a.	n.a.	7
District of Columbia		16	16	16
Florida	10	10	17	10
Georgia	10[1]	n.a.	10	14
Idaho	n.a.	12	14	18
Illinois	n.a.	14	14	14
Indiana	n.a.	12	14	14

	1886 Age	1889 Age	1893 Age	1895 Age
Iowa	n.a.	14	14	13
Kansas	10	18	18	18
Kentucky	12	12	16	12
Louisiana	12	18	n.a.	12
Maine	10	13	14	14
Maryland	10	10	14	14
Massachusetts	10	14	14	16
Michigan	n.a.	14	14	16
Minnesota	10	10	16	16
Mississippi	12	10	n.a.	10
Missouri		12	14	18[2]
Montana	10	10	n.a.	16
Nebraska	n.a.	15	15	18[2]
Nevada	n.a.	n.a.	14	12
New Hampshire	10	13	n.a.	13
New Jersey	10	10	16	16
New Mexico	10	10	14	14
New York	10	16	16	18
North Carolina	10	10	10	10
North Dakota	10[3]	14	14	16
Ohio	n.a.	14	n.a.	14
Oregon	n.a.	14	14	16
Pennsylvania	10	16	16	16
Rhode Island	10[1]	18	14	16
South Carolina	10	10	10	10
South Dakota	10[3]	14	16	16
Tennessee	10	16	16	12
Texas	10	10	12	15
Utah	n.a.	10	n.a.	13
Vermont	n.a.	14	14	14

	1886 Age	1889 Age	1893 Age	1895 Age
Virginia	n.a.	12	n.a.	12
Washington	n.a.	n.a.	12	16
West Virginia	12	12	14	12
Wisconsin	10	14	12	14
Wyoming	10[3]	14[3]	18	18

SOURCES: Benjamin DeCosta, "Age of Consent Laws—1886," *Philanthropist*, February 1886, p. 5; Leila Robinson, "Age of Consent Laws—1889," *Woman's Journal*, April 6, 1889, p. 105; "Age of Consent Laws—1893," *Philanthropist*, June 1893, p. 8; and Helen Gardner, "Sound Morality," *Arena 14 (October 1895): 410*.

[1] Age of consent set at 10 years old by common law.
[2] Considered poor laws.
[3] North and South Dakota were both part of Dakota Territory in 1886. Wyoming was Wyoming Territory until 1890.

When purity reformers assessed their gains in 1895, they noted with pride that Wyoming and Kansas, where women's suffrage had been enacted, were among states with the highest age of consent.[19] They readily inferred a natural connection between women's suffrage and social purity. Among eastern states, only New York had legislated, by 1895, an eighteen-year proviso into their age of consent law. Since new abolitionists were headquartered in New York, their legislative success is understandable. Nevertheless, women's leaders stressed the strong influence of puritan culture in the West to explain their relatively easy legislative victories.

Victories did not come easily in every state. Reformers faced ideological clashes and frequent defeats as well. The New Hampshire governor, for example, frustrated purity reformers by vetoing an age of consent bill. The Reverend Charles Eldred Sheldon organized an Iowa White Cross Society to overcome intensive opposition in that state. In Massachusetts, James Freeman Clark, accompanied by five hundred women, testified before a legislative hearing in 1886 for an age of consent bill. Although the committee permitted the women to testify then, in 1889 a less liberal committee gave women witnesses "leave to withdraw." In Kansas, age of consent legislation was initially disapproved.[20]

Willing to exploit a favorable political climate for allied reforms, social purists used reform enthusiasm to win other cherished legislation. Josiah W. Leeds, rarely a man to miss a reform opportunity, championed an age of consent bill modeled on New York's 1895 law and simultaneously lobbied for stiffer penalties for the dissemination of obscene literature. Connecticut age of consent legislation included compulsory education for children under fourteen and barred children under sixteen from dance houses, concert saloons, roller skating rinks, or variety halls unaccompanied by parents or guardians.

Riding the popularity of the Stead exposé, reformers brought the first phase of American age of consent lobbying to a rapid climax. Public attention was drawn elsewhere and the cause waned almost as suddenly as it had appeared. Without public support, purity reformers experienced political threats to lower the age to fourteen, but an effective protest to the Senate prevented regressive legislation. Opposition persisted, and, a year later, reformers had to counter another maneuver for downward revision. Discouraged by these regressive efforts, Powell despaired, thinking there existed a "Darkest New York" as bad as "Darkest England."[21] New York reformers, as they evaluated the situation, located an unholy alliance between saloon and brothel keepers as the source of regressive legislation. Opponents of reform persisted in their efforts at downward revision just as regulationists had moved to defeat the purity crusade. As late as 1892, the New York Senate considered lowering the age of consent to ten. Two years later, Maryland reformers, alarmed by a well-organized campaign to lower the age, formed the Maryland Purity Alliance and expanded the White Cross League to defend Maryland's social purity.[22]

Frightened by an apparent general trend toward the reduction of age of consent, Aaron Powell regrouped purity forces in 1894, enlisting Dr. Mary Wood-Allen, new National WCTU Superintendent of Social Purity, for a renewed campaign. Powell had discovered a zealous ally in Wood-Allen. Devoting an entire issue of the *Mothers Friend* to publicize age of consent, she underscored the importance of the reform for the woman's movement. Seeking a larger audience, Powell also alerted the editor of *Union Signal* to the renewed crisis.[23] As significant as WCTU journals were in mobilizing women for a new effort, *Arena* was the one that focused national attention on the campaign by opening its pages to purity reform.[24] The use of *Arena* broadened the base of support for the new drive. The 1894-1895 campaign, addressing the general public through *Arena*, excited more public response than previous ones. *Arena* played a major and timely role in spreading the purity gospel.

Helen Gardener, reporting for *Arena*, kept a detailed listing of legislative victories. Evaluating a national poll of more than 9,000 legislators, she discovered only two opponents to the legislation.[25] Age of consent was a popular political issue, and politicians seemed quite responsive to mass pressures. In Nebraska reformers collected more than 5,000 signatures on petitions favoring age of consent legislation. In the sparsely populated state of Montana, reformers collected hundreds of petitions. In

Michigan, leading newspapers editorialized favorably,
making it possible for women's rights advocates to collect
more than 20,000 signatures on a petition. The petition
drive cultivated a new militancy among women who, pur-
suing the campaign with dogged persistence, even stopped
to debate with passengers on trains. Miss Gardener detailed this enthusiasm and tried to explain the factors contributing to success.[26] Reports Gardener received from
Texas indicated the age of politicians was a factor in the
decision-making process. Grey-haired men opposed the bill
while young men favored it. Texas newspapers considered
the age of consent the most important bill in that session of
the state legislature. A full-blown debate on the proposal's
merits appeared in *The Texas Christian Advertiser*
(Dallas), which reprinted the *Arena* symposium. The campaign led to the passage of the bill in 1895.

Age of consent agitation spanned more than fifteen
years and initiated a mass public debate on sex. Even
though the English were more efficient in securing legislation, American reformers gained public support for a new
ideal man-woman relationship through their social education program. By 1895, the American public was well ac-
quainted with the new social morality.

The age of consent battle was a two-fold educational
experience. It was an early venture into mass political action for women and an exercise in social education for the
public, awakening Americans to the importance of purity
subjects. As a social religion, the movement assisted in
framing a new image for emancipated women and a new
morality for the American people.

THE FIGHT AGAINST POLICE COMPLICITY
AND VIRTUAL REGULATION

Not every temperance or moral advocate wanted the prohibition of the saloon or the abolition of prostitution.

Radicals and moderates were divided in their opinions. A temperance faction that splintered from the main movement proposed "high license" rather than prohibition. This idea had special appeal to regulationist-minded reformers since the idea of high license was basically regulatory. The plan was simple enough. By charging high fees for the granting of liquor licenses, reformers might control the number of saloons. Proponents of liquor control shared with regulationists a common view of "human nature." They wanted to control man, not necessarily perfect him. The idea of high license could be applied to the control of prostitution as well, and it was. Omaha, Nebraska, enacted a high-license law for prostitution and Maryland reformers feared that Baltimore might imitate it. Minneapolis resorted to a partial system of licensing by taxing prostitutes ten dollars each per month.

New abolitionists, like their forerunners, were not inclined to compromise with sin or evil by accepting the high-license plan. Joseph May, Philadelphia minister and son of Samuel J. May, exemplified the new abolitionist spirit when he preached against compromising or blurring the ideal. May, a national purity leader reaffirmed the principles of William Lloyd Garrison and the radical abolitionists in his sermon "An Unending Warfare."[27]

The conversion of Lyman Abbot, religious moderate and *Outlook* editor, ranked as one of the more significant gains for new abolitionism. Abbott's conversion to the cause made the recruitment of moderates easier. New abolitionists, however, could claim only a partial victory, for Abbott had committed his pulpit and congregation to the cause (they passed resolutions favoring municipal purity), but he had not opened *Outlook* to the purity message.[28]

Powell, who relied upon the women's movement for continuing support, hammered away at the theme of virtual regulation uncovered in Omaha and other municipalities. As in the St. Louis heresy of the early 1870s, Powell had the opportunity to dramatize his message nationally when, through the insistence of Police Commissioner Pollner, Cleveland, Ohio, implemented informal regulation. Eager to end the practice immediately, Powell decided to throw the revealing light of the reform movement upon the incident. He turned to the WCTU and the *Union Signal* for help. Dora Webb, Ohio Superintendent of Social Purity, led a campaign against Pollner. At first she relied upon the old tactic of mass demonstrations led by women and ministers. Soon a social purity alliance replaced the ad hoc organization, and within a short time the Cleveland Purity Alliance had introduced every aspect of purity reform to the city.[29]

As Powell feared, Cleveland's departure seemed to spread like a "moral contagion." Police Commissioner Sheehan of New York City sent waves of anxiety through purity reformers when he publicly praised Pollner's plan. Fortunately, the plan fell into disrepute. An angry Cleveland citizenry clamored for the removal of Pollner. The mayor and city council capitulated, replacing Pollner with Director Herbert, who immediately abolished the system.[30] Cleveland had restored traditional morality.

Western states adopted high-license prostitution more readily than others. In 1894, Denver businessmen and bankers had advocated licensed gambling and, the *Woman's Journal* noted, licensed prostitution. The editors lamented the growth of vice and sin in America's cities and called for the extension of the ballot to women. The case of Denver proved—at least to women's rights leaders—that morality could be preserved only through female suffrage.[31]

During the 1890s the old pattern persisted: regulationists presented their plans and new abolitionists defeated them. Considering the pattern of regulationist action, reformers were not surprised by the regulationist foray in New York in 1895. They were surprised, however, when newspapers and some legislators endorsed the plan. At this juncture moderates came to the support of abolitionism. Now Lyman Abbott opened *Outlook* to purity reform and editorialized against de facto regulation in Omaha and New York.[32]

TOWARD ACCOMMODATION WITH SOCIAL MEDICINE

In the East, the medical profession had played only a minor part in support of reglementation during the 1890s. As years passed, purity reformers found more to praise than to condemn in medical journals. In 1889, Emily Blackwell applauded the decision of the *New York Medical Record* to join the new abolitionists.[33] The *Record* reflected changes in European medical attitudes, quoting the eminent European researcher August Forel's attack on the sanitarians' fetish for sacrificing every social and economic interest in their single-minded concern with public hygiene.[34] The most significant New York City milestone came in 1891 with Andrew Currier's reading of "The Unrestricted Evil of Prostitution" before the hygiene section of the Academy of Medicine. Purity reformers, pleased with the speech, published it as a purity pamphlet.

New abolitionists had won a regional victory among physicians in the northeastern United States, but medical articles favoring regulation also appeared in other sections of the country.[35] Important urban medical centers had undergone identical transformation, but other medical centers in the hinterland lagged behind. Nevertheless, the national trend was one of accommodation between abolitionists and medical opinion. The Stead-Bushnell exposés had forced physicians to reformulate their attitudes toward prostitution.

Emily Blackwell, understanding the importance of a

converted medical profession, devoted herself to educating physicians to abolitionist perspectives. Since germ theories of disease were winning great support, Blackwell saw a possibility for educating younger physicians to the abolitionist view. Germ theory taught that diseases were caused by the intrusion of external agents rather than by internal bodily processes. Preventive medicine, therefore, emphasized the need to shut out germs before they gained entry to the body. Dr. Blackwell extended the idea through analogy, suggesting that preventive medicine had an additional application in social medicine. Relying on the metaphor of the social body, Blackwell urged physicians to "shut out" reglementation from American society.[36]

Purity reformers frequently had used the metaphors of moral contagion in their literature. As physicians to society, they had acted to protect the basic integrity of culture. They willingly employed germ theory as a device of conservative social transformation: evil must be shut out without disturbing the institutions that preserved an immanent puritan culture. Moralists and social hygienists replaced theologians as physicians to society, but without abandoning the social roles of these stewards. Blackwell discovered germ theory a convenient device in social medicine; purity reformers found it equally convenient as a device in social reform.

Emily and Elizabeth Blackwell, through extensive purity work, gained the admiration of reformers, but James Harvey Kellogg emerged as the national health expert on purity subjects. This can be partially explained by his and his wife's contributions to child rearing literature and to manuals of health that were widely accepted by the purity public. His leadership may be explained, moreover, by Kellogg's special attributes. As a prominent religionist, he was a spokesman for the popular health movements originating in antebellum reform. Amplifying upon Sylvester Graham's diet reforms, the Kelloggs, through experimentation at their Battle Creek, Michigan, sanitarium, invented breakfast cereals, their contribution to the "religion of health." Dr. Kellogg, a medical researcher with an international reputation, possessed charisma for new abolitionists and had the further advantage of being an outspoken temperance and social purity advocate within the medical profession. Kellogg would have agreed with C. C. Bonney, president of the International Law and Order Society, in his advocacy of self-control to restrain individuals and preserve morals and order in society.[37] Dr. Kellogg expressed the theories of personality and sexual attitudes commonly shared by social purists: "The exorbitant demands of the sexual appetite encountered among civilized people are not the result of a normal instinct, but are due to the incitements of an abnormally stimulating diet, the seduction of prurient literature and so called art, and the temptations of impure associations."[38]

Kellogg, one of several advocates of harmonizing natural law and medicine, perceived deviation from law, including the "laws of health," as criminal or delinquent. Paradoxically, he believed law was an educative force in raising a new civilization of men and women. These two conceptions of law led to meaningful contradiction in purity thought. Traditionally, deviation from law required punishment. It would follow, then, that purity reformers, expanding their concept of criminality, also expanded punishments. In practice, as noted in specific cases, western states tended to inflict punishment upon a new class of "sexual criminals." The national purity elite, however, emphasized the curative aspects of their reform, relying upon delinquency rather than criminal classifications. Prostitution was an improper use of function and a breach of the laws of God and hygiene, but, with religion as an ameliorating influence, the prostitute was to remain an object of pity to be rehabilitated into society.

INTERACTION OF SOCIAL THOUGHT AND SOCIAL MEDICINE

Concurrent with a discussion of law, criminality, and delinquency, reformers of the 1880s, as Robert Bremner has
shown, rediscovered poverty in America. Although many
reformers contributed to the discussion, Helen Campbell, a
woman journalist interested in purity reforms, played a
special role in assisting new abolitionists in relating social
and economic forces to poverty and crime.[39]

These two converging influences, the discovery of
poverty and the new decalogue of social health, were at
variance. Disobedience to the laws of health, God, or man,
if willful, would be interpreted as delinquency or
criminality, depending on the severity of the lapse. From
another frame of reference, prostitution might be explained as the result of poverty, with impersonal environmental forces acting upon the individual. Purity reformers
never resolved the tension, although they encouraged the
latter attitude through preventive reforms aimed at improving the urban environment.

Acknowledging that the social evil was rooted in the
inability of society to materially provide for everyone,
purity reformers combatted socio-economic conditions
through limited ameliorative reforms only, rarely engaging
in a fundamental criticism of the system. They chose,
rather, to pressure employers into more humane treatment
of their workers, supporting the payment of a living wage,
humanized working conditions, social control of leisure
time, provisions for vocational education, and the
establishment of labor exchanges.

The remedy for illegal social deviance had been
already proposed by New York women's prison reformers.
Using lessons drawn from the experimental Isaac T. Hopper Home, they extended, with limited success, the curative
principle into the operation of public jails and prisons. Suc-

cess came painfully slowly. Even the inclusion of police matrons on police forces moved at a snail's pace. To prison reformers the urgency of the reform was self-evident. Their empirical studies of station house conditions in 1887 and 1888 indicated immediate reform was urgent. Police matrons were indispensable, they reasoned, since interned women usually were charged with crimes associated with the saloon and the brothel.

Reformers fell short of meaningful achievement in this activity, for conservative images of women hindered extensive implementation. Even the Men's Prison Association of New York opposed agitation for police matrons, contending that women of good character should be shielded from such conditions, persons, and indignities. The Prison Association further contended that municipal police would have difficulty adjusting themselves to women on the force.[40]

Working against the tide of professional opinion, Abby Hopper Gibbons tirelessly lobbied for police matrons and women's reformatories in Albany, New York. After numerous failures, in 1889 she finally shepherded through the New York legislature a bill to fund police matrons sanctioned by previous legislation. Governor Hill, to her bitter disappointment, vetoed it. With his veto, Hill temporarily stopped plans for the construction of a women's reformatory and the hiring of police matrons. Mrs. Gibbons, undefeated and uncompromising, renewed her struggles with typical abolitionist ardor. Carrying the fight to the governor's mansion, she convinced the governor of the reform's importance. Hill finally signed the police matron and women's reformatory bills in 1890.[41]

Reform activities that originated in New York City were broadcast nationally. The woman's movement was helpful in popularizing prison reform issues. Shortly after the organization of the National Council of Women in

1888, the new council standardized police matron efforts by drafting a mandatory police matron bill for use in every town of 30,000 or more.[42]

As Roy Lubove has shown, social work was undergoing a basic transformation and becoming a career for professionals.[43] The police matron movement was part of the broader thrust toward professionalization. At the same time it represented a conscious rejection of earlier techniques for the rescue of prostitutes. With greater emphasis upon social and economic causes of prostitution, social workers abandoned theistic explanations for woman's fall and, concurrently, their tendency toward moral exhortation. They did, however, conserve the underlying religious values inherent in older techniques by stressing cure rather than punishment in their social therapeutics. As social work became professionalized, social workers perceived prostitution as a social pathology.

Women reformers continued endorsing and supporting voluntaristic Magdalen Societies for the rescue of "fallen women," as they had before the Civil War. Like other reforms, the Magdalen Societies became national. Charles Crittenden should be credited for his contributions to that objective. In 1892, Crittenden attended the World's Women's Christian Temperance Union Convention in Denver where he met Frances Willard. Each discovered in the other a "kindred spirit." After their meeting, the WCTU entered into rescue work, with Crittenden financing five homes for "fallen women."[44] Within a relatively brief time, the National Crittenden Homes were a reality.

Moral educationists and women physicians empathized with the downtrodden and dispossessed. Assuming a protector's role for working women removed from the sheltering influences of home and family and placed into a world of business, commerce, and industry, they urged government to use the police power for the protection of women. Foremost in their minds was the threat of sexual offenses against women.

Some aspects of women's reforms seem more amenable to psychoanalysis than others. Occasionally the moral educationists' interest in sexual criminality seemed psychologically abnormal.[45] On closer examination, though, irrationalities become understandable within the context of prevailing social and medical thought. Moral educationists willingly came forward to assist rape victims. Fearful that rapists might be freed either because the victims were reluctant to prosecute or because the testimony of women in courts of law might be disregarded, moral educationists gave moral and material assistance to them. In this instance reformers realistically assessed the unhappy situation and did what they could to end a legal disability of women.

Punishment of criminal sex offenders was not their exclusive concern either. They wanted justice and were also intent upon restoring the criminal to a productive life. But certainly the penalty they advocated—"castration"—was vindictive.[46] Willing to forgive the prostitute, women were less charitable to the sex criminal. Although they were opposed to physiological justifications for licensed prostitution, they relied upon physiological explanations for sexual criminality.

Woman physicians were frequently moral educationists as well, and they wanted to return sexual criminals to society freed from animal drives. Although women physicians noted a connection between psychology and sexual morality, they were still groping toward psychological explanations of criminality.[47] In the interim, they relied upon medical theories predicated upon a physiological basis for the sex drive. Since they distinguished between love and lust, they easily concluded that "no genuine freedom of love can be realized until the tiger

of abnormal amativeness has been subdued and the normal
passion trained into obedience to an intelligent will." They
intended to free the sex offender from criminal drives
through "castration,"—assuring the public of the painless-
ness and simplicity of the operation and its Christian justification.[48] Reformers chose sex theories rationally. As psychological rather than physiological explanations for the
sex drive became more popular, women physicians
willingly changed their thinking.

In fact, women physicians challenged traditional attitudes about sexuality. Elizabeth Blackwell, for example,
contradicted the widely accepted idea of the nonsexual
nature of women. The concept of women as nonsexual,
and therefore pure, was a well-established Victorian view.
When Blackwell proclaimed that women had a sex drive,
Mrs. Josephine Shaw Lowell, prominent New York reformer, vehemently protested. Until convinced otherwise, as
she was in a conference with Dr. Blackwell in London,
Lowell believed the idea a threat to the purity of women
and the very success of the woman's movement.[49] Mrs.
Lowell's fears of rampant animalism were obviously
misplaced, for Elizabeth Blackwell had previously written
that sexual congress was not to be repeated too frequently
since it was a strain on the human body and diverted
energies from human advancement.[50]

Women reformers entertained varying sexual theories. The physician Janet E. Runtz Reese challenged
the ideas of her contemporaries on the criminality of pre-
marital sex: Why was pre-marital sexual intercourse a
crime, yet immediately sanctioned by marriage? Yet, in the
same article, Reese declared prostitution to be a fundamental lawlessness on the part of man and woman.[51]
Reese presented a more permissive attitude towards sex
than normal among her contemporaries. Frances Willard
presented the more conventional ideas of purity reform.

Posing the question differently, Miss Willard asked: "Are our girls to be [as] free to please themselves by indulging in the lawless gratification of every instinct . . . and passion as our boys?"[52] Her answer, and the answer of a majority of the WCTU, was an emphatic "no."

THE MEANING OF SOCIAL PURITY FOR AN URBAN SOCIETY

A SOCIAL RELIGION FOUNDED ON COMMON CONSCIENCE

As they addressed social issues larger than those discussed above, purity reformers defined new social functions for their movement. The national purity elite, a highly educated and inquiring committee, read widely and carefully considered the implications of their reform for American society. They were conscious of a fundamental social transformation in American society. Religious denominations no longer acted effectively as "pillars" of the social system. Secularization, displacing religious values and institutions, had imbued the concept of society with almost sacred attributes. Under these conditions, the symbol of social purity expressed the eschatological hopes of Protestant religionists, permitting the formulation of a common faith. Although interdenominational cooperation was cumbersome, and at times impossible, the purity symbol permitted cooperation across denominational lines and acted as a moral cement for religionists as they applied themselves to social reconstruction.

Traditional Christianity was limited in its capacity to come to grips with the new conditions that arose from industrialization and urbanization. The Social Gospel movement with roots in antebellum reforms, as Charles Howard

Hopkins has shown, had, just prior to the 1880s, explored four basic concerns: problems of the cities, economic competition, business ethics, and the labor question. As religionists criticized these new social conditions, they returned to stricter and older moral codes, driving nails into the coffin of *laissez-faire*.[53] Francis P. Weisenburger, understanding the limits of the Social Gospel, emphasized that by applying Christian ethics to a secular world religionists always confronted the danger of losing religious moorings and becoming secularized social servants.[54]

Purity reformers contributed to the secularization of religious sentiment. Rather than appealing exclusively to religious institutions, they directed themselves toward the "universal" religious sentiments common to all men. As pragmatists, with a religion of morality and humanity, they constructed the religious foundations of modern society. The concept of social purification released religious energies for social tasks. It appealed to churched and unchurched, to traditional religionists and secular progressives. It functioned, therefore, as a force for integrating apparently disparate reforms. Strongly affective, the purity movement defined a role—the reform role—for religion in an urban society. Only by constructing social institutions and agencies might modern society be buttressed. Only through new and transformed institutions might social values be internalized. Briefly, purity reform, in a time of stress and flux, promoted social cohesion and formulated a new social consensus.

Social consensus was essential if the social bond was to be maintained. Atomization and fragmentation worked against the organismic society the purity reformers envisioned. Relying on traditional Puritan ideas of social organization, the large majority of them rejected *laissez-faire* individualism. Unattached individuals were, according to social purists, only social fragments. The family was the basic social unit. Accordingly, their immediate objective was the creation of a "common mind and conscience in social reform." Cooperation was to replace competition in reform and American social life. Since society's cohesion depended upon a relative homogeneity of feeling, temper, and thought in the population, purity reformers emphasized character and fellowship as admirable social virtues rather than freedom. Deemphasizing individualism, they saw every social act as "purposive and progressive," a "reaching toward some desired value."[55]

Purity reformers, again rejecting *laissez-faire* principles, looked backward to "uncommon Jacksonians" for their associationist and cooperative ideas. Although no longer advocating withdrawal into Owenite communitarianism or Fourier associationism, they applied associationist principles within modern society. Associationism became their technique for rebuilding a covenanted society, and utopianism remained an important component of social thought. One reformer, editorializing in the popular health journal, the *Journal of Hygiene and Herald of Health*, reminded his 1895 readers of their obligation to apply Robert Owen's associationist principles on a mass scale.[56] The more secular National Council of Women reinforced this position shortly after it came into existence, defining the woman's movement's special task as the application of associationist ideas to modern society.[57] "Organize, educate and agitate," the slogan of the woman's movement, embodied associationist principles.

Purity reformers who searched for signs of social disintegration discovered an abundance of them. They interpreted the decline in the simplicity of women's dress as a symptom of demoralization, since it symbolized a loss of moral purpose and a loss of social function: "a desperate reaching after . . . an abiding personal identity without which morality itself and all noble sentiments of social existence are but bitter mockery."[58] Fashionable extravagance created false identity, which was contrary to the traditional American ideal of simplicity and led to moral disintegration.

Social existence and personal identity were interdependent in purity thought. According to a Calvinist heritage, purity reformers demanded that the value of one's social existence be proven and demonstrated in action. Morality was, therefore, manifested through personal and social relationships as moral relatedness or social cement. For them, child rearing was the most important device for actualization of the ideal, since it focused on the process of character formation and transmitted their theories of "relation and of life." Character formation, the internalization of values, considered in the aggregate was, above all, the history of man.[59] Social purists believed they had the key to the future. Social perfection depended upon the formation of social character. In turn, the attainment of perfection required intensification of activity, for man's character was formed, tempered, and tested in the crucible of life, and withdrawal from life was not permissible.

As one reformer suggested, either in jest or at a moment of uncontrolled rhetoric, morality kept the planets in place. Antoinette Brown Blackwell did write a book on cosmology, but most purity leaders were more practical and perhaps less mystical, claiming moral education only as a social bond. Maintenance of moral order was a fundamental—but not exclusive—goal of purity reform. Reformers agitated for specific social remedies to protect and strengthen the family institution—a practical enterprise.

Reformers viewed threats to morality and social cohesion as pervasive. Transportation and communications improvements, a higher standard of living, and a higher rate of literacy, they felt, contained both promise and danger. Increased contacts with other cultures might endanger American culture. Americans who lived abroad could become "unAmericanized," carrying back influences that eroded American institutions.[60] These social purists were American exceptionalists. As environmentalists, they perceived culture as a product of controlled education, hindered by random exposure to alien cultures.

They were especially apprehensive that new conditions might encourage the reproduction of French novels for distribution in the nation. Dreading French morality as a contagious disease far worse than epidemic diseases, they were not literary but social critics. "Art is not above morality," Anthony Comstock sternly reminded reformers. Aesthetics and morality were, for him, one. Censors, allied with purity reform, proscribed French literature and art.[61]

Purity reformers used, in addition to the concept of moral contagion, the correlative concept of moral diet. Ideas, like germs, had the power of promoting health or spreading contagion. They measured national health, therefore, by the moral soundness of ideas. Moreover, the national social health was determined by diet. Moral health was a function of literary diet. Pointedly revising a common philosophical aphorism, Dr. J. H. Kellogg advised, "As a man eateth, so he thinketh." Purity reformers, in their role of social hygienists, prescribed preventive moral medicine to stop contagion at its source or to quarantine it.[62] Under these circumstances, purity reformers envied England with its homogeneous population and a simpler task of social purification.[63]

The movement was not monolithic, however. It had within it, variations and competing strategies. One of the more important intellectual divisions was between the literalists and essentialists. The literalists wanted to uphold traditional religious mandates, but the essentialists wanted to conserve the substance, or essence, of religious spirit and were more willing to alter or abandon outmoded codes of inherited religion. This fundamental difference permeated the movement. Alternate responses of reformers to the decline of the "Puritan Sunday" exemplified this attitudinal divergence.

The Puritan Sunday, firmly defended by Sabbatarians, connoted for the literal-minded, order, worship, and church attendance. The seventh day was, according to Scripturalists, for rest and worship. In contradistinction, the "Continental Sunday," usually associated with German-Americans, connoted anarchy, frolicking, and beer drinking. Literal-minded reformers trembled at the thought of a Continental Sunday triumphing, for "if anarchy can have possession of the workman on Sunday, he can laugh at the efforts of law and order to control him during the week."[64] For them, social order depended on the preservation of the Puritan Sunday. The law was a repressive force when custom or mores did not function to conserve traditional culture.

The Reverend A. H. Lewis, purity leader and founder of the Seventh-Day Baptists, like other Sabbatarians, believed Puritan Sunday unsalvageable. He, nevertheless, relied upon an alternative tactic. Only by changing the worship day from Sunday to Saturday might religion be revitalized and the unthinkable prevented.[65] Sabbatarians, regardless of persuasion, considered worship important for the preservation of social order. They contended purity could not be preserved without it.

Liberal and radical religionists had a different view, more acceptable to secularists and essential-minded reformers. Sunday, for them, was to be a day of rest and recreation, not one of compulsory church attendance. William

Channing Gannett expressed his opposition to Sabbatarianism in terms shared by many essential-minded Unitarians and Quakers. A choice between Puritan and Continental Sundays was not necessary. Another alternative existed without dependence on worship. Sunday might be devoted to self-culture, lectures, reading or visiting museums.[66] These were modern functions designed for an urban population.

Essential-minded reformers, even within religious denominations, willingly secularized Sunday and, in the process, transformed its functions. In doing so, they made a religion of culture, further destroying the rigid institutional confinement of religion. Religion was no longer isolated as an exclusively private experience, and essential-minded reformers commingled the religious with the secular. *Kultur* and culture gained in religious significance.

Essential-minded purity reformers revolted against the formalism of denominational religion, but at the same time conserved religious essence. William Channing Gannett, for instance, believed in the efficacy of religious institutions but was also a member of the Free Religious Association.[67] Free Religionists who revolted against theology advocated, in numerous cases, no theology rather than scientific theology. Purity reformers who were members of the Free Religious Association were invariably conservatives within it. They benefitted by stepping outside confining institutions. Often they applied ideas debated in the association to the development of the institutional church. As Social Gospel ministers, they expanded the range of their activities to socialize and democratize Christianity. They ministered to the churched and the unchurched.

In their search for religious essentials, purity reformers reduced the religious sentiment to three components: obedience to authority, reverence, and worship. Attitudes of obedience, reverence, and worship could be redirected toward socially constructive purposes and religious symbols and emotions used to encourage attachment to social institutions. Ethics, accordingly, could be liberated from theology. Appeals to ethical principles would then, returning to a familiar theme, encourage the development of social character.[68] Religious values were thus transformed into social values. Concurrently, the reformers secularized the practice of religion within the denominations. Churches increasingly performed social functions with commitments to social salvation. They assumed supportive roles and functions in society, becoming, for purity reform, institutions among other institutions for the forming of character. Essential-minded reformers (and the majority of purity reform leaders were among them) counteracted the "depillarizing" effects of secularization—the undermining of traditional institutions—through the construction of social agencies and institutions. As one reformer aptly expressed it, they were "Christianizing Democracy."[69]

SOCIAL RELIGION AS UTOPIAN VISION

Obedience proved to be a most important component of the new social religion. Temperance workers had proclaimed the "Law of Obedience" and its complementary requisite "Obedience to Law." They wanted to instill in the American people respect for authority, rules, and regulations. The purity movement, allied with temperance reformers, had the same objective in mind. They favored "law and order." Although relying on education, both movements understood that fear of punishment deterred criminality.[70]

More utopian purity reformers did not want salvation reduced to a matter of conditioning or rewards and punishments. They envisioned a new religio-social system in which the *summum bonum* would be the "Beauty of Holiness" itself and virtue would be its own reward. Happiness, for them, came as a result of living in harmony with law, and unhappiness, as a result to disharmony.[71] From their understanding of religion emerged an ideal of altruistic social service.

Essential-minded purity reformers accepted the idea of worship but wanted it to assume new forms. Worship represented an "instinct toward progress," and an "impulse toward the ideal." Worship of this sort protected society, maintained morality, prevented the growth of religious negativism, and promoted a definiteness of man's relation to society. The young were to be trained to feel the power of reverence within themselves.[72] Worship was to be used to strengthen that religious impulse. In socializing religion, social purists employed reverence, worship, and obedience in new ways. They taught children reverence in order to promote social cohesiveness.

The importance of reverence in secularization and transformation became more apparent in the 1890s. Reformers relied upon the internalization of reverence through child rearing to prepare children for new social life. The public schools were to contribute through the new piety of patriotism.[73] Religious denominations, acting through the Sunday school movement, also instilled attitudes of reverence. Unitarians and Friends proved especially resourceful in assisting purity reform. Episcopalians also gave major support. With the growth of social Christianity, religious denominations were highly supportive of purity and temperance reforms. In 1899 the International Congregational Council defined as its first priority the humanizing of society, opening its churches to the disinherited classes who were entering politics and making larger demands on the educational systems. Thus, the Congregationalists extended the attitude of reverence to a new

constituency, making it a latent force to draw upon in the
work for social betterment.

The woman's movement was part of the general
movement for social perfectionism and accepted as an
aspect of its social mission the cultivation of the religious
sentiment. Through associationist principles, feminists constructed a "Republic within a Republic," a reform apparatus. As a secular movement, social feminism was more
effective than the churches as a force in social reconstruction. It appealed to a larger public without regard to
denomination. Conscious of the social functions of
women's reforms, Elizabeth Blackwell advised substituting
"human" for "Christian" in making public appeals.[74] As
an instrument of reform, the "Republic within a Republic"
revitalized Americans by restoring purpose and meaning to
religion.

SOCIAL RECONSTRUCTION AND SOCIAL CHARACTER: TOWARD AN INTEGRATED URBAN SOCIETY

Reformers over time and after inquiry became conscious of
the central importance for the woman's movement of abolishing prostitution. Prostitution and illicit sex, as unfit objects for human desire, became pivotal concerns for the
woman's movement in their effort to purify society.[75]
Reformers discovered that the social evil affected role relationships within the family, and, consequently, role relationships in society. Women worked for a new image in the
belief that a purified society required the abolition of the
double standard within the family and society. With societal purification, women might enter new professions and
occupations without fear of sexual abuse or discrimination.
Again the theme of social character reappeared, giving
new meaning to the family institution as the crucible of societal advancement.[76] But first, women urged a new marriage ideal. As Elizabeth Cady Stanton, alluding to Henrik

Ibsen, stated, "If men made dolls of their wives, they would turn to courtesans for intellectual companions."[77]

Furthermore, prostitution, an obvious symptom of social disintegration, struck at the roots of religious personality. By unleashing the uncontrolled "animal propensities" of man, it undermined the moral foundations of civilization. The supremacy of the animal over spirit in man doomed religion and civilization. Conversely, to cultivate the human required the repression of the brute in man and the brutal in society. Purity was a denial of sensuality, an ascetic ideal.

Between 1886 and 1895, purity reformers actively engaged in self-examination and evaluation. At parlor meetings, the members of New York Committee systematically examined the nature of their reform and society. New members were recruited on the basis of their specific expertise and their involvement in allied reforms. These new recruits expanded the meaning of the crusade and formed a "communication network" with other national reforms. Functioning as a "reform brain trust," the New York Committee kept the social developments in the nation under surveillance, vigilantly protecting the national morality. When necessary, they could quite easily mobilize the reform community for specific actions.

The New York Committee, from its national vantage point, was sensitive to the benefits of concerted reform activity. Represented on the Nation Council of Women, an informal interlocking directorate within reform, the national leadership was alert to the power of the woman's movement. Through overlapping leaderships, they kept channels of communication within the reform community open. Through appeals using the symbol of social purity they infused new meanings into traditional reforms and integrated reform agencies in the common struggle for a new morality.

Having given symbolic integration to the larger

reform movement, social purists turned to constructionist policies that emphasized child rearing and the family as the basic social unit of society. Institutions had social functions in forging a new social character. Social institutions in the idealized social organization were the scaffolding in the building of men, with the family as a firm foundation. Moving beyond symbolic integration, social purists were unified by the common object of social reconstruction, with the greatest attention given to the reconstruction of the family institution.[78]

The purity and woman's movements were calling for a revolution in social values. Their open-mindedness contributed substantially to their entry into numerous reform activities under the master symbol of purity, but they were fuzzy in the detail of their design. As Robert Wiebe stated, reformers relied upon the rich tradition of village values, placing the mores of the town within a scientific framework. The new man of service, a scientific administrator, had ominous freedom of action with few checks upon his power. He might serve as a national coordinator, an "honest broker," balancing off public demands, or as an aggressive policy formulator.[79]

Purity reformers knew what values they wanted preserved and what social institutions they wanted transformed or constructed. Above all, they wanted social efficiency: the elimination of individual and aberrant action through bureaucratization and the diminution of politics in favor of administration.[80] Since they believed in "eternal" values, men needed only to be "good" and rely on science to serve the public. Morality, an invisible force within men, guided administrators toward just decisions; scientific management guided them toward efficient decisions. New leaders, dedicated to altruistic social service, performed as stewards of morality.

A debate over educational secularization illustrated

reformers' thinking about administration, both in education and government. Upholding the separation of church and state, and church and school, the priest and teacher performed separate social functions. Despite the separation, however, the public school administrator had an obligation, in the moralists' view, to inculcate religious values.[81] Not only educators were to inculcate values, mothers were to perform a similar educational role. Social purists, therefore, saw mothers in a new light. Mothers, anxious for their children in an urban environment, might also be pragmatic instrumentalists, educating a generation to a new sexual morality crucial for the reconstruction of society.

Purity reformers had a pervasive faith in education, in the schools, in the family, and in general society. They were social educationists. Aware of changing societal conditions, they rejected the traditional contention that innocence was preserved through silence on sex subjects. Rather, the family and school had a new role to play in the distribution of sexual knowledge to prevent the spread of sin in an urban society. Self-control remained the best protection against temptations. Increased temptations in the city made it important to internalize new prohibitions to prevent sexual deviations and maintain moral norms. Like Christian ascetics before them, social purists believed that the control of sexual passions was basic to religious personality.[82] Christianity, accordingly, would win or lose in the city depending upon its efficiency in controlling sexuality.

The Tasks of Social Hygiene

Considering the overwhelming nature of remedial action, the best technique to effect changes in social character lay in preventive social hygiene. Top priority was given to the dissemination of child rearing literature through the woman's movement. In a sense they wanted to democratize their life style. Grace Hoadley Dodge became a major spokesman for the new gospel: "Has not the Master given us our larger houses and separate bedrooms, our good localities, our greater education and knowledge, all the purifying and refined influences in our lives, as a trust for the good of the many, in order that we may diffuse a higher standard of living?"[83] Dodge, like other purity reformers, was a self-appointed guardian of culture, and she also believed in the democratization of culture. In quasi-religious language she made of herself an instrument of democratization. Neither her ideas nor her language were uniquely hers. This amalgam of trusteeship and instrumentalist attitudes permeated purity reform. Virtually everything was a trust. The body was a trust, the "Temple of God," to be made a fit vessel for the spirit of God. Wealth was a trust, not intrinsically valuable, but to be utilized for social purposes. Even the child was a trust and, moreover, an instrument of social perfection. In religious language, parents were co-workers with God in the development of "little pilgrims."[84]

The transformation of the family into a socially constructive institution could be accomplished only if mothers changed their self-image to that of altruistic social servant and, additionally, accepted new social roles and duties. Motherhood was to be social religion sanctified through self-abnegation. By stressing mothers' responsibility for "well-born" children, women reformers reinforced the idea that the mother was the "handmaiden of the Lord." In their child development program, which encompassed pre-natal influences, physical nurture and, foremost, moral growth, the mother was ultimately accountable.[85] The program was basically eugenic.

When religious institutions had dominated society,

the family functioned to bring the child into the church. In the new secular order, the family functioned as a social instrumentality for citizenship training, preparing the child for admission into the State.[86] Social responsibility for children went beyond the boundaries of the home. Through democratization, society itself became "homelike" and took upon itself an obligation for every child.[87]

Having established a new ideal, purity leaders searched for techniques to mold the good citizen. They learned to control the child through various techniques, especially dress, sex, and dietetic reforms, but hygiene reform possessed the greatest potential in that it extended beyond child rearing to general health reform.

Obedience to laws of hygiene also meant obedience to values and attitudes considered eternal and universal. Quite simply, obedience to laws led to good health, whereas disobedience led to disease. By injecting the religious factor into popular health movements, hygienic and dietary reforms acquired eschatological meaning and became pregnant with moral purpose. The smallest choice became a matter of right reason. The fusion of morality and salvation in popular health causes had been relatively constant in the nineteenth century, whether assuming religious or social forms. The most minute aspect of behavior was a measure of religiosity. In fact, the control of everyday life was a key to social control. The core value of ascetism, more than anything else, had to be conserved. Hence, obedience to dietary laws became important religiously since the body was a trust. Values, however, were no longer innate but had utility. Man had erred in the past, purity reformers thought, by accepting the false notion of sin originating in the flesh rather than the heart. Purity reformers rejected a harsh ascetism, which warred against the flesh, for a utilitarian version. They did, nevertheless, cling to a muted ascetism.

Reformers in the "Age of Jackson," had pleaded for "Christianity in the Kitchen." They restated the secularized message, following the Civil War, in "Temperance in the Kitchen." As the century drew to a close, purity reformers urged obedience to "scientific laws"—"Science in the Kitchen."[88] Secularization had enlarged the popular health audience. More people read or heard the recurring theme of obedience to law; for religionists obedience to the "laws of God and hygiene," and for secularists obedience to scientific "laws of health." If language varied, social functions were constant, for in either circumstance, deviation from law resulted in injury and disease. Diet reform contributed, undoubtedly, to curing the chronic nineteenth-century complaint, dyspepsia, and may have contained sound nutritional advice, but it also performed a latent social control function by reinforcing the habit of obedience.

Sex reform performed a more manifest social control function. Purity reformers, borrowing from philosophical vitalism and mechanism as it suited their purposes, claimed sex energy as a God-given trust. Hence, sexual intercourse was for procreation only—its vital and religious function. Furthermore, they encouraged moderation, for energies expended in sex were lost to other channels of expression—especially work. The energy system, considered finite and, in accordance with Newtonian physics, running down, had to be conserved. With these apperceptions reformers underscored the importance of sex to good morality. In their advice to mothers they emphasized techniques to avoid sexual deviations in children. They warned mothers of the paramount sin of onanism, the cause of selfishness and the root of self-indulgence. They advised repressing any tendency toward sensuality displayed by the child. They also advised mothers to keep the child active, to work and play him hard. If lucky, a tired child would have escaped the daily temptations that led to damnation. Purity reformers urged sublimation and, perhaps paradoxically, rhapsodized over the wonders of sexuality. They were, indeed, pansexualists.[89]

Dress reform was integral to the purification movement. Social purists, fully understanding women's interest in dress, discovered in the reform an excellent way to educate the mother and child in morality. They exploited dress reform in order to diffuse social purity ideas in and through the woman's movement. Stressing simplicity of attire, purity reformers cautioned, nevertheless, against morbidity in dress. Bright colors might be used but the dress design should reflect republican virtues.[90] Obedience to these principles encouraged good health. Dr. J. H. Kellogg, researching over many weeks, claimed the traditional cinched waist caused many women's diseases. Morality, aesthetics and health were, according to reform ideas, an integrated whole.[91]

Apparently disparate reforms were directed to a similar purpose. Obedience to purity programs led to social salvation.[92] Examined in their interrelationships, the reforms revealed a comprehensive plan, a purity configuration. Individual reformers occasionally disturbed this implicit unity by overemphasizing specific reforms. One health propagandist, for example, seriously urged proper diet upon the public as a way to achieve salvation.[93] Despite occasional ludicrous claims, the purity elite had a clear perspective and a balanced judgment.

Having an idea of what children should be taught, purity reformers required a means for their optimum dissemination to mothers. They located that means in the mothers' meetings. Jenny Duty of Cleveland introduced the idea of mothers' meetings to the movement in 1880. Women conducted instructional meetings for the poor in hopes of reforming urban life. (The idea may have

originated in the Cleveland Moral Education Society.) As
they were apparently successful in Cleveland, reformers
urged the use of mothers' meetings in other cities. Good intentions, sadly, were not enough. The poor did not respond
with great interest. In fact, a report from Philadelphia indicated complete failure.[94] The poor did not respond enthusiastically, but the middle class did. A report of a successful Arkansas meeting described the audience as
"chiefly of the middle classes."[95] Contrary to original
hopes, mothers' meetings appealed predominantly to middle class women.

Purity reformers, nevertheless, earnestly engaged in
organizing mothers' meetings. It was a reform fundamentally in harmony with social feminist objectives, and
reformers quickly incorporated it into their movement after 1886. The WCTU played an important role in its
popularization, serving as a partner to the New York Committee in extending the influence of mothers' meetings.
Purity reformers, having endorsed the idea, had no definite
instructional lessons for the meetings. As pragmatists, they
had solved problems as they arose, not pausing to
systematize their thinking. Social purists urgently needed
an expert on child rearing. They turned to Mrs. J. H.
Kellogg as their logical choice for advice. As the wife of an
eminent physician and as the WCTU Superintendent of Social Purity she had knowledge and status. Although she
had been interested in the subject for years, Mrs. Kellogg
had never crystallized her thinking sufficiently to for-
mulate a course of study. On request she wrote a general
guide to encompass child development from conception to
adult maturity that emphasized sexual and purity factors
throughout child development.[96]

Like the earlier White Cross Society, mothers' meetings were easily attached to churches and other religious
and social agencies. Critical of the exclusiveness of

mothers' meetings, Quakers opened the new reform to fathers as well. They, in the interests of equal responsibility for child nurture, transformed their sessions into parents' meetings. The idea, closer to the meaning of purity reform, was readily accepted. In 1896 the WCTU, impressed with the singular importance of parents' meetings, established a Department of Christian Citizenship.[97] WCTU journals reported the popularity of the meetings and systematically recorded their adoption around the country. The meetings had gained unparalleled national interest. Purity leaders, sensitive to public interest, acknowledged them as potent factors in their work.[98]

Social Control in an Industrial Society: Protecting Women in the City

Social purists took their responsibility for children and women quite seriously. Not only did they urge social responsibility for children and working women, they also actively sought to control the urban environment to avoid their demoralization. Unlike the charity organization societies that stressed investigation and individual treatment, purity reformers were closer to the settlement house ideal. As Roy Lubove has shown, suspicion frequently marked the relation between the settlements and charity organizations. Jane Addams of Hull House, who aligned herself with purity reform and became one of its national leaders in the twentieth century, was disheartened at the outrage experienced by many people coming into contact with the societies.[99] Purity reformers urged preventive social work as more important and economical than remedial. They were, as in the instance of police matron agitation, interested in remedial reforms, but increasingly strengthened the stress points in the social structure with institutions performing functions of a "surrogate parent." The extension of the "mother-heart" into society meant, in institutional terms, the protection of womanhood from the dangers and temptations of an urban society. They were most concerned for the woman traveler and single women living in the city outside the protecting influences of the family. They had ample justification for their fears since brothel keepers recruited primarily from immigrant women and from American women resettling in the city. These women were easy prey for white slavers who used false advertisements and inducements of lucrative employment to lure unsuspecting and unprotected women into the demimonde, from which they rarely escaped.

Greater physical mobility allowed more freedom for women, but it also created more dangers. The public was ambivalent about this new freedom, but not the woman's movement. During the bicycle craze of the 1880s, Frances Willard urged women to take up cycling for increased freedom as well as for healthy exercise.[100] Critics, however, imagined the bicycle as a social vehicle for transporting girls into prostitution. Alarmists even feared the bicycle seat might cause women's moral downfall.[101] Reformers, anxious about the failure of traditional social controls, traced the causes to the transportation revolution. Mobility diminished social restraint. Railroad executives, concerned about demoralization, constructed YMCAs in towns with railroad stations.[102] Josiah W. Leeds, alert to weakened moral restraint, demanded the protection of travelers from widely circulated pernicious literature. Leeds, whose views corresponded to those of railroad leaders, organized the American Railroad Literary Union and Pure Literature Bureau to supervise literature sold at railroad stations.[103]

Moral education societies and other women's agencies took an active interest in the protection of women travelers. Women reformers made themselves available to new arrivals at sea ports and railroad depots to give advice and shelter to women. Initially managed through women's reform groups on a voluntary basis, this impulse was institutionalized in the early twentieth century as the Travelers' Aid Society.[104]

Social purists continued their protection of women who settled in cities. They provided, through clubs, societies, and agencies, lodging and recreation as an alternative for debilitating influences. Working girls' societies, increasingly important in the 1890s, performed a protective function. Outside family influence, confronted by new circumstances, and placed in new situations, working girls were considered unprepared for urban life. They were easy targets for "man's cupidity."

Grace Hoadley Dodge formed the first Working Girls' Society in New York in 1884, modeled on the Philadelphia New Century Guild for Working Women. Meeting for weekly discussions with working girls in a Tenth Street tenement, Miss Dodge became aware of the aspirations of working women and, as a result, dedicated herself to the development of guilds. Within five years she boasted of 3000 members in eleven New York clubs.

The club's functions were simple and corresponded closely with purity objectives: "Co-operation, self-government, self-reliance; these compound words indicate the club principles. Character: this one word has been used to define its life." Miss Dodge preached obedience to law in her talks to working women, and shared her opinions on child rearing and social etiquette, but she stressed that mere obedience to external law was insufficient. She urged working women to actualize the ideal man-woman relationship through education until it became social habit.[105]

Miss Dodge, hoping to transmit her influence beyond

the clubs, published her evening discussions as "Talks to Busy Girls." Within five years, her students published "Thoughts of Busy Girls," basically a restatement of themes previously developed by Miss Dodge.[106]

Working Girls' Societies recruited primarily from religious organizations. A membership survey of 16,713 girls attending society meetings disclosed that 13,998 also attended churches. Of this number, 7,769 listed themselves as Catholics.[107] The survey provided no statistics on Jewish members. Because of denominational pluralism, the society emphasized the commonalities of social morality without undue stress on religion. Miss Dodge purposefully advised leaders to conduct meetings in secular buildings, although the society considered itself "religious" in the broadest sense.[108]

In a decade of nationalization, the Working Girls' Societies also experienced consolidation. The New York society, taking the lead, invited sister organizations from other cities to attend a convention in April 1890.[109] Concurrent with national consolidation, the societies also underwent reorganization on the municipal and state levels. In 1891, New Yorkers unified their societies into a citywide group and Philadelphians combined working girls' guilds into a state group. They, through coordination and consolidation, brought church-affiliated friendly societies, working girls' guilds, and YWCAs together for mutual support and benefit. Conscious of the correspondence in social functions between working girls' clubs and settlement houses (Jane Addams described social work as an expression of a mode of life), Dodge forged a national mechanism to assist her in preserving the morality of girls.[110]

After meeting some reverses, the Pennsylvania Association of Working Women's Guilds never really materialized, since few guilds and societies outside

Philadelphia joined, but the societies were successful in municipal reorganization. Soon, leaders substituted the less ambitious name, Philadelphia Association of Working Women's Guilds. Regardless of minor setbacks, the movement was eminently successful. At its second annual convention held in the Academy of Music, three thousand representatives attended, almost the total of 3,380 working girls enrolled in the organization.[111] Although financial reverses forced postponement of its 1892 convention, the general movement recovered by 1897 with the formation of a National League of Working Women's Clubs.[112]

Although initially the functions of these clubs were limited to protection against urban influences, they did acquire a new function, that of protecting women in the industrial and business world. They lobbied for women factory inspectors, investigated working conditions in mercantile establishments, opened new occupations to women, and generally fought for the principle of equality in the employment of women. Florence Kelley, who had been active in these clubs, branched off into consumer protection and organized the National Consumer League.[113]

Mrs. E. S. Turner, founder of the Philadelphia guild, may be credited with an innovation in social reform worthy of brief mention. She expressed as an ancillary interest to morality and prostitution a deep concern for the "illegitimate" baby. She abhorred the designation and was repelled by the foundling home policy. Turner challenged the concept of illegitimacy entirely. In 1894, she proposed an experiment that had lasting effect—the development of an adoption service to substitute for foundling homes. Working guild members opposed punishment for unwed mothers or stigma for her baby. Once again, purity reformers challenged social theories accepted unquestioningly by the American majority.[114]

Making Society More Homelike:
The Public Censorship

Technology and urbanization expanded opportunities for
social deviation a thousandfold. Defending their ascetic
life-style, purity reformers rose to prohibit deviant
behavior as rapidly as deviations appeared. Traditional
Protestant anxieties about dress, dance, theater, novel
reading, music, and art were transformed and expanded to
include newer anxieties about public amusements, ballet,
opera, and new genres of popular literature. As censors,
purity reformers ranged over a tremendous terrain. Improved printing technologies, the invention of the rotary
press, and the availability of inexpensive paper made mass
advertisement economically feasible and also opened a
new field for censors.

Censorship meant more than the suppression of pernicious literature. Social purists who became prohibitionists wanted to repress deviations in social behavior as
well. Accordingly, they relied upon the ancient Roman
meaning of censorship, placing manners and speech under
their vigilant surveillance. They invariably explained tendencies toward deviation as originating in the aristocratic
behavior of the "upper tenth." Benjamin O. Flower, author
of *Civilization's Inferno*, contended that barbarism came
from above, among the wealthy who had abandoned their
puritanical traditions, not from below, among the im-
poverished. Like the temperance reformers with whom they
were allied, social purists supported both temperance and
prohibition ethics. As Joseph Gusfield suggests, temperance (and, we may add, social purity), was a sign of
life-style commitment.[115] It was, moreover, a way of
defining a middle class status separated from a social psychology of aristocracy. If purity leaders had no aristocratic

class to oppose, they had "aristocratic" modes of thought and behavior to destroy.

Although censorship societies were independent of the purity movement, the two movements had corresponding motivations. Paul S. Boyer, in a reinterpretation of the vice society movement, explained their appearance as a response to drift in urban life after the Civil War. The city seemed to offer nothing to replace familiar sources of guidance and support—family, church, and community. Perhaps, the founders of vice societies reasoned, money and pooled social influence could substitute for the social controls of towns and villages and avert impending social eruptions.[116] Even though institutionally separate, the vice societies and the purity movement corresponded in social function. With the maturation of the movements they coordinated their activities and shared their leadership. Censorship became an aspect of social purification.

How, reformers wondered, was one to maintain moral purity in a modern age? A tension between traditionalist and progressive attitudes towards modernity became manifest. Traditionalists relied upon older, familial role relationships. The father continued the traditional role of protector of his wife and children against intrusions into the household. He protected purity and innocence by shielding the family from the corrupting influences of general society. Progressives opted instead for full participation of women in society. No one, they contended, could stop contamination at the doorway. Only by changing social roles for fathers and mothers within the family and by cleansing society might the home be protected. Without these changes, women remained subordinates to their husbands. While traditionalist and progressive viewpoints both appeared in the woman's movement, the progressive point of view overwhelmingly predominated.

Josiah W. Leeds, who played a dominant leadership role as public censor for the movement, considered literature and reading materials an aspect of the American diet. The national character, the aggregate of individual characters, reflected the literary diet. Leeds occasionally despaired. Once, in a moment of frustration, he considered the compilation of an *Index Expurgatorius*, thinking that in "the present state of affairs, we can not help thinking it could be a blessed invention."[117] Rejecting the idea in favor of educating mothers to the uses of "pure literature" for their children, he turned to prevention. He believed child rearing and education to be the method for saving future generations. Meanwhile, though, he employed repression as a remedial device.

Purity reformers readily accepted censorship as a reform requisite. It was integral to social feminist reform as well. Frances Willard accepted censorship as a national reform and invited Josiah and Deborah Leeds to serve as superintendents of the Department of Pure Literature. In their new position, they launched a national campaign to suppress "blood and thunder" literature.[118] As committed to the conservation of life style as other social purists, Leeds believed traditional literature embodied "truthfulness, honesty, and obedience," while new literature promoted criminality.[119]

With the emergence of mass culture, purity reformers discovered new horizons meriting their attention. Opposing prize fighting, football, the ballet, and nudity in art and photographic reproduction, public censors gained many allies in the woman's movement. Deploring the brutalizing influences of football, Frances Willard even suggested as a debate topic: "Resolved, that differences between Harvard and Yale be settled by arbitration, without resort to football."[120] Aggression she thought, should be channeled into social reform; the brutal and brutalizing should be eliminated from social life.

Among the numerous campaigns Leeds undertook, the campaign for the purification of the daily press was probably most important. He, like other purity reformers, believed that improper reading habits subverted the social order.[121] Newspapers, the daily diet, were the greatest subversive force. Conversely, a purified press, published in the public interest, was an instrument of social betterment. Leeds was quite specific in detailing the characteristics of a clean press. Morality, the cornerstone of reporting, meant articles were to be clean, with no allowance in the paper for frivolities or corrupting advertisements. Leeds and his growing band of devotees favored a "decent . . . commonsense" newspaper.[122]

Attacks against the symptoms of impure reporting were time-consuming and ineffective. Leeds searched for a more efficient technique for the regulation of the daily press. He found a remedy in the use of the muncipal police power. Propelled by a sense of urgency and immediacy, Leeds turned from moral suasion to prohibition politics in 1884. He complained vigorously to the Philadelphia Select Council about the evils of the newsstands around City Hall.[123] Resort to municipal politics resulted in some immediate, but limited, success. The idea used for more systematic repression came from an unexpected source, a newspaper. Favoring Leeds' proposals, the editor of the *North American* further proposed the licensing of newsstands.[124] Thus, freedom of the press would be assured. Although gaining no immediate victories, Leeds, three years later and with the assistance of the Philadelphia Purity Alliance, reapplied political pressures. Again, a specific reform corresponded with purity objectives, for, through the elimination of a particular class of popular literature, they hoped to close a "source of recruitment for the brothels and dives" and protect the family institution.[125]

After failing to stir municipal action in Philadelphia,

Leeds turned to the state legislature in Pennsylvania. Sharing lobbying activities with Anthony Comstock, Josiah Leeds pressured for the passage of state legislation, "little Comstock Acts," modeled on the national act of 1872. Although Comstock's New York bill served as the basic model, Leeds included a clause empowering mayors to act against the spread of "blood and thunder" literature through the use of their executive powers.[126] Clearly paternalistic, the provision allowed the mayor to protect municipal morals much the way a father protected his family against impure literary influences. Comstock and Leeds were highly successful in lobbying for state legislation. A partial listing of states enacting such legislation early in the campaign included California, Connecticut, Maine, New Hampshire, South Carolina, Tennessee, and Washington. [127]

The logic of society-as-family had ramifications for redefining the reform role of editors. Just as the mayor performed paternalistic functions for the "urban family," editors performed corresponding functions for their readers. If social purists could influence editors, the flood of impure literature would be appreciably lessened. Purity leaders wanted to stop this class of literature at its source.

Leeds undertook a campaign to promote pure literature. If he succeeded, external coercion would be replaced by self-regulation in the publishing industry. Leeds, as a natural leader in "prevention," compiled a list of periodical literature for juveniles he considered acceptable, or at least unobjectionable. He mailed the list to 275 editors of religious newspapers, to state superintendents of the WCTU, and to state and national conventions of the WCTU.[128] Leeds' "preventive reform" possessed an attractive quality, seemingly encouraging good. Other purity leaders turned to "prevention" in publishing. Anna Garlin Spencer, deeply interested in social work, encouraged similar experimentation in "moral chemistry." If reform and religious journals printed a "Record of Virtue," reporting only positive achievements, they could eliminate, Spencer argued, the effect of crime news in the daily newspaper.[129]

Religionists, a sympathetic audience for public censors, opened their journals to articles dealing with censorship. After 1891, enthusiastic religionists supported a popular movement to purify the secular press. The Society of Friends set the pace for the action. In October 1891, the Philanthropic Labor Union circulated a petition urging religious societies to ally themselves against the sensational in newsprint. The larger meaning of their agitation was not obscured, however. The Friends were conscious of the relationship between press purification and the purposes of their social purity committees.[130] They were committed and energetic moral soldiers. The Baltimore Yearly Meeting, one of the more active meetings, circulated a purity appeal to one thousand editors throughout the United States and Canada, and also petitioned one hundred educators and editors in Maryland. The woman's movement and the religious associations maintained a steady campaign of public education that paid dividends. In 1894, the *Ladies Home Journal* to the delight of purity reformers, published articles on public and personal purity.[131]

Most censorship activities undertaken by purity reformers during the 1885-1895 time span were directed against the press. In the next phase of action they would branch into areas of censorship arising from the introduction of new technologies—the motion picture, phonograph, and penny arcade—into the entertainment world.

EXPANSION OF PURITY FUNCTIONS
AND NATIONAL ORGANIZATION

By the early 1890s, purity reform had unquestionably become a mass movement. It had expanded so rapidly that the proliferation of specific reforms outran the ability of purity leaders to coordinate them. Social purity alliances were now inadequate organizational structures for the movement. Reformers acknowledged limitations and searched for new institutional forms adequate to new social tasks. Benjamin O. Flower, who had popularized the age of consent agitation in the *Arena*, now devoted himself to preventive aspects of purity reform. Afire with a sense of mission, Flower envisioned an all-embracing plan for universal salvation through Unions for Practical Progress. Like other purity reforms, he advised the union's members to work for character formation. For Flower's followers, society was metaphorically a house for the "Family of Man." They wanted to form a universal social character based upon the social values of Christianity.[132]

Benjamin DeCosta and Mrs. E. B. Grannis, editor of the ecumenical journal *Christian Union*, also experimented with a new organizational structure for the purity movement. In 1890, they started the Christian League for the Promotion of Social Purity, slightly earlier than Flower's union. Its executive board included major leaders of the woman's movement. Aaron Macy Powell, titular head of social purists, withheld his unreserved support of the league. Although he participated in the league, Powell deplored the "narrow views" of Mrs. Grannis and lamented her "injudicious" efforts to gain publicity. He credited his participation to the Mrs. Grannis' "persistence," but felt alienated from her and the league.[133] When Mrs. Grannis promoted a lottery to increase *Church Union* circulation, Josiah W. Leeds, for one, was convinced her league was promoting impurity. He relegated her, metaphorically, to the unregenerate masses.[134] While enjoying a momentary support from the woman's movement, the Christian League never gained permanent or wide-spread support. Both Flower and Grannis failed to sustain the development of their organizations, Flower probably because his union was too secular and without adequate support in the reform community, and Grannis probably because she was too literal-minded and too church-oriented. Despite competition, the purity alliances, with continuing support from the woman's movement, remained the line of important institutional development.

The New York Committee and the WCTU saw an opportunity for further consolidation and coordination in the 1893 Chicago Columbian Exhibit. Since many reformers would attend international conferences in conjunction with the exhibit, they circularized a call for a national purity congress. The most significant gain for the movement was the inclusion of liberal Catholics as social purists. Archbishop Ireland, who had encouraged the use of police matrons, addressed the congress.[135]

Pleased with their publicity, purity leaders contemplated holding more congresses. The congresses had excited interest in major Eastern cities, and reformers determined, in 1895, to reconstitute the purity alliances as a national organization. They convened a National Purity Congress in Baltimore. The new executive board of the American Purity Alliance listed prominent reformers recruited from national reform movements. Aaron Macy Powell was elected president; Emily Blackwell, William M. Jackson, W. T. Sabine, Anna Lukens, Martha Mott Lord, Samuel C. Blackwell, William Emerson, Jr., Elizabeth Gay, and Anna Rice Powell were elected vice-presidents.[136]

Again holding local congresses for the purpose of

building a municipal support base, purity reformers repeated their addresses for the benefit of Philadelphians,
New Yorkers, and Bostonians. As a result of the municipal
congresses, the national leadership formed honorary committees of business, civic, religious, and medical leaders
prominent in municipal reforms. With support in the community, purity reformers effectively gained access to the
widest possible audiences. Although attendance at local
congresses was small, the meetings attracted key local
opinion-makers—teachers, doctors, ministers, and charity
organization workers.[137]

The congresses apparently stirred revival emotions.
An observer at the Baltimore congress, commenting on the
extreme enthusiasm of participants, noticed the personal
satisfaction gained from public discussion of purity topics.
It would, however, be a fundamental error to dismiss
purity reformers as "cranks." Regardless of their personal
idiosyncrasies and apparent psychosomatic disorders,
purity reformers raised topics of real social importance that
triggered highly emotional responses. Young men reporting on the congress for the Baltimore press were sufficiently moved to join the White Cross League.[138]

The congresses broadened the base of public support
for social purity reform and effectively coordinated the
religious support it invariably commanded. Liberal Catholics had joined the movement in Chicago. Jewish
religious leaders joined at local meetings. Rabbi Henry
Berkowitz endorsed the reform during the Philadelphia
Congress, and the New York Board of Jewish Ministers
unanimously approved alliance work during the New York
congress.[139] Purity reform now claimed the support of
the three major denominations. The Purity Alliance immediately exploited its new advantages. New York purity
reformers gathered signatures on a "Ministerial Declaration Against Legalized Vice." Religious leaders were

generous in publicizing their views. Among the signatories were Walter Rauschenbusch, Josiah Strong, and Bishop Henry Potter.[140]

New York physicians also lent unreserved support. After getting the endorsement of the New York Academy of Medicine president, Aaron Macy Powell collected signatures for a Medical Declaration on Chastity, stating that chastity and health were consonant and in accordance with the laws of health. This 1895 Declaration was a milestone for purity reformers in social medicine. They had convinced the medical profession of New York that regulation was inadequate for combatting social diseases and conserving morality, and had further proved to the satisfaction of physicians the efficacy of purity reform for social medicine.[141]

Moreover, the congresses disseminated purity literature to youth groups. Social purists recorded spectacular gains in White Cross membership attached to YMCAs. The Epsworth League sent congratulations and an endorsement for purity work to the Baltimore congress. Later, during the Boston congress, the League reported it had formed a social purity department. Arthur Sawyer, president of the YMCA, graciously informed the New York congress that "your work is our work." The trend continued, and, in 1900, Christian Endeavor Societies endorsed purity reform, making acceptance in Christian youth groups relatively complete.[142]

Purity reform was now a mass movement. Accepted by the woman's movement and municipal reformers, it moved into a new phase of development. With moral municipal reform as the primary focus of its program, purity reform and urban progressivism were converging. Reforms called into being for specific purposes were given greater cohesion through ideological consensus. Institutional separateness, however, seemed to retard the progress of the movement. In the early 1890s feminists no longer were satisfied to work for moral municipal reform exclusively through women's organizations. If their value revolution was to be realized, they had to unify their activities in progressive organizations. If actual unity was utopian, they could at least insist on coordinated efforts in their common struggle for moral uplift. Early in the 1890s reform enthusiasm rose to new levels. Social purists prepared for a new departure in municipal reform.

NOTES

1. E. Moberly Bell, *Josephine Butler* (London: Constable and Company, Ltd., 1963), pp. 177-81.

2. "Dr. Dix on Impurity," *Nation*, March 1888, p. 232; *Woman's Journal*, November 17, 1894, p. 361; and "DeCosta Defends his Plea for Mercy," *New York Herald*, May 1892, p. 4.

3. *Philanthropist*, January 1886, p. 8.

4. *Philanthropist*, February 1887, p. 1.

5. "Nostrums for Vice," *The Independent* 52 (December 6, 1900): 2942-43.

6. Frances E. Willard, *Glimpses of Fifty Years* (Chicago: Women's Temperance Publishing Company, 1889), p. 419.

7. "Another Maiden Tribute," *Union Signal*, February 17, 1887, pp. 8-9.

8. "The Lumberman's Camps," *Union Signal*, March 24, 1887, p. 7; and September 8, 1887, p. 12.

9. *Woman's Journal*, January 26, 1889, p. 1; and C. B. Grant to Frances Willard, January 5, 1888, in *Union Signal*, January 26, 1888, p. 4.

10. *Philanthropist*, November 1888, p. 8.

11. *Proceedings of the Friends Union for Philanthropic Labor, 1890* (Philadelphia: Alfred Fennis, 1891), p. 73.

12. Roy Lubove, "Progressives and Prostitutes," *The Historian* 24 (1962): 300-430.

13. Georgia Mark, "Legal Protection for Purity," *Philanthropist*, January 1887, pp. 1-3.

14. Antoinette Brown Blackwell, "Social Purity," *Philanthropist*, March 1889, p. 5.

15. *Alpha*, October 1, 1886, pp. 8-9.

16. W. C. Gannett, "Social Economics and Ministerial Usefulness," *Lend A Hand* 1 (October 1894): 268-70.

17. Age of Protection Petition," *Union Signal*, March 15, 1888, p. 12. Frances Willard remained indebted to Terence Powderly, Grand Master Workman of the Knights, for his cooperation with the WCTU. She placed his photograph on her desk to share a privileged place beside Josephine Butler's. See Frances E. Willard, *Glimpses of Fifty Years*, p. 423.

18. *Congressional Record: Containing Proceedings and Debates of the Fiftieth United States Congress, First Session, Volume XIX* (Washington: G.P.O., 1888); and *Philanthropist*, February 1889, p. 8.

19. "Age of Consent," *19th Annual Report of the American Purity Alliance, 1895* (n.p.:n.d.), pp. 13-14.

20. *Philanthropist*, May 1895, p. 1; "The Age of Consent in Iowa," April 1894, p. 5; June 1886, p. 1; March 1889, p. 1; and *Woman's Journal*, March 2, 1889, p. 65.

21. *Philanthropist*, May 1890, p. 4; March 1891, pp. 3-4; and April 1892, p. 4.

22. "Department of Purity," *Proceedings of Friends Union of Philanthropic Labor, 1896* (Philadelphia: Alfred Fennis, 1896), pp. 55-69.

23. *Mothers' Friend* 2 (October 1895); and *Union Signal*, April 5, 1894, p. 9.

24. "The Shame of America—The Age of Consent Laws in the United States: A Symposium," *Arena* 9 (July 1895): 192-215.

25. "Opposing Views by Legislators on the Age of Consent: A Symposium," *Arena* 13 (July 1895): 209.

26. Helen Gardener, "The Battle for Sound Morality, Part II," *Arena* 14 (September 1895): 1-32; "A Battle for Sound Morality Part III," *Arena* 14 (October 1895): 213-14; and "A Battle for Sound Morality, Final Paper," *Arena* 14 (November 1895): 409-10.

27. Joseph May, "The Unending Warfare; A Sermon,"

February 2, 1895, in *Woman's Journal*, February 16, 1895, p. 54.

28. *Woman's Journal*, February 27, 1892, p. 71; and Ira Brown, *Lyman Abbott, Christian Evolutionist: A Study in Religious Liberalism* (Cambridge: Harvard University Press, 1953), pp. vii-viii. Abbott played an important role as a moderate in religious battles of the era. He had an uncanny knack for accommodating himself to changes in reform.

29. "The Cleveland Disgrace," *Philanthropist*, December 1893, p. 5.

30. *Woman's Journal*, January 6, 1894, p. 4; and May 5, 1894, p. 137.

31. "Disfranchisement and Prostitution," *Woman's Journal*, December 29, 1894, p. 414.

32. "An Insulting Proposal," *Outlook*, March 16, 1895, p. 423; "The Social Evil," *Outlook*, February 23, 1895, p. 303.

33. *Philanthropist*, December 1889, pp. 3-4.

34. "Editorial," *New York Medical Record*, in *Philanthropist*, November 1889, p. 6.

35. The *Index Medicus* remains the best bibliographical source for this literature.

36. Emily Blackwell, "The Attitude of the Medical Profession in Regard to the State Regulation of Vice," *Philanthropist*, March 1894, pp. 3, 5.

37. C. C. Bonney, *The Present Conflict of Labor and Capital* (Chicago: Chicago Legal News Company, 1886), pp. 1-8.

38. J. H. Kellogg, "Chastity and Health; Delivered at the National Purity Congress, Baltimore, Maryland, 1895," in Collected Reprints, National Medical Library.

39. Robert H. Bremner, *From the Depths: The Discovery of Poverty in the United States* (New York: New York University Press, 1959); and Helen Campbell "Poverty and Vice," *Philanthropist*, May 1890, pp. 2-3.

Aaron Macy Powell had commented earlier upon Miss Campbell's "Prisoners of Poverty," in *Philanthropist*, April 1887, p. 4.

40. *Forty-third Annual Report of the Women's Prison Association of New York* (New York: G. P. Putnam 1887), p. 4; and "New York Prison and Station Houses," *56th Annual Report of the Women's Prison Association of New York* (New York: G. P. Putnam, 1900), pp. 6-7.

41. Abby H. Gibbons to Anna Rice Powell, March 12, and April 26, 1889, and September 30, 1892, in Sarah Hopper Emerson, *Life of Abby Hopper Gibbons* (New York: G. P. Putnam's, 1896), 1: 270-71.

42. Anna Garlin Spencer, reflecting on the history of the National Council, recalled May Wright Sewall's contribution to the idea. The social purity movement, from Spencer's point of view, was the forerunner of the council. Spencer traced the idea of a national council to Elizabeth Cady Stanton who, in 1882, corresponded with English reformers on the subject. The National Woman's Suffrage Association advanced the idea of an international council as early as 1887. Anna Garlin Spencer, *The Council Idea and May Wright Sewall* (NY: Press of J. Herdingsfeld Co., 1930), pp. v, vi, 2, 9. *Report of the National Council of Women, Washington, D.C., March 25-April 1, 1888* (Washington: Rufus Darby Printer, 1888), p. 272.

43. Roy Lubove, *The Professional Altruist: The Emergence of Social Work as a Career, 1880-1930* (Cambridge: Harvard University Press, 1965), pp. 118-156.

44. Otto Wilson, *Fifty Years Work With Girls* (n.p.: Florence Crittenden Missions, 1933), p. 38-39.

45. For an analysis of the "mavericks" of feminism, see Robert E. Riegel, *American Feminists* (Lawrence: University of Kansas Press, 1963), pp. 137-153.

46. "Memorial to the House of Representatives and Senate," *Alpha*, April 1, 1880, p. 9.

47. "Psychology and Sexual Morality," *Alpha*, October 1, 1875, p. 9.

48. "State Association of Spritualists," *Alpha*, September 1875, p. 9.

49. Elizabeth Blackwell, "Cruelty and Lust," *Philanthropist*, December 1891, pp. 1-3; and Josephine Shaw Lowell to Anna Rice Powell, December 13 and 15, 1891, Blackwell Family Papers, Library of Congress.

50. Elizabeth Blackwell, *The Human Element in Sex: Being a Medical Enquiry into The Relation of Sexual Physiology and Christian Morality* (London: J. & A. Churchill, 1889), p. 30.

51. Janet E. Runtz Rees, "Prostitution," *The Medical and Surgical Reporter* 58 (May 26, 1888): 661-62.

52. Frances E. Willard, "Presidential Address," *Report of the National Woman's Christian Union, 1891* (Chicago: WTPA, 1891), p. 128.

53. Charles Howard Hopkins, *The Rise of the Social Gospel in American Protestantism, 1865-1915* (New Haven: Yale University Press, 1940), pp. 24-49; and Henry F. May, *Protestant Churches and Industrial America* (New York: Octagon Books, Inc., 1963), p. 135.

54. Francis P. Weisenberger, *Ordeal of Faith: the Crisis of Church-Going America, 1865-1900* (New York, 1959), p. 121.

55. Anna G. Spencer, "The Dangers of Individualism in Moral Reform," *Index*, March 13, 1884, pp. 438-40; Joseph May, *Jesus, A Study of Ideal Manhood: A Sermon* (Philadelphia: First Unitarian Church, n.d.), pp. 1-4; and A. G. Spencer, "Religious Culture of the Young," *Index*, 1880, p. 346; Antoinette B. Blackwell, *The Social Side of Mind and Action* (New York: The Neal Publishing Co., 1915), p. 93.

56. "Editorial," *Journal of Hygiene and Herald of Health* 45 (January 1895): 25.

57. "National Council of Women," *Woman's Journal*, January 10, 1891, p. 16.

58. Frances E. Willard, "Dress and Vice," *Philanthropist*, May 1887, p. 8 and Martha Schofield to Josiah

Leeds, June 18, 1887, Josiah W. Leeds Papers, Haverford College; and Antoinette B. Blackwell, *The Physical Basis of Immortality* (New York: S. P. Putnam's Sons, 1876), pp. 14-15.

59. J. W. Howe, "Education," November 1881, in Julia Ward Howe Scrapbook, Julia Ward Howe Papers, Radcliffe College; and Charles Roads, *Child Study for Teacher-Training* (Cincinnati: Jennings and Graham, 1907), pp. 13, 15.

60. Frances E. Willard, "The Promotion of Social Virtue," *Philanthropist*, December 1890, p. 2, and January 1891.

61. Anthony Comstock to J. W. Leeds, November 21, 1887, Josiah W. Leeds Papers, Haverford College; *Woman's Journal*, June 24, 1893, p. 195, and September 17, 1898, p. 302; and *Union Signal*, January 12, 1893, p. 12.

62. Women physicians played a special role in preventive medicine. Not enough attention has been given to this special activity of the woman's movement and the function of public hygiene movements in modernization.

63. Walter Wyman, "Government Aids to Public Health," *Journal of the American Medical Association* 15 (July 5, 1890): 1-4.

64. Bonney, *Conflict of Labor and Capital*, pp. 1-8.

65. The Reverend A. H. Lewis was a prolific writer. Throughout most of his writings the predominate theme was religious revitalization through Saturday worship. A. H. Lewis, *Swift Decay of Sunday, What Next?* (Plainfield, N. J.: American Sabbath Tract Society, 1882).

66. William Channing Gannett, *The Workingman's Sunday* (Boston: Free Religious Association, 1877).

67. Anna G. Spencer, Julia Ward Howe, William Channing Gannett, and Aaron Macy Powell belonged to the Free Religious Association.

68. Benjamin O. Flower, "Character-building, the Next

Step in Educational Progress," *Arena* 5 (January 1893): 250.

69. "To Christianize Democracy," *Woman's Journal*, September 30, 1899, p. 312.

70. "Law and Order," *Lend A Hand* 7 (September 1891): 201.

71. Joseph May, *The Beauty of Holiness: A Sermon* (Philadelphia: First Unitarian Church, n.d.), pp. 7-8, and *The Unity of Spirit: A Sermon* (Philadelphia: First Unitarian Church, n.d.); and Elizabeth Powell Bond, "The Elements of Happiness," Elizabeth Powell Bond Papers, Swarthmore College.

72. Joseph May, *The Duty of Worship: A Sermon* (Philadelphia: First Unitarian Church, n.d.); J. W. Howe, "Religious Training of the Young," *Boston Transcript*, April 7, 1899; and Elizabeth Powell Bond, "How to Train Children in Reverence," *The Home Influence Association*, March 26, 1897.

73. Anna G. Spencer, "Social and Moral Education," Anna Garlin Spencer Papers, Swarthmore College.

74. Elizabeth Blackwell, "Christianity in Medicine," in *Things to Come*, ed. G. W. Allen (London: Eliot Stock, 1892), p. 69.

75. Julia Ward Howe, "Address at New England Annual Meeting," in *Woman's Journal*, May 31, 1890, p. 173; "National Council of Women," *Woman's Journal*, February 28, 1891, p. 72; and Anna Rice Powell to Elizabeth Gay, October 17, 1876, Sidney Howard Gay Papers, Columbia University.

76. *Family Culture* 1 (April 1896): 3.

77. Elizabeth Cady Stanton, "On Marriage and Matrimony," *Index*, September 9, 1870, p. 238.

78. *Selections From Mary A. Livermore* (Boston: Massachusetts WCTU, 1892), p. 14.

79. Robert H. Wiebe, *The Search For Order, 1877-1920* (New York: Hill and Wang, 1967): pp. 161-163.

By the mid-1890s purity reform focused on the family as the instrumentality for social reconstruction. Their view of social organization gave the family a vitalistic radiation that flowed outward to influence the remainder of society. Joseph May, *The Ideal Commonwealth and Its Realization* (Philadelphia: Spangler and Davis, 1896), p. 2; and "Editorial," *Family Culture* 1 (May 1896): 1-3.

80. Joseph May, *Conscience in Politics: A Sermon* (Philadelphia: Edward I. Bicking, 1896), p. 11.

81. William W. Folwell, president of the University of Michigan, "Secularization of Education," *NEA Convention, 1882, Saratoga* (Boston: Alfred Mudge and Son, 1882), pp. 42-45.

82. Max Scheler, *Vom Umsturz der Werte* (Bern: 1965), trans. in Philip Rieff, *The Triumph of the Therapeutic* (New York: Harper and Row, 1966), p. 18.

83. *Moral Elevation of Girls: Suggestions Relating to Preventive Work*, 2nd ed. (New York Committee on the Elevation of the Poor in Their Homes, December 1885), p. 12.

84. E. E. Kellogg, *Studies in Character-Building, A Book for Parents* (Battle Creek, Michigan: Good Health Publishing Company, 1905), pp. 11-12.

85. Elizabeth Powell Bond, "The Sacredness of Motherhood," *Philanthropist Series, No. 5* (n.p.:n.d.).

86. In a shorthand method one can consider the emergence of the new nationalism and the new citizenship as a secularization process. Actually the term secularization is too general. More detailed studies are needed to understand the process.

87. "Editorial," *Arena* 2 (September 1890): 508.

88. Sidonia C. Taupin, " 'Christianity in the Kitchen' or a Moral Guide for Gourmets," *American Quarterly* 15 (Spring 1863): 85-9; Mary G. Smith, *Temperance Cook Book* (San Jose, California: Mercury Book House, 1887), preface; and E. E. Kellogg, *Science in the Kitchen* (Battle Creek, Michigan: Modern Medical Publishing Company, 1892).

89. Joseph Flint, *In Potiphar's House: The Young Man in Peril* (New York: J. B. Alden, 1890), p. 32; Elizabeth Blackwell, *Counsel to Parents on the Moral Education of Their Children* (New York: Brentano's Literary Emporium, 1879), p. 111; "Letter to the Editor," *Journal of the American Medical Association* 15 (February 20, 1897): 375-76. For an analysis of the pansexual theories of purity reformers see: David J. Pivar, *The New Abolitionism: The Quest for Social Purity* (Ph.D. diss., University of Pennsylvania, 1965), pp. 127-45; and J. B. Gledstone, "Save the Boys," *Philanthropist*, May 1886, p. 2.

90. Celia B. Whitehead, "Dress Reform," *Alpha*, October 1, 1883, pp. 5-7. "Religion of Dress," *White Cross Library, No. 21, December 1887*, New York Public Library; and B. O. Flower, "Fashion's Slaves," *Arena* 4 (September 1891): 423-25.

91. Dr. J. H. Kellogg toured Indian reservations to prepare anthropometric reports on the natural measurements of the female body.

92. Individual behavior was the foundation upon which the nation operated in the theoretical social organization of purity reformers. It corresponded with the views of Theodore Roosevelt. See "Theodore Roosevelt before The New York Mothers' Convention," *Woman's Journal*, October 28, 1899, p. 340.

93. A reflection of the millenial hopes attached to household reform can be gained from reading "Scientific Cookery," *Journal of the American Medical Association* 22 (June 2, 1894): 857.

94. "Minutes of the Home Influence Association, February 15, 1898," p. 32, in Swarthmore College Collection.

95. *Minutes of the NWCTU, 1893* (Chicago: WTPA, 1893), p. 377.

96. See Appendix B for Mrs. Kellogg's guide.

97. *Report of the NWCTU, 1896* (Chicago: WTPA, 1896), p. 350-51, 395.

98. *Minutes of the NWCTU, 1893*, pp. 381-93; and Willard, *Glimpses of Fifty Years*, p. 419.

99. Lubove, *Professional Altruist*, p. 10.

100. Frances E. Willard, *A Wheel Within a Wheel: How I Learned to Ride the Bicycle* (New York: Fleming H. Revell Company, 1895), p. 20.

101. "John Short Bicycle Saddles," *Journal of the American Medical Association* 32 (March 1899): 653.

102. Thomas C. Cochran, *Railroad Leaders, 1845-1890: The Business Mind in Action* (Cambridge: Harvard University Press, 1953), pp. 174, 177, 210; and Morrell Heald, *The Social Responsibilities of Business: Company and Community, 1900-1960* (Cleveland: Case Western Reserve University, 1970), p. 12.

103. "American Railway Literary Union and Pure Literature Bureau," Josiah W. Leeds Scrapbook, vol. 18, May 31, 1894, Josiah W. Leeds Papers, Haverford College.

104. The relationship of this reform to the social purity movement is stressed in Abbie Graham, *Grace H. Dodge: Merchant of Dreams* (New York: Woman's Press, 1926), p. 216.

105. Helen Campbell, "Working Girls' Clubs," *Public Opinion* 18 (May 30, 1895): 600; "Clubs for Working Girls," *Philanthropist*, June 1889, pp. 1-2; Grace H. Dodge, "Working Girls' Clubs," *Public Opinion* 19 (July 4, 1895): 762; and Grace H. Dodge, "Practical Suggestions Relating to Moral Education and Preventive Work Among Girls, May 1885; Read at the Woman's Christian Association, Cincinnati," p. 5, Grace Hoadley Dodge Papers, National YWCA, New York City.

106. "Review of 'Thoughts of Busy Girls,' " *Nation* February 23, 1893, pp. 148-49.

107. Felicia Hillel, "Working Girls," *The Chautauquan* 10 (December 1889): 332.

108. Grace Hoadley Dodge, "Paper on Association of Working Girls Societies," *Proceedings of the Convention*

of *Christian Workers in the United States and Canada, September 21-28, 1887* (n.p.:n.d.), pp. 9-10.

109. *Associations of Working Girls' Societies Convention, April 15-17, 1890* (New York: Trow's Printing and Bookbinding Company, 1890), p. 7.

110. "Jane Addams to Union Signal," *Union Signal*, March 5, 1896, pp. 4-5. This was a part of a process of forming a national reform elite. This social movement paralleled similar consolidations and mergers in business.

111. *Working Woman's Journal*, February 6, 1892, p. 9; and "Second Annual Meeting of the Association of Guilds and Working Women's Societies," *Working Woman's Journal*, March 1893, p. 22.

112. "Executive Board Minutes of the New Century Guild, January 12, 1894," pp. 48-50; and Mary E. Richmond, Working Women's Clubs," *The Charities Review* 6 (June 1897): 351-2.

113. For the history of the Consumers' League, see Louis Lee Athey, "The Consumers' Leagues and Social Reform, 1890-1923" (Ph.D. diss., University of Delaware, 1965). See, as well, Maud Nathan, *The Story of an Epoch Making Movement* (Garden City, 1926).

114. E. S. Turner, "An Equal Standard of Morals—Some Plain Words on a Forbidden Subject," *Philanthropist*, May 1894, pp. 1-3.

115. Gusfield, *Symbolic Crusade*, p. 30. For an example of the function of censorship or prohibition in maintaining a life style, see Rachel Dunkirk, "Public Censor," *Outlook*, July 6, 1895, p. 21.

116. Paul S. Boyer, *Purity in Print: The Vice-Society Movement and Book Censorship in America* (New York: Scribner's, 1968), pp. 3-4.

117. J. W. Leeds, *Our Free Institutions for the Promotion of Brutality and Burglary* (Philadelphia: Printed by the Author, 1889), p. 7.

118. H. W. Smith to Deborah Leeds, October 17, 1887, Josiah W. Leeds Papers, Haverford College. The campaign

expanded in the 1890s into a major effort to "purify the press." Although the WCTU was involved, reformers of purity persuasion also acted.

119. J. W. Leeds, *Concerning Printed Poison* (Philadelphia: Printed by the Author, 1885), pp. 5-6.

120. *Woman's Journal*, December 8, 1894, p. 388.

121. Anna G. Spencer, *Literature and Vice, Social Purity Series No. 10* (Chicago: WTPA, n.d.). This common view of "appetites" and "diet" points toward a purity reform *gestalt*.

122. Josiah W. Leeds, *The Case of a Friend of the Commonwealth. Versus the Sunday Newspapers* (Philadelphia: Printed by the Author, 1902).

123. "Pernicious Literature," *Philadelphia Inquirer*, June 4, 1884, p. 2.

124. "Printed Poison," *North American*, June 6, 1884.

125. "J. W. Leeds to the Editor," *Public Ledger*, June 13, 1887.

126. J. W. Leeds to George Graham, April 15, 1885, Josiah W. Leeds Papers, Haverford College.

127. A. Comstock to J. W. Leeds, April 20, 1885, April 16, 1885, Josiah W. Leeds Papers, Haverford College.

128. J. W. Leeds, *Juvenile Periodical Literature* (Philadelphia: Printed by the Author, 1888). A notation in the Leeds Scrapbooks provides the mailing list.

129. A. G. Spencer, "The Record of Virtue: An Experiment in Moral Chemistry," *The Century Magazine* 41 (December 1890): 238-45.

130. *Philanthropist*, October 1891, p. 5; and *Proceedings of Friends Union for Philanthropic Labor, 1892* (Philadelphia: Ferris Brothers, n.d.), pp. 51-55.

131. *Philanthropist*, December 1894, p. 8.

132. B. O. Flower, "Union for Practical Progress," *Arena* 8 (June 1893): 78-91, 86.

133. Anna Rice Powell to Elizabeth Gay, November 20, 1892, Sidney Howard Gay Papers, Columbia University.

134. *New York Tribune*, June 1895, in Josiah W. Leeds Papers, Haverford College.

135. "Social Purity Congress," *Union Signal*, June 8, 1893, p. 1; and "Social Purity Congress," *Woman's Journal*, June 24, 1893, p. 195.

136. "American Purity Alliance," *Philanthropist*, January 1895, p. 4.

137. Anna Rice Powell to Elizabeth Gay, January 8, 1895, Sidney Howard Gay Papers, Columbia University.

138. Thomas Beer, *The Mauve Decade: American Life at the End of the Nineteenth Century* (New York: Garden City Publishing Company, Inc., 1926), p. 40; and *Philanthropist*, January 1896, p. 1.

139. K. Kohler to Aaron M. Powell, January 14, 1896, in *Philanthropist*, March 1896, p. 7.

140. "Ministerial Declaration Against Legalized Vice," *Philanthropist*, March 1896, pp. 2-3.

141. Anna Rice Powell to Elizabeth Gay, December 17, 1894, Sidney Howard Gay Papers, Columbia University; and May Wright Sewall, *National Council of Women of the United States, Third Triennial Session, 1899* (n.p.:n.d.), p. 274.

142. *Woman's Journal*, December 14, 1895, pp. 393, 396; *Philanthropist*, January 1896, p. 12; and *25th Annual Report of the American Purity Alliance, 1900* (n.p.:n.d.), p. 16.

5

Purity and the Urban Moral Awakening, 1895-1900

Politics had a high priority on the reform agenda of the
1890s. The woman's movement had constructed its
"Republic within a Republic" and had turned to the
reconstruction of social and political institutions—women
were to purify every place they entered.[1] The Women's
Christian Temperance Union, moreover, had reached
mature institutional development, and its members
seriously yearned for the formation of a third political party of reform. Municipal reformers, after decades of local
political action, also saw an opportunity for consolidation
in the interest of "non-partisan government operated on
an economic basis." Purity reformers, not to be left behind, joined businessmen, new allies discovered in the drive
against prostitution, in municipal reform. Reformers with
diverse interests were arriving at a political consensus, and,
in the early years of the 1890s, they coalesced municipal
reforms into a coordinated movement, a direct response to
mounting pressures for political action. By 1894, Benjamin O. Flower, an astute observer of reform movements,
proclaimed the beginning of a new epoch and called upon
women to "redeem the Republic."[2]

POLITICIZATION OF THE SOCIAL PURITY MOVEMENT

Purity reformers had never seriously thought of their movement as political. They had acted mainly as a pressure group and as an educational agency for moral uplift. Sustained mass political action had never seemed desirable; only limited mass politics for specific limited objectives seemed necessary. The rapidity of change leading into political action left the American Purity Alliance in a momentary dilemma. After unsuccessful efforts to eradicate the brothel and eliminate prostitution, the leaders in the Alliance realized that they had merely attacked the symptoms of social pathology without getting at the causes. With the politicization of reform, Aaron Macy Powell determined, after careful review, that the disease of prostitution was rooted in the body politic and its cure required radical constitutional treatment. Purity reformers had to be counted in reform's political ranks; the Alliance, if it expected to fulfill its mission, had to enter politics.[3] Nevertheless, purity reformers did not think of politics as an end in itself, but rather as a means to an end, the education of the public to a new morality.

Evidence of the accelerating process of politicization already had been duly noted by the purity elite. They located one indication of politicization in the appearance of a Philadelphia reform institution. Purity reformers had, in 1886, assisted in the organization of a "moral committee of one hundred" in Philadelphia. After an abortive beginning, the committee dissolved and was reincorporated into the Law and Order Society. More lasting political involvement came with the development of the Chicago Civic League. As is commonly known, the creation of the league had been accomplished in 1891 after William T. Stead's address, "If Christ Came to Chicago.[4] The address, an exposé of sin and evil in the windy city, revealed Stead's indebtedness to American purity reformers in its footnotes. Stead had borrowed liberally from purity journals and literature.

Stead was not the lone proponent of municipal purification, however. Other purity reformers made contributions as well. Benjamin O. Flower's "Civilization's Inferno," although not as effective as Stead's address, did contribute to Boston's moral reawakening. Philadelphians, less dramatic in their public presentations, assisted in the formation of the Philadelphia Municipal League, which was later affiliated with the National Municipal League.[5] Charles Parkhurst's tour of New York's vice centers exposed police compliance in tolerating commercialized prostitution and led to the formation of the City Vigilance Society. Appropriately, the society almost immediately began a drive for political purification in New York City. In the cities cited, purity reform directly contributed to the organization of "moral municipal leagues." Elizabeth Blackwell, who had dreamed of such leagues, was seeing that dream of municipal purification about to be taken up by the reform community.

The new political zeal for urban revitalization among purity reformers corresponded with their larger goal of citizenship education. Politics, according to a prominent reformer, represented only two things, "national and political housekeeping . . . and national and political child rearing."[6] Purity reformers and social feminists were eminently equipped for political action designed as an exercise in social education. They were encouraged when, in 1893, the Evangelical Alliance distributed patriotic literature to the general public. Directed toward citizenship development, Alliance literature on social purity, temperance, and Sabbath reform repeated the dominant reform themes of the day. Prominent national reformers supported this enterprise with E. E. Hale, John R. Commons, Washington Gladden, Carl Shurz, Albert Shaw, Charles Dudley Warner, and E. B. Andrews writing new morality pamphlets.[7]

Conditions favoring political action were ideal. By the 1890s, reformers, alarmed over crime increases, distressed over the widening social distance between the weathy and the poor, dismayed over moral disintegration, and discouraged by the social irresponsibility of America's wealthy families, came to see American cities as diseased.

In October 1890, the Reverend Charles Parkhurst delivered the first in a series of sermons on urban immorality and police complicity. Seeking moral confrontation, Parkhurst stressed the theme of police complicity as the greatest cause for the continuation of crimes of vice.[8] Purity reformers, familiar with police practices, sympathized with Parkhurst, but the majority of interested New Yorkers, without first-hand knowledge, reacted with disbelief. Parkhurst was a fit man for his job. He, like William T. Stead before him, relied upon journalistic exposés. The Purity Alliance, although not directly involved, saw a golden opportunity to educate the public and, repeating an old appeal, called for an investigation by a municipal vice commission.[9] Parkhurst, however, was more impatient than the Alliance and took independent political action.

The precipitant for political organization came from the New York Grand Jury. Moved to act by Parkhurst's frequent sermons and public pronouncements, the jury, in February 1892, formally denied the charge of police complicity. Interpreting the report as a personal challenge, Parkhurst began his famous tour of New York's vice dens to gather substantiating evidence. As a result of his

investigation, Parkhurst contended the police were drawing dividends from the sexual crime of prostitution and
supporting *de facto* regulation.[10]

Parkhurst carefully prepared a report for the Grand
Jury, but he did not convince jury members. The tours,
however, publicized purity reform and gave it a boost as a
force in municipal reform. In the wake of the Parkhurst
raids, reformers called a mass meeting for May 26, 1892,
at Cooper Union and, at the meeting, organized the City
Vigilance Society. Like earlier law and order societies that
functioned as temperance society enforcement arms, the
vigilance societies functioned as political and legal enforcement arms for social purists. Indeed, the indebtedness to
purity reform was even more direct, since reformers
modeled the New York City Vigilance Society on the Man-
chester City Vigilance League, an institutional invention
of English purity reformers. Municipal reformers learned
an important lesson as they turned to politics: the public
responded more quickly and more emotionally to sexual
than to temperance themes.

After its formation, the New York City Vigilance Society discovered that emotional fervor did not, in itself,
solve urban problems. It did, however, generate public support. With an enlarging scope of operation, the society's
practical problems of social implementation had to be
resolved. Turning to sociologists, the society investigated
and reported on the special requirements of different quar-
ters of the city. Searching for a program to complement the
"New Social Spirit," the Vigilance Society ultimately proclaimed its goal as the "perfection of municipal government."[11] Again, moral perfectionism remained the great
dynamic force in social transformation.

The municipal reform movement, a coalition that
included purity reform, used quasi-religious rhetoric. Although firmly supported by New York churches and

synagogues, municipal reformers asserted their morality primarily in civic, not ecclesiastic, affairs. Appealing for non-partisan support from both major parties, they relied upon a common morality shared without regard to political affiliation. Advocating "civic uplift," the Vigilance Society, like the woman's movement, wanted to extend the attributes of the home into urban life.[12]

Prostitution, the issue that galvanized public support for municipal reform, remained a fundamental municipal issue. Samuel Blackwell, the purity movement's expert on municipal politics, reminded women of the importance of reform to moral personality in his article, "The Lesson of Geneva." If regulated prostitution retained its grip on cities, Blackwell warned his readers, religious personality was doomed. Blackwell pointed to recent events in Geneva, Switzerland, to illustrate his point. Genevans were holding a referendum on reglementation and abolitionists and regulationists had converged upon the city for a final contest in the former stronghold of Calvinism. Abolitionists, including Josephine Butler, threw themselves unreservedly into the campaign, but to their surprise and consternation, the regulationists won.

Blackwell reported the lamentable spectacle that followed a reglementation victory to his American public. Brothel keepers celebrated with a parade through Geneva's streets holding their *lampes rouges* beside them. Entering the Church of Fustèrie (the Great National Church), a demonstrator placed a lantern upon the communion altar and parodied a well-known hymn which they rededicated to the spirit of the red lamp. To Blackwell's further anguish, the victors then proceeded to parody the sufferings of Christ upon the Cross. Continuing their march, they supposedly shouted denunciations of God and De Meuron (the abolitionist leader) and cheered the red lamp. Next they marched to the home of the regulationist leader. Addressing the crowd, the regulationist advised his followers to "Go home now; we have saved our free institutions. From this moment pietism is dead in Geneva. We shall hear no more of it. We shall have peace."[13]

The lesson of Geneva struck home. Purity reformers interpreted it as a signal for entry into municipal politics. The only alternative was defeat. Private life and ideals, they felt, had to be a matter of public concern. Religion, an essentially private experience, had to be extended into municipal affairs in order to survive in an urban age. Religionists could no longer pursue private interests without regard to public concerns. In advancing the idea of the moral state, the reformers symbolically fused the secular and the religious, the public and the private. The moral state, as they understood it, was a political agency for effecting social and moral change.

Resolving the tension between public and private morality was central in reform thought and was illustrated in the political clashes of the decade. The first notable test of the idea in national politics was the 1884 presidential election. Choosing between Republican and Democratic candidates presented a real problem for American moralists, for they were forced to choose between public and private morality. James G. Blaine, who had been unimpeachable in personal morality, was suspect in his public performance as an officeholder. Grover Cleveland, who had been unimpeachable in his public morals, had acknowledged fathering an illegitimate child. Moralists wanted to avoid this decision but could not. In this instance, they chose public morality and Grover Cleveland, but vowed never to be compelled to make such a choice again. Purity reformers vigorously demanded the "same standard of high personal morality" in politics and social life. They were committed to enforcing the principle in politics. When, for instance, Kentucky women learned of Congressman Breckenridge's personal indiscretions, they campaigned against his reelection. Philadelphia women, in another case, responded similarly against a state assemblyman known to consort with brothel keepers.[14]

As reform movements underwent politicization, they strove to change the social functions of the state in other ways as well. Christianizing or humanizing politics had been established aims of the movement. Now purity reformers went a step farther, insisting that the state accept the responsibility for Christianization or humanization. According to their view of society-as-family, the state protected its citizens from immoralities and, in specific cases, also performed social welfare functions. As one proposal for the development of the moral state Frances Willard proposed a secretary of public amusements in the president's cabinet. Anna Garlin Spencer, in a less ambitious proposal, defined the social functions of the state as providing care for dependent children.[15] Whatever the specific recommendation, purity reformers wanted an active, moral state. The comprehensive scope of these plans were so far-reaching as to represent a psychology of totality. Virtually every aspect of behavior came under their scrutiny.

As they strove to implement policies of social education, purity reformers met resistance to the use of political action within their movement. Abolitionists of the antislavery crusade had voiced similar objectives: William Lloyd Garrison, for example, who also believed in the efficacy of education, had objected to political action. Benjamin DeCosta was among the new abolitionists who dissented. He wrestled with the notion of political action, noting the internal conflict between repression and reformation implicit in such a program. Although endorsing

raids on houses of ill-repute, he lamented the consequences
of the raids, the unleashing of strong emotional needs for
even more repression.

One case annoyed him in particular. As a consequence of the Parkhurst revelations, New York police
singled out Hattie Adams, a madam mentioned in
Parkhurst's report, for prosecution. The police apparently
were trying to satisfy public opinion. DeCosta cringed at
what he thought was an injustice. He doubted the probity
of the men who had engineered this sensational political arrest. DeCosta condemned these members of the vigilance
society as stock market speculators and politicians engaged
in reform, men who led "dual lives," immaculate in private
behavior, but tarnished in their public behavior. Hattie
Adams' prosecution represented, for him, a "reform
without reformation." Its main objective was simply
punishment. DeCosta concluded that political action could
only corrupt purity reform.[16]

Although DeCosta's evaluation had some validity,
other purity reformers, excitedly anticipating new gains for
the reform, were more charitable toward Parkhurst. They
lamented Parkhurst's "clear lighted" sight in one direction
and his blindness in others.[17]

The convergence of purity reform with municipal
reform followed a different course in Philadelphia.
Philadelphia purity leaders accepted the same objective as
their New York counterparts—the fusion of reform movements—but were more indirect in their plans. Joseph May,
a second generation abolitionist, used his Unitarian pulpit
to preach the gospels of municipal and purity reforms. As
many merchants were in his congregation, he doubtlessly
successfully influenced businessmen in municipal politics.
Wishing to extend the influence of these sermons beyond
the congregation, his admirers reprinted them for
wide distribution among other reformers.[18] Another

Unitarian minister, William J. Nichols, also preached purity sermons which the Municipal League of Philadelphia thought worthy of republication. Nichols, writing on similar themes, related purity and temperance reforms to municipal problems.[19] Religious and business reformers were ideologically compatible. Businessmen as reformers were perfectly willing to remand both politics and morality to municipal administration.

As municipal reformers in Philadelphia accepted purity reform, they appropriated the style and rhetoric of social purists, giving moral attributes to their own reforms. While businessmen stressed non-partisanship and business efficiency in municipal politics, they shared the purity reformers' religionist interest in promoting municipal moral order. Although organizationally separate from the Municipal League, moral reformers and religionists endorsed the movement. Only May and Nichols participated directly in the Municipal League, with May sitting on its executive board. Other religious leaders joined the Christian League of Philadelphia, whose activities complemented the Philadelphia Municipal League's. They preserved a more traditional separation of magistrates and divines.

In New York, ecclesiastical and secular leadership were commingled, breaking down the traditional separation. Compared with Philadelphia, New York tended to be more theocratic in municipal reform. Municipal reformers in Philadelphia, probably because they were less secular, relied upon a quasi-religious rhetoric. New Yorkers turned to the language of social morality.

Reformers in the two cities also reacted differently to the woman's movement. New Yorkers were willing to give equal institutional status to women in municipal reform. Following Parkhurst's advice in his struggle for municipal purification, Josephine Lowell, a prominent woman reform-

er, organized the Women's Municipal League in 1894.
League members saw municipal reform as transcending
partisan politics and joined willingly in the fight against
Tammany Hall. Not content with political action alone, the
league extended its work into new areas. Its members participated in, or organized, boys' clubs, church societies,
educational clubs, lodges and benefit societies for women,
university extensions, settlement houses, religious and
philanthropic societies, and working girls' and mens' societies.[20] In the 1901 municipal campaign, these women
ardently demonstrated their commitment to purity work,
sending every New York householder a reprint of "Facts
for New York Parents," written by Bishop Henry Potter.
Potter's pamphlet exposed the existence of organized
prostitution in the city and was documented with case
histories of young girls recruited or kidnapped into
brothels.[21]

Philadelphia women reformers pursued a different tactic
in cooperating with municipal reformers. Although they
coordinated activities with the local municipal league, they
did not organize an independent women's political group
for the specific purpose of cooperation. Rather they
depended upon the Civic Club of Philadelphia to direct
them. As a result they campaigned independently of the
municipal reformers, the Democratic or Republican parties, or, for that matter, the prohibitionists. They had not
reached the institutional maturity of the New York movement and relied upon the reform apparatus of the city
woman's movement. Philadelphia women, still more identified with their own cause rather than municipal reform,
were perfectly willing to accept political endorsements in
campaigns for the school board without regard to party
origin.[22]

Businessmen and religionists searched for a new

polity. As Sigmund Diamond has pointed out, the philan-thropic use of great fortunes reestablished the Puritan ideal of wealth as a trust and refurbished the reputation of the American businessman.[23] The purity reform and woman's movements also searched for an accommodation with the business community. While they accepted the businessman for reasons similar to those presented by Dia-mond, their ideas about polity varied from the more theocratic thought of May and Nichols to the separation of reform from politics, analogous to church and state separa-tion, represented in the thought of DeCosta. By the early 1890s, however, political abolitionism was in the ascend-ancy.

At the end of the nineteenth century, New York had become the national leader in social reform. As the un-questioned American financial and shipping center, the city's size, geographical location, and heterogeneous population gave it prominence. Looking toward England, the inspirational font for purity reform, New York reform-ers were usually the first to receive news of European developments. Forced by the enormity of their task to pay attention to organizational factors in reform, New Yorkers built a reform community and consciously delineated the configuration of their reforms earlier than reformers in other cities. Interaction, cooperation, and coordination among reformers accelerated the articulation of social theories applicable to modern social problems.

At the same time that New York became a national leader in social reform, it became an increasingly impor-tant place for entry into national politics. The latter, of course, proved true for Theodore Roosevelt, whose political career had centered around New York City politics. He had been a mayoralty candidate in 1886 and had served as the city's police commissioner. Interested in urban problems, Roosevelt was highly receptive to Progressive reforms, and purity reformers were able to influence him on sexual issues.

Aaron Macy Powell contacted Roosevelt during his tenure as police commissioner and questioned the morality of arresting only the females in prostitution cases. Roosevelt reconsidered departmental policy and issued an order for the arrest of both immoral men and women. He had modified older policies using the standard of equal punishment for sexual offenders.[24] Powell had occasion to contact Roosevelt when he was governor of New York and sent the governor a copy of the *Philanthropist* with the intent of converting Roosevelt to purity reform. Powell happily reported the Governor's reply to purity reformers:

> I thank you for sending me a copy of the *Philanthropist*, but it makes my blood boil to read it. At one time I used to acquiesce when people said that evil should be licensed for the purpose of controlling it (although I had always regarded this merely as what would be desirable though impractical). Since you called my attention to the result in Paris and Belgium (of State Regulation), I have made some inquiries and I can not sufficiently express my horror of the system.[25]

Powell claimed Roosevelt as a purity convert. Encouraged by his achievement, he proposed that the *Philanthropist* be distributed to other state and municipal authorities to influence their opinions.

Roosevelt went well beyond verbal endorsement. As governor, he proved himself an ardent ally of social purists. As a concession to the Purity Alliance, he proposed the introduction of vagrancy laws to eliminate procuring. As

Roosevelt expressed it, vagrancy laws were a technique to get at the "bully" or "souteneur" rather than at the wretched woman. He further expressed the depth of his commitment when, in his legislative message, he recommended punishment for immoral men and expansion of reformatory work.[26]

THE VICE COMMISSIONS

Purity appeals to the public had made an appreciable difference in attitudes toward prostitution. Purity reformers discovered an awakened public interest in the social evil, although it was not always manifested in a form acceptable to them. When, in 1887, the new abolitionists called for a National Vice Commission to investigate the traffic in women, Congress had not acted on the appeal. In the 1890s, special investigating committees did examine, under emergency conditions, the charge of a white slave traffic. Finally, in 1900, New York authorized an investigation by the Committee of Fifteen. As the New York investigating committee performed its work, the American Purity Alliance exerted a quiet and indirect influence upon it. Providing expert advice and investigatory assistance, they contributed substantially to the final report. Quite happy with their achievements, purity reformers endorsed the Committee of Fifteen report. Furthermore, the New York Committee of Fifteen received assistance from English purity reformers, too. E. R. A. Seligman, prominent member of the committee, queried Maurice Gregory of the Friends Association for the Abolishing of State Regulation of Vice (England) about the policies of the Association. Perfectly willing to provide Professor Seligman with literature, Gregory sent a parcel of purity pamphlets quite similar to the American variety.

The formation of the Committee of Fifteen was only

one indication of a growing interest in public morality in the city. In 1900, the New York Moral Committee appeared. With seven locals and a central committee, the Moral Committee performed both watchdog functions, to protect public morals, and educative functions, to disseminate the ideas of social purity. The city-wide organization was composed of a cross-section of New York reformers.

WORLD POLITICS:
PURITY AND THE MILITARY SPIRIT

The entrance of abolitionists into international politics was triggered by their concern over the British army's policy of regulation. New abolitionists had failed to influence military sanitarians, among whom regulationists remained strong, and who persisted in defending reglementation when other physicians had abandoned it. Citing statistics gathered from the Asian Naval Stations, they claimed regulation was operating efficiently.[27] Although new abolitionists, remembering the contagious diseases acts introduced by the military into England, did not condone the system used by the American Navy, they opposed military sanitation in another way. In cooperation with British abolitionists, they attacked military regulation in India.

Anglo-American abolitionists understood that defeating military regulation in India was important to the future of their movement, but they were motivated by other reasons as well. Their most immediate fear was that colonial regulation might eventually contaminate England. Moreover, new abolitionists opposed colonialism. Licensed prostitution symbolized, for them, a new form of slavery and a wrong policy in their relationship to underdeveloped nations. American reformers were anxious about one other issue: military sanitation struck at the family institution. If the military was not compelled to reform, military regulation might contribute to a new system of polygamy.[28]

Colonialism complicated the task of social hygiene in various practical ways. Elizabeth Blackwell noted that sixty percent of the soldiers returning to England from their tours in India had contracted venereal diseases. Their return to the mother country was a medical problem of major proportions since they carried contagious diseases. It was also a social problem, for they perpetuated attitudes negatively affecting the progress of the woman's movement. Arousing her public, Blackwell located a remedy for military transgressions in temperance and self-restraint. To armor young recruits against immorality she recommended education in the benefits of continence. To further protect them during their tours of duty, she recommended they be removed from idleness, which encouraged sin.[29]

Josephine Butler was similarly interested in the medical threat to England and voiced equal concern for the status of Indian women. Colonialism raised fundamental social questions for her. How were colonials to be treated? Suffering civil disabilities and subjugation themselves, English women reformers empathized with colonial peoples. Accepting the idea of Empire, Josephine Butler defined the correct relationship to colonials as one of guardian or teacher rather than master or conqueror.[30]

The Anglo-American woman's movement exhibited a lively interest in Indian regulation, with American women agitating for its dismantling by collecting signatures for an "Appeal to Queen Victoria." When British military leaders denied the existence of the system, an American, Dr. Kate Bushnell, went to India as an investigator for the English purity movement. She had previous experience in the Michigan lumber camp incident. Bushnell, with the assistance of another World's WCTU missionary, gathered the data that proved the existence of the system to the satisfaction of a parliamentary commission.

The "Appeal to Queen Victoria," the investigation by Bushnell, and the commission report proved successful. The British Army changed its policies. In April, 1898, Lord Wolsey issued a "General Order for Army Morality," an expansion of an earlier memorandum. Thus, the British Army supposedly abandoned regulation for troops stationed in the colonies. Women reformers proclaimed a "new era in Army life." In practice, the system continued in modified form.

This exercise in international politics came at a fortuitous moment. Shortly after the incident, the United States, as a result of the Spanish-American War, became an important world power and a ruler of colonies. Powell, watchful as usual, employed the lessons of India well by alerting the American public to the dangers of colonialism.[31]

American involvement in the Spanish-American War divided not only the public over imperialism and colonialism, but purity reformers as well. The reform community's reaction to the war foreshadowed a future division over the United States entry into World War I. Interventionists and non-interventionists among the leadership seemed evenly split. Immobilized by uncertainty, reformers debated many of the issues in the *Woman's Journal*.

Julia Ward Howe and Anna Garlin Spencer wrote for the interventionist position. They accepted the idea of an American international mission and, denying that sin and evil were national, urged the American people to correct evils and wrongs outside the nation's borders. No newcomer to the interventionist camp, Howe had previously expressed her zeal for international adventure in

1896, when she urged intervention on behalf of Christian Armenians.[32] Neither woman endorsed aggression, but each cast the United States in the role of international protector of the weak. They acknowledged the pitfalls of intervention but believed Americans should have no reservations about participation if war was forced upon them. Nevertheless, they warned Americans to be alert to moral dangers created by a standing army inevitably having close contacts with "undeveloped" and "immoral" natives of newly acquired tropical islands. Remembering the Blackwell message, interventionists warned against possible national contamination.[33]

Non-interventionists presented their case, not only within the *Woman's Journal*, but in other journals and pulpits as well. Joseph May, later a vice-president of the Anti-Imperialist League, spoke and wrote against intervention, believing it would foster a colonial policy. Searching for the causes of the overseas adventure, May located it in a false concept of patriotism. If the moral system of purity reformers was to be preserved, it required a redefinition of patriotism. In keeping with a belief in absolute moral values, May preached that the patriot was the man who conformed to law and obeyed it under every circumstance. This man would realize that "justice was always justice, purity was always purity, murder, theft, the violation of womanhood were always crimes." He would feel guilt and shame when others were robbed of their freedom.[34]

Joseph May further developed his view of world politics. Society-as-family was projected into world-as-family, for May considered mankind a unit and the world the family of man. In an imperfect world, moral leaders possessed civilization as a trust and were obligated to protect weaker members of the community. This was the principle to govern the relationships of weak and strong nations. The denial of the principle led to the defeat of

Republicanism and the victory of militarism. Self-government, essential for Americans, was equally important for the remainder of the world. In a perfect society, May continued, militarism was an atavism with as much justification to exist as the duel. Civilization meant the building of schools, not armies.[35] May was emphasizing the principle of nurture applied to international affairs. He was an early advocate of what Sondra R. Herman has named "communitarian internationalism."[36]

As emotionalism waned, most purity reformers and women's rights leaders saw intervention as an error that had brought about temporary rupture in reform ranks. Reformers confessed their error adequately without explaining the causes of the schism. Purity reformers, reaffirming their ideals, proceeded as if nothing had divided them. Above all, they did not question their own social theories, supposedly a foundation for the new civilization, despite the failure of these theories to keep even the reform movement together.

Regardless of whether they were interventionists or non-interventionists, purity reformers united against the "new militarism." Elizabeth Blackwell, anticipating new colonial problems as America entered the Spanish-American War, astutely forwarded a copy of the British "General Order on Army Morality" to President William McKinley. Purity reformers who agreed with her saw the new militarism as potentially resulting in the enslavement of womankind. It had happened in India through reglementation and it was happening in the Philippines and Cuba. It could also happen in the United States.

Purity reformers knew that moral transgressions were already rampant among the military. William Lloyd Garrison, Jr., reported to the *Philanthropist* on gambling and immorality at the army camp in Tampa, Florida. A YMCA physician independently reinforced social purists' apprehensions in his reports to Aaron Macy Powell.[37] Immediately, purity reformers contemplated a new wave of regulationist schemes appearing throughout the country. Their worst fears were realized when General Davis implemented a "rigid regulation and restriction of prostitution" in the American Army Camp in Havana. Shortly thereafter, women's rights leaders heard rumors of licensed prostitution being planned in the Philippines. To their consternation, later reports indicated the reglementation was actually being implemented.[38]

Believing that a crisis situation existed, purity reformers reviewed the history of military sanitation during the Civil War to strengthen their position. To their surprise and dismay, they discovered the army had resorted to legalized prostitution for 40,000 troops stationed near Nashville, Tennessee.[39] New abolitionists, who viewed the Civil War as a milestone in moral history, were temporarily thrown off balance. They were reassured, however, when they learned that Dr. Dio Lewis, a noted public hygienist, had offset these bad effects by proposing camp libraries and sanitary camps for bathing, swimming, and recreation for the Union Army. He intended the camps to preserve the chaste life of the soldier and to provide lessons in personal hygiene.[40]

Purity reformers, reviewing the contemporary situation, returned to an older device to curtail these moral deviations—alerting the public to the problem. After publicizing the lessons of India, they addressed "An Open Letter to President McKinley," calling his attention to the "Sodom of sin" in Tampa and Jacksonville.[41] To ensure the broadest possible support, the National American Women's Suffrage Association joined with purity reformers in memorializing President McKinley.

The assassination of the president placed the responsibility for the decision on military hygiene on Theodore

Roosevelt. Previously, he had looked with favor upon purity reform. He continued to do so. Granting an interview to Dr. O. Edward Janney, successor to Powell as president of the American Purity Alliance, Roosevelt, in 1899, restated his opposition to regulated prostitution. Later he followed through with his pledges and ordered the suppression of vice among the troops in the Philippines, an act which brought hearty congratulations from purity reformers.

A NEW GENERATION OF PURITY LEADERS

Until the mid-1890s, the New York purity elite performed an important role in coordinating purity reforms. Intent on developing a consciousness of reform configurations in the woman's movement and on reawakening moral consciousness among urbanites, social purists primarily provided symbolic integration for many reforms undertaken by the woman's movement. Once engaged in mass education, purity reformers better understood the importance of institutionalizing the reform. In the process of institutionalization, essential elements of purity reform attained independent status and existence. By 1900, purity reformers were returning to the earlier functions pursued by new abolitionists—a narrower interest in sex education, control of venereal diseases, and campaigns against prostitution—but not before an institutional consensus had been forged. In converging with urban Progressivism, purity reform lost its independent existence. The purity movement therefore had had a transitional function within social reform. These changes between 1895 and 1900 came at a moment of leadership change as well. Purity reform pursued its core objectives under a highly professional new leadership recruited from the scientific community.

In retrospect, social hygienists pinpointed the change. Anna Garlin Spencer, remembering the reform turmoil of the 1890s, saw purity reform as part of a greater movement in the development of the "religion of social service." In the late 1890s, she recalled, reform was in the "middle of a Bach fugue," but reformers were convinced that harmony would follow if only they persisted in their efforts.[42] A few years later, in 1902, O. Edward Janney reported to the American Purity Alliance that he anticipated an early actualization of a "service character" among the American people.[43] Janney and Spencer, as utopian visionaries, anticipated a new society with a high degree of socio-cultural integration. A common social morality, giving cohesion to the American people, would ease the task of mobilizing the nation for the final crusade to achieve social perfection.

By 1899, a new generation of purity leaders had taken control of the American Purity Alliance. Anna Garlin Spencer, a spokesman for social work, was among the most prominent. Originally a Unitarian minister, she had broken with the denomination to become spiritual leader of the Bell Street Chapel in Providence, Rhode Island, a free church. Spencer ministered to free religionists who still required an institutional shelter. The free church was only a temporary shelter for Spencer. Next, she broke with organized religion altogether and devoted herself to the education of social workers at the New York School of Social Work of which she was a co-founder.

Although Janney's career was no secular pilgrim's progress, he too symbolized new attributes of social leadership. Purity reformers, after reviewing his qualifications, turned to Dr. Janney as the new president of the Alliance after Aaron Macy Powell's death in 1899. He was young, he had had medical training, he was a Quaker dedicated to social service, and he was not "fettered by evangelical limitations."[44] A physician and religious leader, Janney was a prime advocate of the "Christian medicine" for which Elizabeth Blackwell and her followers had striven. Janney seemed a logical choice of the older leadership to serve as a "physician to society." Janney, as a social hygienist, and Spencer, as a social worker, represented the new professionals in purity reform. They partially reflected the changing nature of the reform and its continuing secularization.

The emergence of new leadership also occurred in the WCTU wing of purity reform. In 1895, Frances Willard selected Dr. Mary Wood-Allen to succeed her as Superintendent of Social Purity. Like Janney, Wood-Allen symbolically represented the fusion of social reform with medicine.

Clearly understanding the consequences of secularization and bureaucratization, Anna Garlin Spencer, in 1902, advised purity workers to enter social work and "to provide the leaders . . ." in the new field.[45] Again, she valued secular social reform over religious revivalism. Purity reformers may have yearned for a revival, but they doubted the efficacy of evangelical religions in 1902. They longed for a religious revival that year but did not think it imminent. Rather, they placed their faith in moral education.

THE DEVELOPMENT OF PURITY PROGRAMS

SOCIAL WORK AND EDUCATION

Education and social work were more and more the secular forces expected to complete the job of purifying the nation. Since social purists saw teachers and social workers as technicians who implemented social hygiene policies, they encouraged professionalization. Through the reform

of school curricula and through the education of professional social workers and teachers, they expected their social values to be effectively perpetuated. They had reason
to be optimistic, since the techniques of moral education
had already served the National Divorce Reform League,
an agency concurring with purity objectives, quite well.
The league had excellent success in its campaign to in-
corporate the study of the family into college and university curricula.[46]

Anna Garlin Spencer and Grace Hoadley Dodge
cooperated in order to improve the education of teachers
and social workers, with Dodge devoting her energies
primarily to professionalizing teachers' education and
Spencer to social work. In the summer of 1894, Spencer
participated in her first summer conference for the professional training of social workers. After the conference
Dodge and Spencer met to evaluate the endeavor. Dodge,
satisfied with the results, pledged financial support and
enabled Spencer to become co-founder of the New York
School of Social Work.[47] Dodge also interested herself in
education, continuing her work with the working girls' societies and extending her interests to the education and
training of young people. Experimenting with the Kitchen-
Garden Association, she and Emily Huntington adapted
the infant school or kindergarten idea to vocational
training of girls. The experiment did not meet her expectations and she moved in new intellectual directions. Over
time she and others transformed the society. Ultimately,
the society combined with other reform associations to
establish Teachers College at Columbia University.[48]

Although purity reform disintegrated through specialization and turned to professionals, it still pursued mass
reforms. Social purists remained keenly interested in social
education, paying special attention to the revitalization of
the family institution. In fact, reformers paid more atten-

tion to child rearing and education than in the past. Reflecting this expanded interest, the National Divorce Reform League changed its name, in 1896, to the League for the Protection of the Family. Two other innovations within purity reform reflected an interest in family reforms. First, the Reverend Mary T. Whitney, a Massachusetts purity reformer, founded the Institute for Family Culture in 1895 and began publication of *Family Culture* to stimulate women into reforming the social institution. Second, the WCTU initiated a massive campaign to educate women in new child rearing techniques, and, in 1896, commenced publishing the *Mothers' Friend* with the intention of coordinating mothers' meetings and promoting interest in the family and child rearing. The WCTU, as in the past, depended upon purity leaders for guidance. Dr. Mary Wood-Allen, the editor, borrowed freely from purity reform literature.

The mothers' meetings, as has been mentioned, were enormously popular. With growth this aspect of purity reform followed an independent course, culminating in the formation of the Mothers' Congress. Mrs. Theodore Weld Birney, a purity reformer and wife of James G. Birney's grandson, believed the reform deserved wide-spread attention from American mothers. Attending an 1895 mothers' meeting at Kellogg Hall in Chautauqua, New York (the hall was built with contributions from Dr. and Mrs. J. H. Kellogg to disseminate purity knowledge), Birney was struck with the notion of "Saving the race" through the child. She saw in character building, beginning with infancy, a method for stopping the "wild, mad worship of Mammon."[49]

Acting upon her idea, Birney circulated invitations to prominent educators and philanthropists for a Mothers' Congress to be convened in 1896. The congress decided on annual meetings, and state branches sprang into being. After a rapid development, the congress became the National Parents-Teachers Association. Although a similar organization, the Parents' National Education Association, developed earlier in England, Birney formed the American organization independently, and without knowledge of the English association's existence. Birney first learned of the English organization after the Mothers' Congress. In fact, this time American reformers influenced the course of English reform. Maurice Gregory, an English purity reformer, studied the reports of the Mothers' Congress and liked the cooperative feature of the American movement. He resolved to introduce the idea into England.

From its inception, the Mothers' Congress was committed to the purity ideal. Papers read at the first sessions clearly repeated purity themes, and resolutions passed by the congress supported purity programs. Furthermore, the congress adopted a program of censorship. In 1903, it even followed Josiah Leeds' emphasis upon pure literature and preventive reform applied to censorship by preparing a "List of Books for Mothers."[50] The Mothers' Congress, in its early years, resolved to cleanse homes, schools, streets, popular amusements, or anything producing evil thoughts or conduct. In brief, its members wanted to control the urban environment. It endorsed a single standard of morality, resolved to raise the age of consent, favored dress reform and advocated physical education for girls. Naturally, it encouraged further use of mothers' meetings.

The Mothers' Crusade, like purity reform before it, was elitist in its initial conceptualization and final organization. Its history was a recapitulation of the purity story. A small band of women with a common interest in a specific reform and unlimited ambition formed a national organization. Success followed quite easily; in 1899, the Mothers' Congress could boast 50,000 members, who undoubtedly contributed to its rapid institutional growth.

In 1900, the Illinois Congress of Mothers, after careful consideration, proclaimed its purpose to be the control of the child's total environment. The social purity ideology had been extended to its logical conclusion. The Illinois proclamation was no mistake, for Birney restated the instrumentalist mission of the Mothers' Congresses only four years after the first national congress. She believed mothers, through collective action, would "purify the press, pioneer in sex education, lobby for child welfare legislation, and realize the single standard of morality.[51]

The Mothers' Crusade was a movement with much political appeal. Theodore Roosevelt, with an appreciation for its political significance and, undoubtedly, sympathy for its objectives, addressed the New York Mothers' Congress in 1899. On that occasion, he directed attention to the responsibilities of fathers in child rearing. The governor thought child rearing was the foundation of national character, for, as he explained it, the parent-child relationship created attitudes that determined the nature of the social system. Warming to his audience, Roosevelt called upon mothers to adopt an education and training to make heroines of girls and place boys on the side of right.[52]

Although Roosevelt enjoyed immense popularity among reformers, his bellicosity aroused suspicions among pacific purity reformers. These gentle reformers were substantially in agreement with Roosevelt's perceptions, but they distinguished between a spirit or psychology contributing to social control and one resulting in social regimentation. For them, true patriotism meant the development of peaceful men and women. Nevertheless, factions within the movement were united as nationalists. The woman's movement was a prime mover in social education for patriotism, requesting the placement of a flag in each classroom.

Interest in the protection of the family assumed

various forms. In reforming public school curricula, women reformers inordinately emphasized "household and domestic science." Starting with traditional roles for women, they now declared them sanitary experts within the home. Reformers believed household science and domestic economy lent dignity to woman's work and presented a new image for women in a modern age. In conservatively extending the traditional purifying role of women, they confused being a good housekeeper with being a good mother. The idea of two roles for women, career and mother, was not ignored but was certainly minimized.

Citizenship education was not limited to the home and classroom. Mrs. Cornelius Stevenson, a co-founder of the Mothers' Congress and an active member of Philadelphia's New Century Guild of Working Women, enrolled 3,000 children from the seventh ward into a League of Good Citizenship.[53] Later, the guild introduced the idea into the public schools. If the family failed to inculcate purity values into children, social purists willingly became surrogate parents.

With the enactment of the Pennsylvania compulsory education law in 1895, the drive for compulsory education in the United States was almost completed. As a consequence, educators had a special problem to solve. Children, willfully absent from school, broke the law. Technically, they were delinquents. To return them, if they were habitually truant, to regular schools seemed inappropriate since the schools had failed to adequately socialize them in the past. Moreover, these children could not be sent to prison. Searching for an alternative, purity reformers found one in the George Junior Republic. These boys' republics, organized according to the reformatory spirit, tried to teach good citizenship to the "deprived" young men of the 1890s. Camp instructors disciplined young men and attempted to create an *espirit de corps*. As

they marched, these young men often sang the following
song:

> Down with the boss, down with the tramp;
> Down with the pauper; down with the scamp;
> Up with the Freeman, up with the wise;
> Up with the thrifty; on to the prize;
> Who are we? Why, we are,
> Citizens of the GJR:
> We love our land and we would die,
> To keep Old Glory in the sky.[54]

Other aspects of the republic were less regimented. Self-
government was encouraged. Trying to recapitulate
republican government, William George, the founder,
allowed students to manage their own affairs to the greatest
extent possible. Despite the liberality of the camps, they
were half-way houses between reformatories and conventional schools.

Purity reformers, in this situation, faced a glaring
paradox in their thought. Although dedicated to an ideal of
voluntarism, they resorted to techniques of forced socialization. Committed to free choice, they made non-
conformity criminal or, at least, delinquent. Only their
curative impulse saved them from the harsh implications of
the paradox.

CENSORSHIP

Pressures for the purification of the press that had begun in
the early 1890s continued and grew stronger, as public
opinion was most favorable to press purification. Mrs. Emilie
Martin, the Josiah Leeds' successor as WCTU superintendent of purity in literature, reported an endorsement for
pure literature from the National Editorial Association in

1895. The association reaffirmed its endorsement at its 1896 convention. Reformers made other gains among professional newspapermen. In 1898, the president of the International League of Press Clubs, Henry D. Vaught, endorsed the campaign for purity of the press. In the same year, the executive board of the American Newspapers Publishers' Association unanimously approved the reform.[55]

Endorsed by publishers and editors, the movement also gained wide public acceptance. More than 3000 people attending the Swarthmore conference of the Friends Philanthropic Labor Union listened to an address on "The Press and Purity" in 1897. This was not an isolated phenomenon, for the *New York Evening Post* commented on the mass involvement of people in the crusade for press purification.[56]

Indeed, censors seemed to possess a voracious appetite for their work, calling for ever-expanding prohibitions against "anti-social behavior." Affluence and a decreased work week caused literal-minded reformers anxiety over increased leisure time. When, in 1887, the New York legislature enacted the Saturday Half-Holiday Act, prominent New York reformers inquired into the possible consequences. Although they favored a reduction in the work week, they feared the masses would turn to "dancing, carousing, low behavior, rioting, shooting, and murder."[57] To purity reformers, rationalized leisure seemed the best alternative to anarchy. Purity reformers and religionists hoped to remove the "Devil's sting" from entertainment. They were attempting to desexualize and sublimate.

The indomitable Josiah W. Leeds lengthened his list of public censorship activities with the discovery of leisure-time activities. According to Leeds, prize fighting, like dueling, slavery, lotteries, and polygamy, deserved repression. They were atavisms from a by-gone age. Leeds, relying on the assistance of Philadelphia District Attorney George Graham, prohibited the Sullivan-McCafferty fight in April 1885.[58] Not content with stopping actual fights, purity reformers, in 1896, pressured Congress for a national prohibitory law against transmission of any description or picture of prize fighting through the mails or interstate commerce. Conscious of technological changes, Senator George Hoar (R-Massachusetts) submitted a bill to prohibit mechanical reproductions of prize fights by "Kinetoscope or kindred devices."[59]

Prohibition, an eastern phenomenon, did not appeal to westerners. High-license policies, previously applied to the sale of alcohol in the West, were also applied to prize fighting when Nevada licensed it in 1897. Eastern purity reformers immediately protested the act as the "Nevada disgrace." For purity reformers, licensing prize fighting, gambling, prostitution, or saloons was as unthinkable as licensing murder, robbery, or other crimes.

Gambling was antithetical to the purity life style. When expressing mild opposition, reformers considered gambling a "moral loss." When emotion dominated reformers, they more strongly associated gambling with both speculation in stocks and bonds and "speculation in sex."[60] Moral reformers worked to remove chance from life and to minimize their risks. In their highly structured world, they put a premium upon purposive, rather than speculative, behavior.

In their on-going struggle with gambling, they had reason to celebrate, but they remained discontented with their ability to control social development. The National Anti-Lottery Act of 1890, a case in point, drew applause from purity reformers but also stirred dissatisfaction. Leeds, not trusting to chance, wrote to Postmaster General John Wanamaker urging strict administration of the law.

Wanamaker assured him the law would be administered broadly and comprehensively.[61] Despite prohibitory legislation against gambling, Leeds fought a rear-guard action as gambling became more acceptable to Americans. Going beyond opposition to lotteries, Leeds lobbied to prohibit legalized horseracing. Lobbying in Pennsylvania prevented legal licensing, but in New Jersey the legislature overrode a governor's veto to legalize horseracing.

Leeds expended more time as a public censor, since technology, by permitting new forms of popular culture, created new censorship activities. Purity reformers reported with alarm that for merely two cents New York boys and girls could listen to "indecent" phonograph records. They also discovered that advances in motion picture technology permitted the reproduction of prize fights and immodest dances.[62] Social censors rededicated themselves to the prohibition of these entertainments.

Leisure time and greater affluence allowed other deviations in entertainment forms to either be developed in or introduced into the United States. One English import, the "living picture," shocked both American and English reform communities. The living picture, the staging of sparsely dressed actors and actresses in artistic representation and their rearrangement in other poses after the curtain drop, was introduced into New York City in 1894. The entertainment, to use a purity metaphor, spread like a plague. The WCTU determined to abolish the entertainment. Purity reformers urged passage of prohibitory state laws. In Philadelphia, Leeds, with the backing of Mayor Stuart and Superintendent of Police Linden, suppressed the performances. Isabel Wing Lake, national superintendent of rescue work for the WCTU, led the prohibitory campaign in Chicago. Lady Somerset, who was in the United States at the time, was reported to be the leader of the campaign. She denied it, but did indicate that the

WCTU had undertaken a national campaign. In New York City, Parkhurst, still popular after his investigations, hinted at new reforms to follow the repression of the living picture.[63]

Social purists were alarmed over the public acceptance of nudity. For this reason, Leeds was adamant in his opposition to the introduction of ballet into the United States. Convinced the wearing of tights was the equivalent of nudity, he labored to stop ballet performances at the Philadelphia Academy of Music. Morality, for Leeds, was supreme over art. He therefore acknowledged no basic difference between the low dancing halls across the street from the Academy and the ballet. He worked diligently to close both. Nor was he alone in this endeavor. To his joy, he learned that WCTU and religious leaders in other cities acted to suppress the ballet company's performances as the company went on national tour.[64]

Theatrical performances, like motion pictures, were reaching a mass audience and, as a consequence, came under the censor's surveillance. Frances Willard, eager to experiment with devices to conserve moral purity, advised temperance workers to establish local review boards to preview plays before public performances.[65] Highly successful in gaining censorship legislation on state and local levels, purity reformers had less to satisfy them in national censorship legislation.

Purity reformers were not only interested in repression; they turned to reforms to control and sublimate. In Philadelphia, the Working Girls' Guild agreed in 1895 to permit supervised social dancing at their meeting hall. It was feared that if girls were not given an opportunity to socialize with their young men, they would frequent low dance halls. The guild's executive board also introduced the "Theater Blanc," an experiment based on a Parisian innovation—the presentation of purified theater to young people. Later, in the early twentieth century, social hygienists encouraged the building of public dance halls, the regulation of private dance halls through licensing, and the municipal encouragement of public amusements, of which Coney Island was an example.

Technology also made possible the mass reproduction of art that could threaten moral purity. In 1887, when a *New York Telegram* salesman hawked reproductions of Blanchard, Cabanel, and Serestre in Philadelphia, Leeds had the peddler arrested. Anthony Comstock and Leeds paused to review the incident, reassuring each other that they had defended public morals against degenerate Parisian art. The two men had a theory of moral aesthetics. In the language of Comstock, "art is not above morality."[66]

In 1891, Leeds' private concern for art became public through an incident that commanded the reformers' attention. The inclusion of two nude canvasses by Alexander Harrison in the sixty-first Annual Exhibit of the Pennsylvania Academy of Fine Arts occasioned a political encounter humorously referred to in the press as the "war of the righteous women."[67] The incident unleashed a wave of moral indignation.

Five hundred prominent Philadelphia women protested the nude paintings, condemning Academy President Edward Coates' decision to hang the canvasses. Unexpectedly, their action triggered a public response favoring their viewpoint. The Philadelphia Purity Alliance meeting, usually poorly attended, overflowed with people listening to a paper on "The Nude in Art." The issue, seized upon by the press, remained in public view long enough to change decisions.

Coates, adamantly protecting his artistic integrity, took to task those who saw only immodesty, indelicacy, and indecency in the human figure. Not deterred by an attack on his motivations, Leeds again led in the fight against impurities. Lamenting Coates' audacious defense, Leeds, in a letter to the newspapers, equated nude paintings at the Academy with paintings decorating saloon walls. Uncompromising in his ideal of moral stewardship, Leeds insisted upon a single standard of morality without concessions to artistic license. The public apparently sympathized with Leeds. Coates, sensing his precarious position, capitulated with assurances that future exhibits would cause no objections.[68]

Purity reformers, quick to exploit a propaganda opportunity, capitalized on public sentiment. The local Purity Alliance conducted a city-wide campaign against the indecent in art. The national WCTU, picking up the issue, propagandized throughout the country, getting thousands of "prominent Americans" to sign a "Protest against Indecent Pictures."[69]

However, social purists no longer enjoyed an attitudinal consensus on nudity. By 1896, some purity leaders thought nudity in art might serve good purposes. Rejecting the notion of a dichotomy between body and spirit, they preached the beauty of the body and accentuated the psychological, not the physical, aspects of immorality. They saw the advantage of changing perceptions through sublimation rather than isolating the phenomenon of nudity and prohibiting it. How were the values of the purity movement to be internalized within the American people? Education, an article of faith among purity workers, was the proper vehicle, but not just education within the schoolroom. In this regard, popular hygiene causes and public health work had meaningful educative significance.

SOCIAL HYGIENE

Popular hygiene, in particular, had combined physical and moral hygiene into social medicine. The social hygiene movement was heir to this medical tradition. In the interests of public health, social purists championed the construction of public baths to promote health *and* morality. If people learned to be clean, they would also learn temperance habits. The campaign for public baths had latent functions of teaching obedience to health laws and educating the good citizen. If people associated dirt and filth with the values of the saloon and brothel, they associated cleanliness with morality. Hence, social purists, for health and moral reasons, advocated municipalization of the water works to make water free.[70] Temperance reformers had emphasized a similar point in their agitation for public drinking fountains. Without them, intemperance and the saloon were the beneficiaries. Not only were the masses to be educated to the cleanliness ethic, special lessons in cleanliness were advocated in child rearing. Celebrating the cause of "clean lips," the Reverend Mr. Gledstone contended that soaping the mouth was more effective than caning a child as punishment for swearing.[71] Social purists were learning the importance of substituting psychology for physical force.

Social education as a preventive technique promised much for the future of reform. Social hygienists were depending upon the lessons of preventive social medicine. They wanted to build a hygienic society, in moral and physical harmony. Thus the institution of public baths, as preventive social education, excited social workers. William Tolman, sociological adviser to the New York Association for Improving the Condition of the Poor and the City Vigilance Society, did much to popularize the reform. Remembering earlier experiments in public hygiene and knowing the limits of voluntarism, the association recommended municipal funding for baths.[72] As the reform enthusiasm spread, the Philadelphia government financed public baths in 1898.

Women reformers who involved themselves in bath

reform appreciated the urgency of educating youngsters to cleanliness at an early age. Hoping to reach a mass audience, women reformers introduced the notion of free baths into the public school system to internalize the value of cleanliness in the child. Schoolboards were convinced. Springfield, Massachusetts, introduced the first free "rain-showers," and New York introduced them into the schools in 1900.[73]

INDUSTRIAL PURIFICATION

Since cleanliness was a cornerstone of purity morality, moralists pursued various tacks to instruct the American people. The social education of the working man was especially attractive to them. An exuberant claimant contended that public baths might save the working classes. More realistic reformers saw it as only an instrument of social education. William Tolman, who coordinated many of these reforms, urged employers to provide cleaning services so working men could return home at the end of the day looking like gentlemen. Keeping industry compartmentalized might prevent the values of the shop from destroying the home.

By ameliorating socio-economic tensions, purity reformers hoped to extend values of the home and religion into the general community. As social purists became political, they moved into economic and political life with evangelical design. In trying to find a new consensus, they deemphasized conflict and encouraged compromise. Fully aware of the threat of industrial conflicts to a consensual society, purity reformers feared purification of family, school, church, and politics would be in vain as long as the industrial environment, physical and social, remained impure. They resolved to "purify and idealize industry." Without cooperation and sympathy among classes, they were doomed to failure.[74]

Many progressive reformers proselytized for industrial betterment and industrial peace. The National Civic Federation, the Chicago federation grown large, stressed industrial cooperation and the National Municipal League contributed toward the same end. New York reformers, however, thought it important to coordinate and publicize these programs through a League for Social Service. With Josiah Strong as president and William Tolman as secretary, the league was a "clearing house" for reform and worked for the realization of new ideals of industrial betterment nationally. Although appealing to the profit motive by indicating the importance of social environment to productivity, Strong and Tolman hoped for altruistic motivation from businessmen, but pragmatically accepted compliance regardless of motivation since they thought industrial betterment mutually beneficial to employer and employee. Some large corporations not only accepted the program, incorporating social welfare into their operations, but also instituted profit-sharing as an aspect of the New Industrialism. Intended for industrial betterment, social welfare frequently was used manipulatively by personnel directors.

More concerned with idealizing existing enterprise than changing industrial or governmental structure, the Municipal League did, on a small scale, encourage trade unionism through a Toynbee society.[75] There were exceptions to this generalization, of course. A few purity reformers dabbled in third party politics, and they allied themselves with reform candidates in mayoralty campaigns. Frances Willard, supposedly sympathetic to socialism, did advocate the "nationalization of industry" during the New York City Tailor Strike of 1895.[76] But these were exceptions. The majority of purity reformers advocated a form of communitarian cooperativism akin to the company town. In fact, many admired the cooperative town of Bolsover, England. They were interested in

equalizing opportunity, not in expropriating wealth.[77] To
the contrary, they wanted societal revitalization—a
triumph of the values of social religion over the values of
the market place.

FURTHER INSTITUTIONAL DEVELOPMENT OF PURITY REFORM

A study of social processes raises distinct problems in
periodization. Where may one end a study of a movement
continuing beyond the scope of investigation? There are
justifications for terminating this study with 1900 since
changes in the institutional development and leadership of
the movement occurred about then. The appearance of the
American Purity Alliance represented, moreover, the culmination of nineteenth-century purity reform and marked
the beginning of a modern social hygiene movement. As
the movement gained new leadership between 1895 and
1900, it assumed new meaning. Social purists turned from
the experimental voluntarism of earlier days to a reliance
upon professional expertise and administration. Although
faith and morality remained important to them, they abandoned quasi-religious language as education gained ascend-
ency over moral exhortation.

New social hygienists willingly assumed the mantle of
leadership. They vigorously implemented reforms that
obliterated former distinctions between physical and spiritual salvation. Now allied with the medical profession, they
proceeded with greater efficiency than older moralists.
Having educated physicians to society's moral expectations, purity reformers anticipated a future in which physicians would respond automatically to moral requisites,
rather than act through external compulsion.[78]

In the twentieth century, institutional consolidation,

an aspect of the organizational revolution, enlarged the authority of the social hygiene movement. In the interest of consolidation, O. Edward Janney called a convention of five purity associations in 1901, but it had disappointing results. At that moment of disappointment, however, social purists received an unexpected organizational assist from Dr. Prince Morrow, a leading New York physician. Morrow's reputation, from the purity point of view, was tarnished after he attended an 1899 medical convention on venereal diseases. The international congress raised reformers' apprehensions of a resurrected regulationist movement. Morrow, however, underwent an attitudinal change. After further investigation of venereal disease problems at the 1902 Brussels international congress, he accepted a policy of moral prophylaxis and issued a call to physicians for the establishment of hygiene societies. Moving slowly, physicians finally organized the New York Society of Sanitary and Moral Prophylaxis in 1905.[79]

Five years later, Dr. Morrow reported that the medical profession was awakened to the interrelationships of venereal diseases and morality. He further stated that character and health were dependent upon each other; that is to say, that the primary cure for the venereal diseases was "impersonal interpretation of physiological laws of man and nature as developed by science and confirmed by human experience." Consensus and control were clearly interdependent. One could not succeed without the other. Morrow and purity reformers now agreed on the purposes of social medicine and condemned the idea of "sexual necessity" as a fallacy. Morrow's societies rapidly gained membership, and, in a few years, the society claimed locals in New York, Philadelphia, Baltimore, Chicago, Denver, Indianapolis, Jacksonville, Mexico City, Milwaukee, Portland, Spokane, and St. Louis.[80]

The social hygiene and social medicine movements

partially converged in 1906 with the formation of the National Vigilance Committee. At last, local committees
formed in 1876 had achieved national status. Formed at a
special meeting held at Grace Hoadley Dodge's home, the
committee included Charles W. Eliot, Prince Morrow,
Grace Dodge, Seth Low, Cardinal Gibbons, James Bronson Reynolds, and Dr. Robert N. Wilson.[81] As a watchman over national morals the committee relied upon in-
direction to influence legislation. Its effect was extensive,
reaching into the highest national councils. Reynolds, for
example, served as liaison between purity reformers and
President Theodore Roosevelt. By 1910, the committee
had gained more permanent status as the National
Vigilance Society.

Another important and independent institutional
development was the funding of the Bureau of Social
Hygiene by John D. Rockefeller, Jr. The bureau collected
data on social purity questions and funneled information to
the numerous urban vice commissions springing up in the
Progressive Era. The bureau and assorted independent
groups reorganized in 1910 into the American Society for
Sex Hygiene. Finally, in 1913, the National Vigilance Society for Sex Hygiene combined into the American Social
Hygiene Association.[82] The association, which has been
in existence ever since, is known today as the American
Social Health Association.

Other social functions previously performed by the
municipal vice committees and social purity alliances were
transferred to new national agencies. The Traveller's Aid
Alliance, formed in 1904, undertook responsibility for protecting women travellers. The Working Girls' Societies
were, predominantly, absorbed into the Women's Trade
Union League of the United States. And, of course,
mothers' meetings came under the aegis of the National
Parents-Teachers Association.

Although purity reform as a social movement disintegrated, it contributed its ideology to progressive reforms. It endured through secularization and contributed to a new social consensus at the foundation of modern social institutions. Beginning as a cultural response to the effects of urbanization and industrialization, purity reform directly influenced the development of a modern social system. Contributing to the formation of social morality, it educated Americans to common social values. Quietly assisting in the channelling of social reconstruction, it continued a new asceticism as a variant of social Puritanism.

NOTES

1. "National Council of Women," *Woman's Journal*, February 28, 1891, p. 72, and Isaac Clothier, "Protection of Young Women in Stores," *Philanthropist*, July 1896, p. 19. By the end of the century a unity of sorts had been achieved for the woman's movement. By 1890 club women, suffragists, purity reformers, and other women's rights groups had affiliated into the National Council of Women. Women were organized in every state, and an interstate organization had been formed to coordinate activities. Municipal councils of women were formed in the cities.

2. "National Reform Conference," *Union Signal*, July 11, 1895, p. 9; Frank Mann Stewart, *A Half Century of Municipal Reform* (Berkeley: University of California Press, 1950), pp. 11-12; Samuel C. Blackwell, "The Municipality in its Relation to Vice," *Papers and Speeches of the National Purity Congress*, pp. 110-17; and Benjamin O. Flower, "Crucial Moments in National Life," *Arena* 6 (July 1894). For Parkhurst's call to politics, see *Union Signal*, July 5, 1894, p. 8.

3. Anna Rice Powell, "The American Purity Alliance and its Work," *Woman's Journal*, December 21, 1895, p. 402. Available evidence gives no indication of planned political action among purity reformers. Rather, they were swept into political action along with other reformers by a general politicalization.

4. Anna Gordon to Frances E. Willard, November 6, 1898, Frances E. Willard Papers, WCTU Headquarters, Evanston, Illinois.

5. For a more detailed account of the founding of the National Municipal League, see David J. Pivar, "Theocratic Businessmen and Philadelphia Municipal Reform,

1870-1900," *Pennsylvania History* 33 (July 1966): 289-307.

6. "From the Home Standpoint," *Woman's Journal*, July 14, 1894, p. 218.

7. "Campaign for Good Citizenship," Josiah W. Leeds Scrapbook, vol. 12, p. 106.

8. *Philanthropist*, April 1892, p. 4, and October 1892, p. 1; and Charles Garner, *The Doctor and the Devil* (New York: Warren Publishing Co., 1894), p. 14.

9. "Editorial," *Philanthropist*, May 1892, p. 4.

10. Charles Parkhurst, *Our Fight with Tammany* (New York: Charles Scribner's Sons, 1895), p. 154.

11. William Tolman, "Municipal Reform," *Arena* 16 (October 1896): 734; "Prospectus," *City Vigilance*, January 1894, p. 1; and W. H. Tolman, *Municipal Reform Movements* (New York: G. Nevell Co., 1895), pp. 18-19.

12. Tolman, *Municipal Reform*, pp. 17, 20-21; "Our Aim is to Uplift our City," *New York Vigilant*, January 29, 1901, p. 1; and "The New York Society for the Prevention of Crime and the City Vigilance Society," *New York Vigilant*, December 11, 1900, p. 1.

13. Samuel Blackwell, "The Lesson of Geneva," *Woman's Journal*, August 22, 1896, p. 268.

14. "Massachusetts Women's Suffrage Association, Resolution 8," *Woman's Journal*, January 12, 1895, p. 12; and "Editorial," *Philadelphia Evening Ledger*, January 7, 1899.

15. Anna Garlin Spencer was chairwoman of the International Congress of Charities and Corrections (Chicago) section of care of dependent and neglected children. *Woman's Journal*, July 15, 1893, p. 217. For a statement on dependent children, see "Declaration of Principles," *Woman's Journal*, March 11, 1893, p. 87. For Frances Willard's proposal, see *Cleveland Evening Record*, November 16, 1894.

16. "DeCosta Defends his Plea for Mercy," *New York Herald*, May 14, 1892, p. 4; and B. J. DeCosta, "The

White Cross in Politics," *Philanthropist*, December 1894, p. 8.

17. Samuel May, Jr. to Elizabeth Gay, February 19, 1897, Sidney Howard Gay Papers, Columbia University.

18. Joseph May, *Conscience in Politics: A Sermon* (Philadelphia: First Unitarian Church, n.d.).

19. William J. Nichols, *Duties of Citizens in Reference to Municipal Government* (Philadelphia: Municipal League, 1892).

20. Josephine Shaw Lowell, "Women's Municipal League of the City of New York," *Municipal Affairs* 2 (September 1898): 465-66.

21. W. R. Stewart. *The Philanthropic Work of Josephine Shaw Lowell* (New York: MacMillan Company, 1911), p. 417.

22. Herbert Welsh, *The Relation of Women to Municipal Reform* (Philadelphia: Civic Club, February 23, 1894); Mary Mumford, *The Relation of Women to Municipal Reform* (Philadelphia: Civic Club, 1895); and Mrs. Talcott Williams, ed., *The Story of a Woman's Municipal Campaign, A Paper Submitted to the American Head of the Academy of Political and Social Science by the Civic Club of Philadelphia* (Philadelphia: Published by the Academy, No. 150, 1895).

23. Sigmund Diamond, *The Reputation of the American Businessman* (New York: Harper Colophon, 1965), pp. 178-79.

24. Theodore Roosevelt to Aaron M. Powell, June 21, 1895, in *Philanthropist*, July 1895, p. 8.

25. *Proceedings of the Friends' Union of Philanthropic Labor, 1900* (Philadelphia: Ferris Brothers, n.d.), pp. 370-72.

26. "Governor Roosevelt on Regulation," *Philanthropist*, July 1900, p. 8; and Theodore Roosevelt to O. Edward Janney, August 4 and September 19, 1899.

27. "Report of the Committee on the Prevention of Venereal Diseases of the American Public Health Asso-

ciation," *Public Health: Reports and Papers, Volume VI, 1880* (Boston: Houghton Mifflin, 1881), p. 411.

28. Josephine Butler, "Appeal Concerning British Regulation in India," reprinted, *Philanthropist*, June 1890, p. 1; and " 'Regulation' in Practice," *Woman's Journal*, June 26, 1897, pp. 204-5.

29. Elizabeth Blackwell, "Responsibility of Women Physicians," in *Woman's Journal*, July 31, 1897, p. 248; and August 7, 1897, p. 256.

30. *Woman's Journal*, July 10, 1897, p. 220.

31. Aaron Macy Powell, "The Lessons from India," *Philanthropist*, July 1899, pp. 10-11.

32. Julia Ward Howe, "Shall the Frontiers of Christiandom be Maintained against the Turks?" *Forum* 22 (November 1896): 321-26.

33. *Appeal for Purity: The American Purity Alliance to the Men and Women of America* (n.p.:n.d.).

34. Joseph May, *The True Patriotism: A Sermon* (Philadelphia: First Unitarian Church, March 27, 1898), pp. 11-12.

35. Joseph May, *Mankind A Unit: Civilization A Stewardship* (Philadelphia: First Unitarian Church, 1899), pp. 14-16; and *The Peril of our Republic: A Sermon* (Philadelphia: First Unitarian Church, 1899), p. 14; Anna Garlin Spencer, "Is the Declaration of Independence Outgrown?" *Woman's Journal*, January 14, 1899, p. 12; and Joseph May, *Militarism—The Enemy of Civilization: A Sermon* (Philadelphia: First Unitarian Church, March 26, 1899), pp. 11-12.

36. *Eleven Against War: Studies in American Internationalist Thought, 1898-1921* (Stanford, Calif.: Hoover Institution Press, 1969), p. ix.

37. William Lloyd Garrison, Jr. to Elizabeth Gay, January 14, 1898, and Aaron M. Powell to Elizabeth Gay, October 20, 1898, Sidney Howard Gay Papers, Columbia University.

38. William Lloyd Garrison. Jr. to Elizabeth Gay,

January 14, 1898, Aaron M. Powell to Elizabeth Gay, February 2, 1899, Sidney Howard Gay Papers, Columbia University; "A Philippine Evil," *Journal of The American Medical Association* 33 (August 19, 1899): 467; and *Chicago New Voice*, August 23, 1900, in *Philanthropist*, October 1900, p. 4.

39. Charles Smart, Deputy Surgeon General, to J. W. Leeds, March 10, 1899, in *Woman's Journal*, April 15, 1899, p. 118.

40. "Military Hygiene," *The Journal of Hygiene and Herald of Truth* 48 (July 1898): 190-92.

41. "Army Immorality—An Appeal to President McKinley," *Philanthropist*, January 1899, p. 6; and *Philanthropist*, October 1900, p. 6.

42. Anna Garlin Spencer, *Remarks, Free Religious Association Proceedings, May 27 and 28, 1897* (New Bedford: Free Religious Association, 1897), p. 106.

43. O. Edward Janney, "The Child of the Twentieth Century," *31st Annual Meeting of the American Purity Alliance, 1906* (New York, 1907).

44. Anna Rice Powell to Elizabeth Gay, December 14, 1899, Sidney Howard Gay Papers, Columbia University.

45. *27th Annual Report of the American Purity Alliance, 1902* (New York, 1903), p. 6.

46. Mary Livermore was the purity reformer most active in cooperating with the National Divorce Reform League. Her view on divorce closely approximated that of the league. The league changed its name in 1896 to the League for the Protection of the Family. In the mid-1890s it launched an effort for the inclusion of the study of the family in college and university curricula. See Mary A. Livermore, "Women's Views of Divorce," *North American Review* 398 (January 1890): 110-17.

47. Anna Garlin Spencer, "Pilgrimage: Over the Roads of Moral Reform, 1851-1921," Anna Garlin Spencer Papers, Swarthmore College; and *Woman's Journal*, June 16, 1894, p. 185.

48. Lawrence Arthur Cremin, David A. Shannon, and Mary Evelyn Townshend, *A History of Teachers' College,*

Columbia University (New York: Columbia University Press, 1954); and Edwin Williams, "What Grace Hoadley Dodge has done for the Working Girl," *The World Today* 18 (December 1910): 1363-66.

49. Mrs. Theodore Weld Birney, "The Work of the Mothers' Congress and Clubs," *The Coming Age*, September 1899, p. 253.

50. *National Congress of Mothers, List of Books for Mothers* (n.p.: prepared by the Committee on Literature, 1903).

51. *Illinois Congress of Mothers, 1900* (Chicago, 1900), pp. 7-8, 20-21, Library of Congress.

52. "Theodore Roosevelt before the New York Mothers' Convention," *Woman's Journal*, October 28, 1899, p. 340.

53. "League of Good Citizenship of Philadelphia," *Lend A Hand* 17 (July 1896): 51-54.

54. William J. Hull, "The George Junior Republic," *Annals of the Academy of Political and Social Sciences* 10 (July 1897): 85.

55. *Union Signal*, February 13, 1896, p. 1; and Anna Rice Powell, "The Purification of the Press," *Philanthropist*, April 1898, p. 24.

56. *Philanthropist*, April 1897, p. 1.

57. J. W. Leeds, "The Wage-Earners Half-Holiday," *Banner and Herald*, July 1887, Josiah W. Leeds Papers, Haverford College.

58. *Philadelphia Ledger*, April 1, 1885.

59. Leeds Scrapbook, vol. 12, pp. 33, 51-52, Josiah W. Leeds Papers, Haverford College.

60. J. W. Leeds, *Horse Racing: The Beginning of Gambling; The Lottery* (Philadelphia: By the Author, 1895), p. 6; and Blackwell, *The Human Element in Sex: Being a Medical Enquiry into the Relation of Sexual Physiology and Christian Morality* (London: J. & A. Churchill, 1889), p. 16.

61. Leeds Scrapbook, vol. 6, p. 65, Josiah W. Leeds Papers, Haverford College.

62. *Philanthropist*, September 1894, p. 1. The National

Board of Motion Picture Censors was organized in 1903 by New York reformers.

63. "Decency Again Vindicated," *Episcopal Recorder*, October 4, 1894, p. 9; *Chicago Mail*, September 29, 1894; "Against Living Theater," *New York Sun*, November 28, 1894; and "Lady Somerset's Plans," *New York Sun*, November 29, 1894, p. 1; and *New York Press*, November 28, 1894.

64. "J. W. Leeds to the Editor," *Philadelphia Inquirer*, January 25, 1887; "Against the Ballet," *Banner and Herald*, February 1887; and *Christian Statesman*, June 16, 1888.

65. Frances E. Willard, *Annual Address Before the National WCTU, 1894* (Chicago: WTPA, 1894), p. 127.

66. *Philadelphia Evening Bulletin*, November 18, 1887; Anthony Comstock to Josiah W. Leeds, November 21, 1887, Josiah W. Leeds Papers, Haverford College; *Union Signal*, January 12, 1893, p. 12.

67. Leeds Scrapbook, vol. 6, pp. 108-9, Josiah W. Leeds Papers, Haverford College.

68. *Philadelphia Evening Bulletin*, March 9, 1891; Josiah W. Leeds, "Purity in Art Exhibits," *Philadelphia Inquirer*, March 6, 1891; and "Edward Coates to the Editor," *Philadelphia Inquirer*, March 6, 1891.

69. Joseph May and William McVicker to Josiah W. Leeds, April 20, 1891; *Christian Statesman*, March 12, 1891; Eunice Macy (WCTU) to Josiah W. Leeds, March 20, 1891; and "Protest against Indecent Pictures," February 28, 1893, Leeds' Scrapbook, vol. 7, p. 37; all in Josiah W. Leeds Papers, Haverford College.

70. Charles Shepard, "Public Baths, A Prevention of Disease," *Journal of the American Medical Association* 19 (October 8, 1892): 429-32; Francis S. Longworth, "The People's Baths," *The Charities Review* 2 (January 1893): 180-83.

71. J. P. Gledstone, "Clean Lips," *Philanthropist*, November 1886, p. 1.

72. William Tolman, "Public Baths, Laundry and

Public Comfort Stations in New York City," *Annals of the American Academy of Political and Social Sciences* 8 (July 1896): 205-9.

73. "The Pupil and the Bathtub," *Woman's Journal*, July 23, 1898, p. 234; "Baths in New York Public Schools," *Charities Review* 10 (March 1900): 4-5.

74. "Mothers' Congress," *Woman's Journal*, February 4, 1899, p. 36; and Anna G. Spencer, "Marriage and Social Control," *Harvard Theological Review* (n.d.), in Anna Garlin Spencer Papers, Swarthmore College; and William Tolman, "The Social Unions of Edinburgh and Glasgow," *Charities Review* 3 (April 1893): 332. The operation of this program in Milwaukee is analyzed in Gerd Korman, *Industrialization, Immigrants and Americanizers: The View from Milwaukee, 1866-1921* (Madison: State Historical Society of Wisconsin, 1967), pp. 87-109. A real tension existed between International Harvester's idea of social welfare and that of the social worker hired as director of social welfare. The company view ultimately prevailed.

75. Herbert Welsh Scrapbook, 1895, Herbert Welsh Papers, Historical Society of Pennsylvania. The Reverend W. I. Nichols formed the Toynbee Society to assist labor in organizing and to work toward industrial peace.

76. *The Journal of Hygiene and Herald of Health* 47 (July 1897): 194.

77. "A Cooperative Town," *The Journal of Hygiene and Herald of Health* 44 (November 1894): 303-4.

78. Elizabeth Blackwell, *The Influence of Women in the Profession of Medicine* (London: George Bell and Sons, n.d.); and "The Medical Man and his Morals," *Journal of the American Medical Association* 29 (July 10, 1897): 86-88.

79. Prince A. Morrow, *Society of Sanitary and Moral Prophylaxis—Origin of the Movement, Its Object, Aims and Methods of Work*, New York Public Library, Uncatalogued Pamphlets.

80. Prince A. Morrow, *Results of the Work Accom-*

plished by the Movement for Sanitary and Moral Prophylaxis (New York: Fred H. Hitchcock, 1910) pp. 4, 8-9.

81. Anna G. Spencer, "Those Who Blazed the Trail," *Anniversary Luncheon, American Social Health Association, January 19, 1929,* Anna Garlin Spencer Papers, Swarthmore College; and *31st Annual Report of the American Purity Alliance, 1906* (New York: 1907), pp. 6-7.

82. Mrs. T. P. Curtis, *The Traffic in Women* (Boston: The Woman's Suffrage Party, n.d.), p. 12; Wilson, *Fifty Years with Girls*, p. 24; and Charles Walter Clarke, *Taboo: The Story of the Pioneers of Social Hygiene* (Washington: Public Affairs Press, 1961), p. 74.

6

Purity Reform in Perspective

Purity reformers played a major role in changing American sex attitudes. Introducing a tabooed subject into general society, they reeducated Americans to a new morality, proclaimed a woman's right to her own body, and denied licensed prostitution a place in society. Believing in conservative birth control and eugenics, they paved the way for Margaret Sanger's future ideas on planned parenthood. Quietly and unobtrusively they instructed a generation of mothers in sex education, affirming their life style and simultaneously reinforcing social structure during a particularly stressful transition. Thus, purity reformers were the originators of modern sex education.

They failed, however, to achieve their goal—the triumph of love over lust. Commercialized vice merely changed forms in an affluent age—the call girl replaced the ancient courtesan.[1] Social purists fell far short of "ultimate" reform, but they did raise new ideals of social morality.

As Henry May has correctly averred, a history of American morals closely approximates a history of

American thought.[2] Purity reformers accepted the sup-
position, believing sexual morality to be the underpinning
of social morality. In this regard they were conservatives
and their excursion into a massive sex reform performed a
latent social function of developing a new social consensus
that relied upon the core values of traditional religious
morality. Firmly committed to social service, purity reformers reaffirmed social asceticism—self-abnegation—to
encourage good citizenship. They envisioned a new social
character for mankind, one molded and tested in everyday
life. New conditions compelled them to abandon the traditional view of innocence, since knowledge and intelligence
on sexual matters were requisites in an urbanized society.
In destroying the "conspiracy of silence," they broke down
sexual segregation and prepared society to accept women
on a more equal basis with men.

As pansexualists, purity reformers thought almost
everything in social behavior originated in sex. In application, the interpretation of the ascetic heritage varied appreciably with reformer and situation. Although reformers
described sex as the generating force of everything
beautiful in human experience, they also described it as the
origin of sinfulness. More extreme purists associated sexual
incontinence with love of gambling and speculation on the
stock markets.

In application, theories of sex were primarily directed
at abolishing prostitution and changing child rearing.
Through limited applications to business, commerce, and
industry, purity reformers encouraged sexual repression
for the protection of women. They sloganized "no sex in
politics and no sex in industry."[3] Businessmen and the
general public had to be convinced that women could work
in factories, offices, and retail stores, and participate in
politics without being abused. Women under these circumstances rebelled against being sex objects but not
against sexuality itself.

More modern sex theorists overcame contradictions stemming from an intrinsic analysis of sex, which made of the sexual impulse the source of both good or evil, by turning to the utility theory. Anna Garlin Spencer, borrowing from that theory, urged an extrinsic evaluation of sexual behavior upon social hygienists.[4] By relating sex to society, Spencer's theory approximated libido theory in its acceptance of an energy system, while abandoning Augustinian or Lockian views of human nature. She accepted sex not as a biological act, but within a cultural context. Like contemporary neo-Freudians, purity reformers chafed at the limits of libido theory used for physiological explanations of the sex drive.[5]

Without adequately resolving conflicting attitudes toward sex, reformers tenaciously held to the curative ideal in the reconstruction of society. In the reconstruction of the family institution, social purists formulated a liberal alternative between "free love," on the one hand, and strict divorce laws on the other. Although contributing to greater repression and/or sublimation, they were more remissive in accepting liberal divorce as a rational alternative rather than letting marriage become a source of societal discontent. Initially opposed to liberal divorce, even conservative and moderate women's leaders had, by the 1890s, accepted the reform.[6]

Purity leaders, in channeling women into tasks of social purification, defined conservative social objectives for the woman's movement. Initially only a humane interest in rescuing prostitutes and suppressing reglementation, purity reform became the symbol of a totally purified society. In the transformation, reformers moved from a defense of traditional morality to an aggressive attempt to control the social environment. In its symbolic phase the reform contributed to the ideational development of social reform by emphasizing the relationships among reforms and their social functions in society. After enlisting the woman's move-

ment to its cause, the expanded purity movement converged with the municipal reform movement—urban Progressivism. It provided the moral consensus critical to the
political awakening of the middle classes.

The two convergences, first with the woman's movement and then with urban Progressivism, diminished the
importance of the woman's movement as a radical movement. The conservative integrative tendencies of the social
hygiene movement limited women in significant ways. As
early as 1912, Spencer lamented the effects of domestic
education upon the image of women.[7] Confusing the roles
of mother and housekeeper, Spencer contended, denied
women the expansion of their freedoms. Women, because
of this confusion, were neither liberated to play better roles
as mothers and wives in the family nor play newer roles in
American society. The projection of the maternal role of
women into society, making of her a national and political
housekeeper and child rearer, defined women's social roles
quite conservatively.[8] A glorified and idealized woman
became an agent for spiritualization.

What the woman's movement lost, Progressivism
gained. Within Progressive reforms, purity symbols bound
apparently unrelated activities into an integrated whole.
Diet, sex, hygiene, age of consent, and dress reforms
popularized and politicized the woman's movement and
contributed to a secularization process. Purity reform functioned for religionists and social feminists as an integrating
symbol during social transformation, reminding them of
their Puritan heritage. Without fail, it drew attention to the
ideal of character and related sexual morality to the ideal.

Purity reform performed, then, a transitional function
in social reconstruction. It allowed moralists to restate
their ideals for an urban covenanted society. Going beyond
symbolization, purity reformers utilized social institutions
to create a new ethical culture, upon which, they conjec-

tured, all religions were founded. The ultimate test of a higher civilization was, for them, the character of citizenship. The new citizenship, a logical complement to the new nationalism, required the internalization of purity values if a transvaluation of religious values was to be achieved.

Within a relatively short time, reformers had changed medical thought on prostitution and related sex issues. Medical men could no longer dismiss purity reform as utopian, nor could they manage prostitution on an exclusively sanitarian basis. By 1900, the two independent movements, one coming from moral reform and the other from the medical professions, had drawn closer to each other ideologically and had combined in limited ways institutionally to constitute a modern social hygiene movement. Even as purity reform disintegrated as a social movement, it infused the social and sex hygiene movements with its spirit.

The Mother's Crusade, an heir of the movement, accepted, as its social mission, saving the republic through the child. In the process, it borrowed child rearing ideas and theories of sex education from social purists and introduced sex education into high school curricula. Manuals on sex and family life coming from the purity movement exerted continuing influence upon Americans well into the twentieth century.

These social educationists, as they assessed conditions in the late nineteenth century, relied upon three criteria for determining their course of action. They measured the human condition against their cultural ideals and their expectations, and further assessed those ideals and expectations against actuality. For them, actuality was a network of commercialized vice—including prostitution—sustained through police complicity and corrupt machine politics. They could not accept actuality without sacrificing their ideals. If, as in the case of literal-minded reformers, they merely tried to reimpose their ideals upon society without understanding the genesis of problems, they would be compelled to resort to repressive policies and actions. Essential-minded purity reformers discovered an escape from the dialectic of the actual and the ideal in new social theories. Preserving their ideals and expectations, they abandoned theological and even philosophical ontologies and re-engaged themselves in an effort to transform actuality. They turned to the social sciences, especially social work as an applied social science.

Using Christian sociology as the conserver of law and the ultimate authority for social practices, they accepted the religious sentiment as sociology's cornerstone and emphasized a new ideal of human relationships and the attainment of perfection within those relationships through radical reconstruction.[9] Starting from these premises and these instruments, they relied upon physiology, psychology, and sociology in the defense of civilization and the reconstruction of the American character. Social purity, as Antoinette Brown Blackwell reminded her colleagues, was educational, giving social orientation to the nation.[10]

Purity reform, in summary, was a stabilizing force, a brake on a social locomotive moving at ever accelerating speeds. It provided, in a period of acute social stress, social identity for urban dwellers. It reaffirmed the religionists' confidence in morality by offering a common value system that was authoritative, and substituted social for religious institutions diminished in authority by secularization.[11]

Purity reformers wanted a new social equilibrium but did not think beyond it. As urban reformers, they envisioned a "city of Hygeia," but never were overly specific about the nature of this utopia. Although purity reform assisted in social transformation through a transcendental credo, the reform became increasingly interested in maintaining the status quo after it had been insitutionalized. In a new socio-historical situation its functions were fundamentally changed.

Purity reform, as a social movement, played a positive role in the emergence of Progressivism, but it had negative aspects as well. Purity reform tended toward coercion as well as toward social constructiveness. When examined closely, it is clear the reform involved the building of an organic, or monistic, society. Voluntarism, as a result, could be lost to citizens under specific conditions, and individual choice could be severely restricted. Wrestling with cultural transformation, purity reformers reconstructed their world view to permit control of their destinies and reassert the dominant role of man, or at least certain men, in the historical pageant. What emerged from the endeavor was a total view of society. It is the nature of this totality that causes pause. To understand it let us turn to the writings of Erik Erikson.

As Erik Erikson illustrates the psychology of totality (classified by him as normal psychology), a patient undergoing therapy relates himself totally to the past and environment. This quite beneficial experience allows the patient to rethink his life in more positive ways. The inherent danger of the therapy is the possibility of the patient's crossing the thin line separating the psychology of totality from the psychology of totalitarianism.[12] Purity reform, when measured against Erikson's therapeutic psychology of totality, was beneficial and healthy for the purity elite. It did permit preservation of life style through complex social change. The consequences of the movement are, of course, another matter.

The ugly side of reform was not opposition to prostitution or the brothel, but the totalitarian implications reflected in its elitism and contributions to censorship. In censorship, the reform's prohibitory aspects were manifested explicitly; in censorship, its most coercive and even totalitarian characteristics appeared. Furthermore, censorship, rather than an isolated or peripheral activity, was integral to purity reform and readily adopted by the woman's movement. With the convergence of the purity movement with urban Progressivism, municipal reformers and the National Parents-Teachers Association accepted the censorship role, making it integral to moral reform in the Progressive era.

Despite an apparent latitudinarian or pluralistic point of view, the movement, as suggested in its censorship functions, was basically monistic. While ends were already determined, variations in technique were encouraged. In laboring for an American character which internalized their values, social purists tried to standardize and rationalize American social life. Accordingly, they emphasized child rearing and education for the protection of innocence in an urban environment.

The new moralists eagerly resorted to censorship in character development. Character performed two functions: it helped to repress "bad" thoughts originating in the subliminal unconscious, and it censored or warded off temptations emanating from a corrupt world. Believing in the unlimited possibilities of education, these elitists claimed that even optimism, an ideological imperative for the movement, might be incorporated into the second nature of man.[13] To mold the new man, obedience to the law was critical in the cultivation of self-control. True to the idealist tradition, alter-ego would finally triumph over ego—they intended keeping "the soul on top."[14] With the cultivation of social man, virtues learned in everyday life would become ascendant, while sins, evils, and vices would atrophy through disuse.

Standardization also meant control, coordination, and planning. Self-control meant the internalization of values and implicitly referred to individualism as expressed within their social units. In regulating social life, social purists relied upon social conditioning and habituation—the internalization of morality—to create a court from which there was no appeal. Reformers tried to inculcate a new generation with the spirit of selfless social service. As social religionists, they applied revitalized but traditional concepts of purification to American society. As they de-mystified and abandoned theology, they mystified social life by subtly infusing the religious emotion of reverence into secular forms, establishing preconditions that tended to legitimize manipulation and control on a massive basis.

Like any complex social movement ideational tensions over voluntarism, coercion, compulsion, and freedom were evident, with coercive factors plainly manifested in the management of delinquency or criminality. These inherent tensions appeared in the definition of "education." Ellen Guillot, in an admirable study, *Social Factors in Crime, 1860-1885*, unveiled tensions within the compulsory education movement. Relying on the philosopher-educator William H. Harris' definition of education as the inculcation of respect for society and a feeling that society represented the substantial good for the individual, she underscored the quandry created for the delinquent student: "Crime was, therefore, a reaction on the part of the individual against the very object of education. It attacked the necessary forms of social life, and asserted for itself the right to persist in the form of the non-social individual."[15] Social educationists' ideas, which were similar to Harris', created a similar dilemma when applied to the rehabilitation of the prostitute. Prostitution, whether it was explained as a result of impersonal economic and social forces acting upon the individual or as willful disobedience to the laws of hygiene and man, classified the prostitute as a criminal. Purity reformers, however, tended to be forgiving, placing the "fallen woman" in rescue homes, socially between prison and general society, a halfway house amalgamating curative and punitive impulses.

A similar paradox appeared in the care of school truants. Young truants who disobeyed compulsory education laws were too young to be remanded to prison or reformatory. Although technically a criminal, the truant received less harsh care. Putting truants into prisons made hardened criminals their schoolmasters. To prevent this obvious disaster, moral educationists again opted for a halfway station between the reformatory and the school, the George Junior Republics. These schools enrolled delinquents and truants, training them through military discipline and principles of self-government to republican social values. Since the inmates were trained to social service, social purists did not think of the training as regimentation; nevertheless, like prostitutes, truants were undergoing forced or intensified socialization.

Social prevention—child rearing and education—remained the shining hope of the movement. On the face of it, the reformers' aim to raise a generation of children committed to social service may seem laudable. The unintentional consequences of their actions, however, require examination. Purity reformers, like William James, searched for "moral equivalents to war." In the process, they wanted to channel aggressions into socially useful tasks. Since they relied upon utilitarian criteria for gauging their achievements, behavior seemed the only valid index of success. Raising children to withstand urban temptations meant a higher frequency of negations in growing up and a dependence upon ascetic values. It followed from an ideal of self-abnegation that man had to be freed from his animal nature and be reborn. Therefore, purity reformers advised mothers to repress childhood sexuality. J. H. Kellogg, for instance, contended that sexual appetites had been artificially stimulated through the increased tempo of civilization and were not natural. He justified repression.[16]

Alice Ryerson, who studied medical advice on child rearing over several centuries, concluded that child rearing advice being given at the end of the nineteenth century intensified competitiveness. Abram Kardiner, an early contributor to the study of child rearing, indicated that as incidents of conflict increased for children so too did frustrations.[17] Thus, purity reformers, although convinced that they used aggression for good purposes, actually contributed to the intensification of competitiveness within society. While ostensibly promoting cooperation, they expanded the militant spirit with crusading fervor in the 1890s. Believing that civilization required less reliance upon instincts and more upon learned social roles, they became more forceful in their demands upon children.[18] They used the language of duty, responsibility, order, and stability, but rarely mentioned happiness. As reform social Darwinists interested in adaptation, they implied, however, that the happy citizen was one who lived in harmony with the law.

Without fanfare, purity reformers conscientiously looked for ways of preserving the social bond and allowing social nurture. If they failed, or erred, they should not be categorically condemned. They displayed an enthusiasm, hope, and confidence rare among contemporary reformers, tired by the vastness of their social responsibilities. In a sense, contemporary reformers have inherited problems stemming from the earlier reform, for as social purists conserved the religionists' interest in personality and character, they applied these principles of social education more widely and with more effect than religious denominations

had previously. They gave new impetus to the social perfectionist impulse and gained wider support for it among
the general public because they had fused the secular and
spiritual.

In effect purity reform gave new meaning to Protestantism. Continuing the retreat from otherworldly "cities of God," they liberated the religious sentiment from its
institutional bonds. Although more than a social gospel
movement, reformers did rely upon the Word. In its fuller
meaning, purity reform came closer to social engineering.

Purity reform drew its social ideal from Protestantism. Reformers were, on the face of it, moral individualists
crusading against an immoral society, questing for actualization of ultimate values. Their faith in the perfectibility of the social world through applied Christianity
was, and continues to be, criticized by social theorists. In
the mid-1840s, the Reverend Merritt Caldwell, after
analyzing the consequences of perfectionism, saw in it a
potential threat to social organization. Citing Oneida and
Oberlin Perfectionism specifically, Caldwell raised other
objections to perfectionism, but he deferred final judgment until history could prove the perfectionist ideal detrimental to human society.[19] Paul Tillich, the existential
theologian, returned to the persistent problem more than a
century later. He located in perfectionist yearnings the
basis of authoritarian systems. Troubled by master trends,
Tillich questioned whether Protestantism could survive
modern collectivism—a nagging fear of totalitarianism.
that had been implicit also in the writings of Caldwell and
William Channing Gannett. Tillich, in expressing his
solicitude for the Protestant cause, had a different meaning
in mind than did purity reformers. He criticized
nineteenth-century Protestantism's social perfectionist
goals, and sought to restore Protestantism as a force of
"protest" against evil, of existential "decision" for justice,

as a critical and "prophetic" voice. In brief, he rediscovered in Protestantism an opposition to newly emerging principles of social organization.[20] Clearly he would have been unsympathetic to tendencies within purity reform, both its search for social perfection and social control.

Regardless of their high ideals, purity reformers had utilized authoritarian techniques to construct their purified society. In giving new social expression to Protestantism, they overstressed social order at the expense of liberty. Lacking the knowledge of Freudian psychology, the new moralists tried to provide institutional mechanisms as social safety valves, but did not challenge their premises. Rather, they moved from crisis to crisis and event to event. Later, an understanding of Freudianism by Progressives raised hopes for a less repressive civilization—a hope shared by Herbert Marcuse in our own time, who through his exploration of the philosophical meaning of Freudian psychology has reawakened an interest in the implications of Freud for social organization.[21]

PURITY REFORM AND URBAN PROGRESSIVISM

Early in the history of the purity movement its leaders chose a pragmatic strategy. When, in the 1860s, the Free Religious Association debated strategy, William Channing Gannett (later a purity leader) clarified his point of view. Gannett and like-minded theologians who maintained formal affiliation with religious bodies utilized religious symbols for new social and secular purposes. Gannett did not lose sight of the inherent dangers within pragmatism. As a liberal, he anguished over the possible unintended effects of a strategy that, in the final analysis, depended upon manipulation and control. Freedom, the objective essential to the meaning of purity reform, might be lost if reform energies were mobilized for coercion, however subtle, of a mass audience by an all-seeing but unseen elite. Gannett resolved this dilemma for himself by distinguishing between liberal and conservative uses of the strategy. Liberals informed people of the changed nature of religious symbols; conservatives—including many purity reformers—did not.[22]

Joseph May was even more apprehensive than Gannett about the dangers inherent in purity reform strategy. The very idea of "freedom" as used by the reform required refinement, since May feared social transformation would reduce man to an automaton in the name of freedom. Both men had touched the philosophical contradiction within the movement. By manipulating religious symbols and ideals to gain support for reform, social purists made man an object to be acted upon; that is, in the cause of freedom, they denied the "free nature" of man. May dismissed these fears, consoling himself with the belief that man might still choose how to serve. While ends were defined, means remained undefined. Not totally restricted, therefore, man chose within a limited range of alternatives; thus, man preserved his freedom of choice within socially acceptable limits.[23] The meaning of individualism was being redefined.

Although premonitions of danger were voiced from the early years of the movement, the purity elite, not at all naive, accepted the risks of this pragmatic strategy and its possible threat to freedom. They proceeded with their reform with reservations and caution. In the Progressive era, however, reformers had a fuller understanding of consequences, and many regretted earlier decisions made by older leaders. For purposes of illustration, let us explore the reactions to reforms flowing from the purity movement of key Progressives: Edward Devine, an editor of *Survey* magazine and a spokesman for the "New Health"; Benjamin Orange Flower, muckraking journalist and a former member of the American Purity Alliance; John Collier, major spokesman for motion picture censorship and an associate of the People's Institute; David Starr Jordan, president of Stanford University and the American Vigilance Association; and Jane Addams, renowned social worker and a director of the American Social Hygiene Association Board. Each of these reformers was interested in social organization, but each responded differently to purity reforms in the Progressive era. With bureaucratization and professionalization in the early twentieth century, purity reform had undergone substantial changes. In a new socio-historical situation, reforms that had formerly been attractive now took on new, and at times threatening, meanings.

Edward Devine, the most optimistic of the spokesmen under examination, promoted the "new health" as a social ideal. Like purity reformers of an earlier period, Devine believed health to be an aspect of every reform, "an index of our civilization," and that the greatest victory was over vice in all its repulsive or seductive forms.[24] Unlike earlier reformers, Devine now related the new health to a national corporate feeling and founded it upon science. In doing so, he accepted, in large measure, both bureaucratization and professionalization, never fearing that they endangered progress. Indeed, these forces might make for more efficiency than earlier reform techniques in achieving the goals of the social hygiene movement.

Benjamin Orange Flower, although essentially in accord with purity ideology, lacked Devine's sanguine viewpoint. The two reformers differed in their evaluations of the implications of bureaucratization and professionalization for reform. Flower, characterized, with some validity, as a populist in reform, was far from a conservative social Darwinist, but he was an individualist about social organization, ardently opposing the licensing of professionals.[25] He rejected the notion of expertise. On the other hand, he had no qualms about using counter-bureaucracy to fight bureaucracy, and he turned to a tactic of countervailing power. Aware of the financial difficulties of reform and religious journals—there had been many bankruptcies—Flower communicated with Lincoln Steffens to urge the establishment of a Progressive communication network to get the reform message to the general public rapidly and to compete with regular news services and papers.[26] As inconsistent as Flower may have seemed, favoring individualism in one instance, and bureaucratization in the other, he came to grips with the changes in institutional arrangements confronting social Progressives. He was not isolated in this regard.

John Collier, the third of the figures to be discussed, had engaged in antivice activities through the People's Institute, contributing to the organization of the National Board of Censorship of Motion Pictures in June 1909. When, from 1913 to 1915, Congress considered enacting censorship of the motion pictures, Collier and his associates argued persuasively that private and informal censorship through the voluntaristic National Board was already effective and precluded the necessity of federal legislation. By 1916, John Collier had stepped back from censorship, shocked by its implications. Federal censorship, which Collier opposed, was the stumbling block. Collier now considered censorship important only on an interim basis. Furthermore, he saw in federal censorship of the motion pictures an intimation of a more general and sinister attempt by the few to control the thought of the many.[27] He still hoped, however, to provide alternate entertainment suitable for American democracy. Like Benjamin O. Flower, he turned to the idea of countervailing power, becoming active in the community theater movement.

David Starr Jordan, a man of enormous reform energies, persistently struggled against the collectivistic tendencies of his day. Jordan, vitally interested in social hygiene, exercised his judgment on sports. As president of Stanford University, he prevented the university's adoption of football until 1920. Unlike other college presidents, some of whom had met at Columbia University in 1907 to refine the rules and regulations of the sport to make them acceptable to civilized men, he disliked the sociological implications of football. The sport promoted "mass play" and was contrary to principles of individualism.[28] Jordan, clearly opposed to what, in contemporary language, might be called "massification," restated policies on football enunciated earlier by Frances Willard. Jordan's attitude toward massification was evident not only in his opinion of football, but in his idea of the nature and function of education. For him,

> The masses, the mobs of men are never free. Hence the need of the hour is to break up the masses. There should be masses no longer, but individual men and women. The work of higher education is to put an end to the rule of the multitude, to turn the multitude into men.[29]

This phenomenon of massification was not a figment of Jordan's imagination. The general secretary of the American Social Science Association, Frederick S. Root, favored football because it related men as a unit to the mass, a relationship involving the subordination of self.[30]

As our final example of Progressive reformers wrestling with problems of bureaucratization and professionalization in a modern age, we may profitably turn to

Jane Addams. Though she had participated fully as a national Progressive leader, Jane Addams, seeing militarism as a desertion of reform ideals, broke the institutional solidarity of the movement with the coming of World War I. Her Woman's Peace Party represented a return to the mass politics characteristic of the purity movement in earlier development. In a romantically noble effort to end the war she rallied women to the white banner of peace. Her attempts, however, were futile. In 1916, Jane Addams lamented the failure of the movement for purification, for the war had challenged women's view of politics, specifically their view that government was an agency for the nurture of human life. Addams, explaining the failure of the woman's movement, believed she had forgotten the "primitive functions" of the state.[31] Savage and aggressive tendencies in man had broken through the layers of civilization. She had not taken into account the persistence of "barbarism" within man.

Thus, in assorted ways a new leadership found fault with the course of American social development. English purity reformers, viewing the American situation from a physical and social distance, made similar criticisms. At one point, they even disclaimed the movement for the suppression of prostitution. The editors of *Shield*, a journal of social and moral hygiene, shuddered, in 1919, at the news that California's new abolitionists had arrested twenty-one apparently innocent working women, placed them in a "quarantine" under the public health laws, and denied them legal counsel under the pretense of abolishing prostitution. The authors wondered how Josephine Butler and older abolitionists would have responded to this abomination. English purity reformers cautioned against neo-regulationism in America and Canada masquerading as abolitionism.[32]

Nevertheless, abolitionism seemed triumphant in the Progressive era. Almost every major city in the United

States had a vice commission and enacted red light abatement laws. In 1910 Congress passed the Mann Act, prohibiting the interstate traffic in white slaves. On the face of it, abolitionists seemed to have swept the field. Political critics, however, believed the sex issue had been co-opted for political purposes.

One critic, writing at the peak of the municipal drive against prostitution in 1913, charged that white slaves had to be produced since John D. Rockefeller had financed the Bureau of Sex Hygiene. William Marion Reedy, the critic, pointedly belittled the movement as an "anti-vice crusade, financed by Standard Oil money." In denying the charge, William Burgess described the campaign leaders as "sane, conservative people, statesmen, medical authorities, scientists and businessmen with a conscience, and eminent educators."[33] He described an apparently objective and disinterested elite. Nevertheless, the contention that Rockefeller and J. P. Morgan financed the antivice campaign had some validity.[34]

In any case, reform politicians introduced sex into municipal politics with telling effect. During the 1901 New York mayoralty campaign, Bishop Potter, assisted by the Women's Municipal League, mailed antiprostitution literature to every householder.[35] New York reformers exploited the vice issue. They published political cartoons showing the red lamp tied to the neck of the Tammany tiger.[36] Politicians had found in purity ideology consensual political issues. In repressing prostitution and breaking the informal Tammany complicity with the police and vice rings, they furthered reform politics. Something had happened during politicization. Purity ideas became instrumentalities devoid of value. Political technique became an end in itself. The narrowly repressive aim of municipal reformers in their way of suppressing prostitution was alien to the earlier movement.

Purity ideology, co-opted by political leaders, was co-

opted as well by businessmen. Some reformers dedicated
themselves to industrial "purification." (Others, it should
be noted, encouraged unionization.) Improvements in the
industrial environment, as William Tolman had expressed
it, could increase workers' efficiency. Environmental improvement might have been, and ideally should have been,
altruistically motivated. In the absence of an altruistic
spirit, businessmen might accept the reform for motives of
enlightened self-interest—that is, because it was prof-
itable.[37] As in the case of politics, moral reformers lost
control of the movement for industrial purification. Efficiency interests eventually reduced the ideal of humanization to the impersonal assessment of a "human factor." As
a result, the direction of the reform, despite sweet pieties,
was toward scientific management. As these "purifiers"
turned to ameliorative palliatives, they continued to compromise until they were led further from their original intent. In fact, their reform, which was no longer controlled
by them, legitimized practices they probably would have
opposed.

What had begun as a simple movement to repulse
regulated prostitution had, with other influences, crested
into a moral movement for social purification. At the moment of apparent success, the purity movement underwent
basic transformations that permitted new alternatives in its
future evolution. As society became more complex, so too,
did the reform. Some of its proponents learned to deal with
this complexity through compromise and accommodation;
others persisted in reaffirming what had, too quickly,
become a worn ideology. As late as 1924, Charlotte
Perkins Gilman at a symposium on "Our Changing
Morality" reiterated ideas astonishingly similar to those of
the 1890s woman's movement.[38]

The movement's inner circle had witnessed the harsh
and seamy side of industrialization and had reacted with

humanity and compassion. While others amassed great fortunes, they tried to extend the benefits of industrialization
to the millions. In their failures, we all failed, since the effects of their decisions have persisted, in many instances,
into the present. Settlement houses, even Jane Addam's
Hull House, did not conserve or transform urban
neighborhoods. Nor did purity reform, as social work,
transform the nation.

The victory of home and church values over those of
the saloon and brothel became, for purity and temperance
reformers, a struggle between the forces of light and
darkness. As idealists, they failed to assess the influences of
the material world on value formation. With technology
undermining the authority of the family, they simply tried
to extend the spirit of the home into the community. To
borrow the language of George Herbert Meade, the
parents as significant-others were being displaced by
authoritative-others—journalists, teachers, and reform
leaders, to mention a few—a shift from significant- to
authoritative-others explainable as a direct consequence of
an on-going technological and organizational revolution.
Daily newspapers, journalistic gurus (the muckrakers for
example), and, later, radio and television commentators
with easy entry into the home undermined the authority of
the significant-others, the parents. With the family institution weakened by the urban environment and paradoxically a more significant dependency of youth upon the
family in an industrial society, Americans were ill-
equipped to contend with the enormity of new tasks.[39]

The social hygiene movement, encouraging, among
its programs, the development of parents-teachers associations, sex education, age of consent legislation, institutions for the protection of young women, a new national
literature for purposes of "uplift," improved industrial
conditions, and new techniques for helping the criminal

and delinquent, touched upon the vital social reforms of the Progressive era. The woman's movement, never detached from larger social questions of the day, joined with social hygienists to extend the "mother's heart" into social reform and cause a revolution in social values. In the process, the social hygiene movement subsumed the woman's movement.

Nor were the converged hygiene and woman's movement immune to influence. Values, as they came from the business and industrial world, dominated the conservative and moderate wings of the woman's movement. The home, church, hygiene, and woman's movements not only influenced but were, in turn, influenced. Purity leaders allied with the Progressives willingly accepted the notion of expertise and its implications for social and professional organization. Through social transformation, social hygienists, almost imperceptibly, became managers of American social life. The slogans of freedom, social justice, and love, to which they appealed, had great emotional attraction, but told little about intellectual content as expressed in organizational forms. Earlier purity leaders, still using quasi-religious language, thought of themselves as moral stewards, dispassionately and objectively constructing a good society. With secularization, social hygienists, a managerial elite, imagined themselves above partisan interests dispassionately and objectively constructing a good society.

As Randolph Bourne stated in his "Twilight of Idols." pragmatic philosophy may be inspiring in a society at peace, prosperous, and with a fund of progressive goodwill. Under those conditions, intelligence, especially in the educational sphere, even verged on gaining control within the schools. Under conditions of war and crisis, however, pragmatic intellectuals seemed unable to contain the taste for power or militaristic values.[40] Undoubtedly Bourne's criticisms apply to the social hygiene movement as well. The criticisms remain pertinent today. Goodwill in an industrial and post-industrial society must be a prerequisite for social reformers, but it is not sufficient. Intentions must also be gauged against consequences and values considered in relation to social organization. Purity reformers never paid enough attention to consequences or ends. Certain in their values, they pursued the politics of belief, not the politics of reason. Concerned with social control, they contributed substantially to conservative moral reconstruction.

NOTES

1. In his study of prostitution, Fernando Henriques states that prostitution has been transformed into the call girl racket. Henriques assumes the permanency of prostitution but does allow for cultural transformations. See Fernando Henriques, *Prostitution in the Old and New World* (London: MacGibbon & Kee, 1963).

2. Henry May, *The End of American Innocence: A Study of the First Years of Our Time, 1912-1917* (New York: Alfred A. Knopf Company, 1959), p. 10.

3. This was the slogan of the Women's Christian Temperance Union.

4. Anna G. Spencer, *Work and Character* (Boston: Press of Cochrane & Sampson, 1884), p. 5.

5. For an interesting treatment of this theme, see J. A. C. Brown, *Freud and the Post-Freudians* (Baltimore, Maryland: Penguin Books, 1961).

6. Much of the opposition to more radical feminists in the 1870s and 1880s stemmed from a rejection to divorce reform. In many instances "free love" really meant the acceptance of divorce. For an early defense of liberal divorce, see Andrew Jackson Davis, *The Genesis and Ethics of Conjugal Love* (New York: A. J. Davis Co.

[Progressive Publishing House], 1874), pp. 72, 100; for a recent study of divorce, see William L. O'Neill, *Divorce in the Progressive Era* (New Haven: Yale University Press: 1967).

7. Anna Garlin Spencer, "The School and the Feminine Ideal," *Forum* 47 (May 1912): 589-605.

8. "From the Home Standpoint," *Woman's Journal*, July 14, 1894, p. 218.

9. Samuel Zane Batten, *The New Citizenship* (Philadelphia: *Union Press*, 1898), pp. 16, 19, 20; and "American Institute of Christian Sociology," *Union Signal*, September 7, 1893, p. 8.

10. Antoinette Brown Blackwell, "Social Purity is Educational," *Philanthropist*, March 1889, p. 5.

11. *Woman's Journal*, August 29, 1891, p. 279; Joseph May, *The Perils of Our Republic: A Sermon* (Philadelphia: First Unitarian Church; May 26, 1899), p. 10; and Elizabeth Blackwell, *The Influence of Women in the Profession of Medicine* (London: George Bell & Son, 1889), pp. 19-20.

12. Erik H. Erikson, "Wholeness and Totality—A Psychiatric Contribution," in *Totalitarianism*, ed. Carl J. Friedrich (Cambridge: Harvard University Press, 1954), pp. 160-62.

13. "Mental Intemperance," White Cross Library, June 1887, New York Public Library Pamphlet Collection; Benjamin O. Flower, "Mastery of Temper," *The Coming Age* 1 (May 1899): 584-85; and Martin Luther Holbrook, "Some Thoughts on Personal Hygiene and the Waste of Life's Forces Through the Emotional Nature," *Journal of Hygiene and Herald of Health* 46 (June 1896): 148.

14. *Union Signal*, April 22, 1886, p. 2.

15. Ellen Guilot, "Social Factors in Crime, 1860-1885" (Ph.D. diss., University of Pennsylvania, 1943), p. 84.

16. J. H. Kellogg, "Chastity and Health: Delivered at the National Purity Congress, Baltimore, Maryland, 1895," Collected Reprints, National Medical Library.

17. Alice Judson Ryerson, "Medical Advice on Child Rearing, 1550-1900," *Harvard Education Review* 31 (Summer 1961): 302-23; and Abram Kardiner, *The Psychological Frontiers of Society* (New York: Columbia University Press, 1947).

18. Elizabeth Powell Bond, "High Ideals of Social Purity," *Philanthropist*, October 1887, pp. 1-2.

19. Merritt Caldwell, *The Philosophy of Christian Perfectionism* (Philadelphia: 1849).

20. Paul Tillich, *The Protestant Era* (Chicago: University of Chicago Press, A Phoenix Book, 1963), pp. 222-33.

21. For an analysis of sex manipulation, see Herbert Marcuse, *Eros and Civilization: A Philosophical Inquiry into Freud* (New York: Vintage Books, 1955), pp. 94-95, 202.

22. "Address of W. C. Gannett," *Free Religious Association Proceedings of the Sixth Annual Meeting, 1873* (Boston: Cochrane and Sampson, 1873), p. 43.

23. Joseph May, *A Treasure Hid in a Field: A Sermon* (Philadelphia: First Unitarian Church, n.d.), pp. 13-14.

24. Edward T. Devine, "The New Health," *Survey* 32 (July 4, 1914): 376-78.

25. Christopher Lasch, *The Agony of the American Left* (New York: Alfred A. Knopf, 1969), pp. 13-15.

26. Benjamin O. Flower to Lincoln Steffens, February 9, 1910, Columbia University.

27. *Survey*, March 4, 1916, p. 688.

28. Note contained in David Starr Jordan Collection, 1909, Stanford University.

29. David Starr Jordan, "The University and the Common Man," *The Independent* 51 (January 19, 1899): 171-73.

30. Frederick S. Root, "The Ethical Element in College Football," *The Independent* 51 (October 5, 1899): 2681-83.

31. Jane Addams, "War Time Challenges Woman's Traditions," *Survey* 36 (August 5, 1916): 475-78.

32. *The Shield*, May-June 1919, p. 119.

33. "A Wave of Sex Hysteria?" *Vigilance*, September 1913, pp. 8-9.

34. Paul S. Boyer, *Purity in Print: The Vice Society Movement and Book Censorship* (New York: Scribner's, 1968), pp. 5-6.

35. W. R. Stewart, *The Philanthropic Work of Josephine Shaw Lowell* (New York: MacMillan Company, 1911), p. 417.

36. Vigilance Pamphlets, New York Public Library.

37. William Tolman, *Industrial Betterment*, Monographs on American Social Economics 16, ed. Herbert Baxter Adams (New York: Social Science Press, 1900), p. 3.

38. Charlotte Perkins Gilman, "Toward Monogamy," in *Our Changing Morality*, ed. Freda Kuchweig (New York: Albert and Charles Bond, 1924), pp. 53-68.

39. George Herbert Meade, *Mind, Self and Society* (Chicago: University of Chicago Press, 1934).

40. Randolph Bourne, "Twilight of Idols," *The Seven Arts* 2 (October 1917): 688-702.

Appendix A

MEMBERS OF THE EXECUTIVE BOARD OF
THE AMERICAN PURITY ALLIANCE, 1895[1]
(Asterisk indicates no information available)

Ackerman, Jessie A.
Angell, Mrs. C. D.*
Bailey, Hannah J.
Baily, Joshua L.
Blackwell, Antoinette Brown
Blackwell, Elizabeth
Blackwell, Emily
Blackwell, Samuel C.
Bogue, Mrs. M. L.
Bond, Elizabeth Powell
Bonney, Charles C.
Branson, Ann B.
Burt, Mrs. Mary T.
Carpenter, Mrs. Julia H.
Chapman, Mariana W.
Clothier, Hannah
Coale, Elizabeth H.
Collier, Mrs. Eva W.*
Comstock, Anthony
Cornell, John J.
Davis, Mrs. Naomi Lawton*

Dodge, Grace Hoadley
Dodge, Mrs. L. M.*
Dorr, Sara J.
DuBose,
    Mrs. Miriam Howard
Edholm, Mrs. Charlton
Emerson,
    Mr., Mrs. William
Flint, Joseph F.*
Fliteraft, Allen J.
Flower, Benjamin O.
Fox, Sara C.*
Gannett,
    Mrs. M. T. Lewis
Gannett,
    William Channing
Gardener, Helen H.
Garrison, Francis J.
Gavett, Andrew J.*
Gavett, Cornelia A.*
Gay, Elizabeth

281

Gerry, Elbridge T.
Gibbons, Abigail Hopper
Harper, Frances E.
Hildrith, Susan W.*
Holbrook, Martin Luther
Holmes, Pauline
Howe, Julia Ward
Howland, Emily
Humphreys, Mrs. S. G.
Hull, Angie S.*
Huntington, Arrie S.
Jackson, Anna M.
Jackson, William M.
Janney, O. Edward
Kellogg, Mrs. J. H.
Kellogg, J. H.
Lake, Isabel Wing
Lapham, Mrs. H. J.*
Leavitt, Mary Clement
Leeds, Deborah C.
Leeds, Josiah W.
Levering, Joshua
Lewis, Alfred H.
Lewis, Charlotte S.
Livermore, Mary A.
Lukens, Anna
McVicker, William N.
May, Elisabeth Justice
May, Joseph
May, Samuel (Jr.)
Miller, Sarah T.
Mosher, Eliza M.
Nichols, Benjamin F.
Nichols, Lauretta H.

Phillips, Mrs. Katherine M.*
Pierce, Sarah H.
Plummer, Hannah A.
Plummer, Joseph W.
Powell, Aaron M.
Powell, Anna Rice
Powell, Marcia C.*
Prindle, A. L.
Ripley, Martha G.
Roads, Charles
Roberts, Isaac
Robinson, Alice C.
Sabine, William T.
Satterthwaite, Laura H.
Schofield, Martha
Severance, Carolina M.
Seward, S. S.
Smith, Mary G.
Spencer, Anna Garlin
Starr, Anna M.
Stearns, Mrs. Sarah B.
Stebbins, Mrs. C. A. F.
Thompson, E. H.*
Travilla, Mary
Underhill, Mrs. E. G.*
Vaughan, Anna M.
Virgin, S. H.
Walton, J. W.
Webb, Mrs. Dora
Welty, J. B.
Whitney, Mary T.
Willard, Frances E.
Wood-Allen, Mary
Woodnutt, Thomas W.*

ORGANIZATIONS REPRESENTED ON EXECUTIVE BOARD OF THE
AMERICAN PURITY ALLIANCE[2]

WCTU

President; World Missionary (2); National Superintendent of Department of Peace and International Arbitration; National Superintendent of Rescue Work; National Superintendent of Impure Literature; National Superintendent of White Cross Work; President of Non-Partisan WCTU; President of California WCTU; National Superintendent of Social Purity Department; National Superintendent of Mothers' Meetings; Chairman Corrupt Literature Committee of Society of Friends (also State Superintendent of Impure Literature).

Religious Organizations

President Baltimore YMCA; Corresponding Secretary of American Sabbath Tract Society; Friends Philanthropic Labor Union (6); Friends Superintendent of Social Purity; Dean of Swarthmore College.

Reform Societies

President of Society for the Prevention of Cruelty to Children; Vice-President Universal Peace Union (2); Executive Committee of National Reform Association; Executive Board New York State Charities Aid Association; President International Law and Order Society; Vice-President International Law and Order Society; President World's Congress (Chicago 1893); Treasurer, Teachers' College, Columbia; President Pennsylvania Society for Prevention of Vice and Crime; President New York

Women's Prison Association; Secretary New York Women's Prison Association; Vice-President Free Religious Association (2); Vice Chairman Citizens Representative Committee (Philadelphia); Secretary Florence Crittenden Missions.

Women's Societies

President Women's Congress; President International and National Council of Women (2); Vice-President Women's Congress (2); President New England Moral Education Society; Dean of Women, University of Michigan; Vice-President National-American Women's Suffrage Association; President New York Women's Suffrage Association; Vice-President Georgia Women's Suffrage Association; President Minnesota Women's Suffrage Association; President Kentucky Equal Rights Association; Chairman New York Moral Education Committee; President Working Girls' Society; President New Century Guild of Working Women; President Massachusetts Moral Education Association; President Scientific Family Culture Institute; and President Women's Educational and Industrial Union.

Editors

Woman's Journal; Medical Temperance Quarterly; Good Health; Modern Medicine and Bacteriological World; Arena; American Sentinel; American Spectator; The Coming Age; Herald of Health and Journal of Hygiene; Health Reformer; Sabbath Recorder; Sabbath Outlook.

PHILADELPHIA HONORARY COMMITTEE FOR
PURITY CONGRESS OF 1895[3]

Honorary Committee: William McVicker, Isaac H.
Clothier, Rev. C. D. Foss, Joshua L. Baily, Rev. O. W.
Whittaker, Bishop W. R. Nicholson, Rev. George D.
Baker, George Griffiths, Arthur Burton, Rev. Joseph May,
J. Chester Morris, M.D., Edward P. Davis, M.D., Josiah
W. Leeds, Rev. H. L. Wayland, W. H. Parrish, M. D., Rev.
Joseph Kraushopf, Rev. Henry Berkowitz, Robert M. Jan-
ney, Robert C. Ogden, B. B. Comegys, Rev. Charles
Roads, William P. Henszey, John H. Converse, Mary
Crow, Mrs. Enoch Lewis, Mrs. Isaac Clothier, Mrs. Eliza
S. Turner, Mrs. Emma J. Bartol, Mrs. Horace Vassitt, Mrs.
William P. Wilson, Mrs. Joseph P. Mumford, Miss Sarah
H. Pierce, Mrs. W. W. Frazier, Mrs. Cornelius Stevenson,
Mrs. Elizabeth J. May, Mrs. W. G. Moorehead, Mrs. Susan
I. Lesley, Mrs. Edith Longstreth.

[1] Aaron M. Powell, ed., *The National Purity Congress: Its Papers, Addresses, and Portraits* (New York: Cauley Press, 1896).

[2] This listing of organizations was compiled from biographical data collected about members of the American Purity Alliance Executive Board. Although no criteria were stated for selecting the board, it may be safely concluded, after examining the data, that members were selected because of their involvement in national reform.

[3] *20th Annual Report of the American Purity Alliance, 1896* (n.p.: n.d.).

OCCUPATIONS OF PURITY ELITE

(If a woman was married and no occupation was given, she is included in her husband's occupation.)

Occupation	Women	Men	Total
Business	4	2	6
Reformers	29	5	34
Ministers or related occupation	5	11	16
Physicians	8	3	11
Educators	4	1	5
Journalists	3	2	5
Sanitation	0	1	1
Total	53	25	78
No Information	23	5	28
			106

RELIGION OF PURITY ELITE

Friends	36
Unitarian	15
Episcopalian	4
Agnostic	1
Minor	7
Baptist	2
Methodist	3
Total	68
No Information	38
	106

EDUCATION OF PURITY ELITE

	Women	Men	Total
Graduate			
Lawyers and Physicians			
included	14	14	28
Undergraduate Plus	3	2	5
Undergraduate Degree or			
Training beyond			
High School	5	3	8
High School	12	2	14
Elementary School	1	0	1
Total	35	21	56
No Information	41	9	50
			106

Appendix B

Since it should be our purpose in the study of the subject of Social Purity to grasp, if possible, all the various influences which tend in the direction of sexual morality and purity we have planned our program to cover the life of an individual from its beginning, through the years of development to maturity.

1. *Ante-natal Influences*

Suggestions: Since without doubt many are predisposed to vices by inheritance, let the physical and mental conditions of parents at the beginning of the new life, and those of the mother during its development be studied, together with such unhygienic surroundings and other untoward influences as have a bearing upon the subject.

2. *Early Perverting Influences*

Suggestions:
1. Juvenile flirtations.
2. Sexual precocity.
3. Promiscuous associations.

288

3. Predisposing Causes

Suggestions:
1. Personal habits, Self-Abuse, etc.
2. Bearing of clothing, exercise, sleep and diet of children on the subject.
3. Effects of the use of highly seasoned and stimulating foods and drinks upon the passions.

4. Dangers to Our Girls

Suggestions:
1. Effects of luxury.
2. Bringing up girls to idleness, and dependence.
3. Ignorance upon sexual subjects.

5. Dress and Vice

Suggestions:
1. Love of dress, extravagance in dress, etc.
2. Dress a temptation to vice, among the poor.
3. Desolate dress.
4. Physical bearing of tight clothing.

6. Pitfalls For Our Boys

Suggestions:
1. Lack of respect for women.
2. Mental unchastity.
3. Loafing, aimlessness, etc.
4. Fashionable dissipation.
5. Obscene conversation.

7. Stimulants and Narcotics and Vice

8. *Aids to Impurity*

Suggestions: 1. Undue familiarity of the sexes.
                          2. Modern methods of Courtship,
                          "Sitting up nights," etc.
                          3. Flirtations.
                          4. Skating rinks, Round dances,
                          etc.

9. *Bad Hygiene Vs. Virtue*

Suggestions: 1. Diet vs. chastity.
                          2. Nervous irritability a result of
                          modern modes of life.
                          3. Bearing of exercise, rest, etc.

10. *Literature and Vice*

Suggestions: 1. Obscene and Impure Books.
                          2. Novel reading, sentimental lite-
                          rature, etc.

11. *Responsibility of Parents*

Suggestions: 1. Wrong ideas of life taught to
                          children.
                          2. Lack of instruction on important
                          topics.

12. *The Legal Aspect of the Question*

[4] Mrs. J. H. Kellogg to Elizabeth Gay, February 14, 1886, Sidney
Howard Gay Papers, Columbia University.

A Note on Sources

The text of this book is amply documented and may serve as a guide to the literature on this subject. Rather than duplicating these listings in a conventional bibliography, it seems wiser to comment upon the available and significant primary and secondary sources.

Unfortunately, no single source may be referred to for institutional development. The *American Bulletin*, published between 1879 and 1885, apparently is not extant. The Fawcett Library in London, deposit for the records of the English movement, has only limited references to the American movement. Were it not for Elizabeth Gay's chronic absences from committee meetings, there would be no important source materials for the early period. Members of the New York Committee for the Suppression of State Regulated Vice regularly informed her of decisions reached in committee. The letters are located in the Sidney Howard Gay Collection at Columbia University. Furthermore, the journal *Alpha* may be consulted for these early years.

More specialized accounts covering the early period

may be found in various places. Henry J. Wilson kept detailed diaries and corresponded relatively frequently with his wife during the Gledstone-Wilson Mission to the American Abolitionists. These letters and diaries are held by the Sheffield Public Library in England. Gledstone and Wilson also published their observations in *Report of a Visit to the United States* (Sheffield: 1876). Although Aaron Macy Powell left no important manuscript collection, he did write a history of the early efforts to introduce reglementation into the United States, *State Regulation of Vice: Regulation Efforts in America* (New York: Wood & Holbrook, 1878). For the implementation of reglementation in St. Louis the William Greenleaf Eliot Papers at Washington University, St. Louis is a good source. The William Lloyd Garrison, Mary A. Livermore, and Samuel J. May Papers at the Boston Public Library may be helpful for information on the continuity between old and new abolitionism.

Purity reform's institutional line is easier to follow after 1886. The *Philanthropist*, official journal of the movement, is the richest source of information. The Annual Reports of the New York Committee and American Purity Alliance are in the Library of Congress. Both the *Union Signal* and the *Woman's Journal* are invaluable.

The Frances E. Willard Papers maintained by the National Woman's Christian Temperance Union in Evanston, Illinois is a rich source of primary information. Although mainly interested in the reform within the temperance movement, Frances Willard corresponded with important Anglo-American purity leaders. Her presidential addresses delivered at the national conventions of her organization are especially important for understanding the purity ideology.

Alpha, official journal of the Moral Education Societies, reported on numerous aspects of the movement for social purification. Edited by Caroline Winslow, an early pioneer in medical sociology, *Alpha* reported not only on the antiregulation movement but on sex reform and moral education.

The Josiah W. Leeds Papers at Haverford College are valuable for tracing censorship activities of the purity associations. The Benjamin DeCosta Papers at the New York Historical Society, although sparse, are the main records for the history of the White Cross movement in the United States. For the student of municipal reform, the Herbert Welsh Collection at the Historical Society of Pennsylvania will be of general interest. Welsh, like many other municipal reformers, was involved in purity reform and corresponded with Philadelphia Purity Alliance leaders on a fairly regular basis. Grace Hoadley Dodge's papers at Teachers' College, Columbia University, and the New York Young Women's Christian Association are a mine of information on working girls clubs, vocational education, and social work. The Anna Garlin Spencer Papers at Swarthmore College complement the Dodge papers and show the connection between social reform and social work.

Various manuscript collections were used to reconstruct the ideology of the purity reform. The Blackwell family's contributions to medical sociology and social reform were a fount of vital data. The Blackwell Family Papers can be found at the Library of Congress, which holds the major portion of the collection; Radcliffe College and Columbia University also have significant holdings. The William Channing Gannett Papers, another important source for the writing of this history, is located at the University of Rochester. The Julia Ward Howe Papers are at the Library of Congress and Radcliffe College. Although the Aaron Macy Powell Papers at Swarthmore College were a disappointment, the location of the Elizabeth Powell Bond Papers at Swarthmore compensated for the disappointment.

Less important sources for the reconstruction of ideology were Joseph May's sermons, held by the Historical Society of Pennsylvania, and miscellaneous letters in the Notable American Women Collection, Radcliffe College, and in the Friends' Historical Library, Swarthmore College.

Periodical literature was a major source for this study. Beyond the women's journals previously cited, journals and magazines deserving special mention are: *Arena, Coming Age, Nation, Forum, Independent, Lend A Hand, Family Culture, Working Woman's Journal, The Mothers' Friend,* and the *New Century Journal.*

Proceedings of voluntary organizations were critical to this study. Probably most important were the *Proceedings of the Friends' Union for Philanthropic Labor.* The Society of Friends was most influential in purity work. Its libraries in Philadelphia and London probably had the most materials pertaining to purity reform. The minutes and reports of the National Woman's Christian Temperance Union were also very useful. Other proceedings of importance were: *American Public Health Association, Reports and Meetings,* 1876-1900; *Reports of the National Congress of Mothers,* 1895-1900; *Reports of the National Council of Women,* 1888-1900; and *National Divorce Reform League Reports,* 1880-1900.

Among the many books and pamphlets written by purity leaders, Elizabeth Blackwell's *Wrong and Right Methods of Dealing with Prostitution* (Hastings: D. Williams, n.d.); *The Laws of Life* (New York: G. P. Putnam's, 1852); *On the Religion of Health* (New York: S. W. Partridge, 1869); and *The Human Element in Sex: Being a Medical Enquiry into the Relation of Sexual Physiology and Christian Morality* (London: J. & A. Churchill, 1889) are certainly important for understanding purity ideology. Josephine Butler's *Personal Reminiscences of a Great Crusade* (London: Horace Marshall and Sons, 1896) remains the most important source for connecting the English and American movements and reporting upon international aspects of the purity movement. Benjamin F. DeCosta wrote a brief account of the White Cross movement: *The White Cross: Its Origins and Progress* (Chicago: Sanitary Publishing Co., 1887). Other important materials may be located in the edited papers of Abby Hopper Gibbons, Sarah Hopper Emerson, ed., *The Life of Abby Hopper Gibbons,* 2 vols. (New York: G. P. Putnam's, 1896). Early biographies and autobiographies containing social purity materials are Anna A. Gordon, ed., *What Frances E. Willard Said* (Chicago: Fleming H. Revell Co., 1905); Ida Husted Harper, *The Life and Works of Susan B. Anthony*, 2 vols. (Indianapolis: Hollenbeck Press, 1898); Mary A. Livermore, *Selections from Mary A. Livermore* (Boston: Woman's Christian Temperance Union, 1892); Aaron Macy Powell, *Personal Reminiscenses* (New York: Caulon, 1899); and Frances E. Willard, *Glimpses of Fifty Years* (Chicago: Woman's Temperance Publishing Company, 1889).

A convenient and succinct summary of purity views may be found in Aaron Macy Powell, ed., *The National Purity Congress: Its Papers, Addresses and Portraits* (New York: Caulon, 1896).

General histories of prostitution, sexual morality or social hygiene are few, and, at best, only adequate. An easily accessible summary of the history of regulated prostitution may be found in Vern L. Bullough, *The History of Prostitution* (New Hyde Park, University Books, N.Y.: 1964). Other accounts of European prostitution are in C. J. Lecour, *La Prostitution à Paris et*

à Londres, 1789-1870 (Paris: P. Asselin, 1870); Yves
Guyot, *Prostitution under the Regulation System*,
translated by Edgar Beckit Truman (London: G. Carpenter, 1884); and Benjamin Scott, *A State Iniquity: Its
Rise, Extension and Overthrow* (London: Kegan, Paul,
Trench, Trubner and Co., 1890). For the American
history consult Howard B. Woolston, *Prostitution in the
United States Prior to the Entrance of the United States into the World War* (Montclair, N.J.: Patterson Smith,
1969); and Charles Walter Clarke, *Taboo: The Story of
the Pioneers of Social Hygiene* (Washington: Public Affairs, 1961). For an intellectual history of continuing
worth see Sidney Ditzion, *Marriage Morals and Sex in
America, a History of Ideas* (New York: Bookman,
1953).

Recent scholarship has gone a long way toward recti-
fying earlier shortcomings in the analysis of sexual
morality and related themes. Emil Oberholzer, Jr., *Delinquent Saints, Disciplinary Action in the Early Congregational Churches of Massachusetts* (New York: Columbia
University, 1956) may be read with benefit. Among the
new literature on the woman's movement, one may
discover a provocative analysis of sexual morality in
William L. O'Neill, *Everyone was Brave: The Rise and
Fall of Feminism in America* (Chicago: Quadrangle,
1969). For one of his earlier books of equal importance,
see *Divorce in the Progressive Era* (New Haven: Yale
University Press, 1967). Another history of feminism giving sexual morality important attention is Andrew Sinclair,
The Emancipation of the American Woman (New York:
Harper and Row, 1965). Although not about American
feminism, a work also giving important attention to sexual
morality is Christopher Lasch, *The New Radicalism in
America, 1889-1963: The Intellectual as a Social Type*
(New York: Vintage, 1965). A recent interpretation of

the career of Margaret Sanger is David M. Kennedy, *Birth Control in America: The Career of Margaret Sanger* (New Haven: Yale University Press, 1970).

Monographs of related interest have been published on the temperance and censorship movements. On temperance reform Joseph R. Gusfield, *Symbolic Crusade: Status Politics and the American Temperance Movement* (Urbana: University of Illinois, 1963), provides an important interpretation of temperance reform from the perspective of "status anxiety." A more conventional history is Morton Mezvinsky, *The White Ribbon Reform, 1874-1920* (Ph.D. diss., University of Wisconsin, 1959). For a reinterpretation of censorship, one may profitably turn to Paul S. Boyer, *Purity in Print: The Vice-Society Movement and Book Censorship in America* (New York: Scribner's, 1968). Of course, the standard work on the American family remains Arthur W. Calhoun, *A Social History of the American Family*, 3 vols., (1917-1919; reprint ed., New York: Barnes and Noble, 1960).

Several articles were quite helpful in writing the history of purity reform. Among the more important were John Chynoweth Burnham, "Psychiatry, Psychology and the Progressive Movement," *American Quarterly* 12 (1960): 457-65; "The Medical Inspection of Prostitutes in America in the Nineteenth Century," *Bulletin of the History of Medicine* 45 (1971): 203-18; Roy Lubove, "Progressives and Prostitutes," *The Historian* 24 (1962): 300-430; Fred W. Baldwin, "The Invisible Armor," *American Quarterly* 16 (1964): 432-44; James R. McGovern, "The American Women's Pre-World War I Freedom in Manners and Morals," *The Journal of American History* 55 (1968): 315-33; Robert E. Riegel, "Women's Clothes and Women's Rights," *American Quarterly* 15 (1963): 390-401; Charles E. Rosenberg, "Science and American Social Thought," in *Science and*

Society in the U.S., edited by David D. Van Tassel and Michael G. Hall (Homewood, Illinois, 1966), pp. 135-162; Alice Judson Ryerson, "Medical Advice on Child Rearing, 1550-1900," *Harvard Educational Review* 31 (1961): 302-23; Richard Shryock, "Sylvester Graham and the Popular Health Movement, 1830-1870," *Mississippi Valley Historical Review* 18 (1931): 172-83; Lloyd G. Stephenson, "Science Down the Drain," *Bulletin of the History of Medicine* 29 (1955): 1-26; and Sidonia C. Taupin, " 'Christianity in the Kitchen' or a Moral Guide for Gourmets," *American Quarterly* 15 (1963): 85-9.

Index